this much
country

a memoir

KRISTIN KNIGHT PACE

GRAND CENTRAL
PUBLISHING

NEW YORK   BOSTON

Grand Central Publishing
Hachette Book Group
1290 Avenue of the Americas, New York, NY 10104
grandcentralpublishing.com
twitter.com/grandcentralpub

First edition: March 2019

Grand Central Publishing is a division of Hachette Book Group, Inc. The Grand Central Publishing name and logo is a trademark of Hachette Book Group, Inc.

The publisher is not responsible for websites (or their content) that are not owned by the publisher.

Artist credit: Sarah Glaser

Library of Congress Cataloging-in-Publication Data has been applied for.

ISBNs: 978-1-5387-6240-0 (hardcover), 978-1-5387-6239-4 (ebook)

Printed in the United States of America

LSC-C

10 9 8 7 6 5 4 3 2 1

For Mom and Dad

Race Trail

2016 IDITAROD
Anchorage to Nome

DETAIL

Koyukuk River

NOME
WHITE MOUNTAIN
ELIM
KOYUK
NULATO
GALENA
RUBY
SAFETY
KALTAG
SHAKTOOLIK
UNALAKLEET

Norton Sound

Yukon River

CRIPPLE
OPHIR
TAKOTNA
NIKOLAI
MCGRATH

Kuskokwim River

ROHN
RAINY PASS
FINGER LAKE
WILLOW
SKWENTNA
YENTNA

ANCHORAGE

- ● **CHECKPOINTS**
- ● **Hospitality stops**
- ● Other Towns
- *Rivers*
- Roads

Bristol Bay

Gulf

Routes

2015 YUKON QUEST
Whitehorse to Fairbanks

CENTRAL
CIRCLE
Eagle Summit
Mile 101
Slaven's Roadhouse
Trout Creek
EAGLE
TWO RIVERS
FAIRBANKS
DAWSON CITY
Scroggie Creek
PELLY CROSSING
Stepping Stone
McCabe Creek
CARMACKS
BRAEBURN
WHITEHORSE

ALASKA

Yukon

Fortymile

of Alaska

Ferry
Tanana
Nenana
Denali National Park & Preserve
Healy
McKinley Park
Cantwell
Denali 20,310 ft
Susitna River

PROLOGUE

Yukon Quest Trail

Where Woodchopper Creek met the Yukon River, blown snow whipped across the ice like big white sheets curling and unfurling on a mile-long clothesline. Trail markers lay like fallen soldiers, splintered by the dogsleds that had come through before me. We were traveling on the frozen Yukon River, and I was in the first stages of a gripping panic. Miles ago, Lance and his team had been just ahead of me. But now they were a long, dark ghost in the far distance, already across the entire river valley from us. The next team was a day behind us, and the trail was disappearing. At the head of my twelve-dog team, my lead dog Solo hopscotched from one patch of snow to the next, linking them together over slippery, wind-polished glare ice peppered with sharp shale. His nose was to the ground as he sniffed for the scent of teams who had come before us, giving him hints about where to go. But the wind was blowing away their trail one gust at a time. It was a chinook—incessant and warm, heralding a new weather system that was sweeping in and erasing the extreme cold of the past week. My giant white windbreaker flapped loudly, whipping against my body, catching air like a sail. But as we hugged turns in the river and thus became sheltered from the wind, last week's remnant –40°F cold seeped up from the Yukon—a bitter reminder of the fickle flux of this place. Alongside the frozen ramparts of jagged, jammed-up ice, the dogs' ears perked up and they stared down at the trail. Out of the wind, it was quiet enough that they could hear water pulsing a few feet below us, under the ice. It was frightening, and I imagined my sled crashing through the ice and falling into the river. And now that Lance was leaving me behind, there would be no one to help us. Ahead, the Yukon was a cracked and expansive sea, claiming the entire landscape.

As Lance's team surged and disappeared into the distance, my team kept stopping for one reason or another. The dogs found prior teams' snacks on the ground and stopped to chew them out of the ice. They mouthed their booties, ripping off the Velcro fasteners, and the booties had to be replaced. They played with their partners and then got tangled. I became unreasonably short with them, telling them we needed to keep up. I began panicking about falling too far behind and being alone. The more I worried, the less motivated the dogs became. I stopped and pulled on my parka, realizing a reset was needed as the insidious cold infiltrated my layers. Attitude was everything, and I knew that I needed to believe in my dogs. And seven hundred miles into a one-thousand-mile race, I had no reason not to. We had all gotten ourselves this far, hadn't we?

As the sun descended behind a gunmetal wall of lenticular clouds, shards of light glowed on the distant mountains behind us. But for us, it would be into the dark. Into the clouds and into the wind. For us, it would never be the easier of two ways. Hadn't I learned by now that nothing worth doing was easy? The dogs faced forward as another gust ruffled their fur. They were silent, patient, composed, self-possessed. They were on an adventure. They were on a new trail. They were not scared. I looked at my sled and saw that it had everything we needed to survive out here. Everything I had learned in an entire lifetime was within my power. I was capable. We needed no one.

I stood on the runners of my sled and looked forward. I snugged my fleece neck gaiter up around my nose and it smelled like my unbrushed teeth, raw meat, dog shit. Before us stretched some of the most lonesome country on earth. It was huge and thrilling, and we were a part of it. An understanding rippled like a current from the dogs to me, and from me back to them. Without a word, they jolted forward, leaning into their harnesses as we glided into the coming night. The only witnesses to our silent transformation were the wolves who traveled wraithlike on the periphery, welcoming us in their way to a lone wildness.

PART 1

Alfred

B efore there was Alaska, there was Alfred.
    I was eighteen years old and madly in love with a boy I'd never met.

The first thing I loved about Alfred was his handwriting. The angular letters written by a man's hand that spelled out my name. The sign-offs in swift, half-print half-cursive. The whimsical, swaying "A." After six months of letter writing, the envelopes now came addressed to hilarious nicknames: Kristin "Strawberry Thunder" Knight. Kristin "Big Panties" Knight. I'd rush to the door every day when the mailman came, hoping to see a letter addressed to me from Montana, and later, Washington. Craving the next dispatch of a vagabond lifestyle I had never known. I was a senior in high school who lived with my siblings and my parents in the suburbs in Fort Worth, Texas. And Alfred's stories of getting drunk and crawling into manholes with his buddies, running from the cops in purple climbing shoes, competitively racing mountain bikes in the Cascades, and climbing peaks in Glacier National Park's majestic backcountry painted the picture of a life I wanted to experience. He pulled me in like a magnet.

Here's what I knew of Alfred: He was five years older than me. He loved the Montana sky. He was Native American—his mother was Tlingit and his father was Sioux—and he had brown hair and heavy-lidded, blue-green eyes. He was self-conscious about the eczema that dappled his abdomen and about the extra weight he had gained over the winter but confident about his sense of humor and his outdoor skills. He had tattoos that were intricate and meaningful—parts of his heritage. He had friends who let him sleep on their couch and they had a weekly poker game. They called him Fredo.

I knew all of these things even though I had never heard his voice.

Some months into our correspondence, he called me from a pay phone somewhere in Montana. I imagined him sitting on a sun-washed curb, chrome cable hanging stiffly down from the blue "Public Phone" box; wind shuffling long, green blades of sweetgrass; mountains far in the distance, painted against a robin's egg–blue sky. Semitrucks pulled in and out of gas station pumps, bound for North Dakota or Seattle. My heart pumped hard as I strained to make sense of it. A stranger's voice. "Where are you off to next? I'm out of change, I'll send you a letter. I'll call again, as soon as I can."

After nearly a year of contact, we were in love. *I love you*, he had said on one of his nightly phone calls. And I laughed in disbelief. "Say it again."

"Kristin, I love you."

"I love you, too! I can't believe this is happening!"

One night after dinner I told my parents that I planned to move to Montana to be with Alfred in May, right after I graduated from high school.

This news crushed my parents. They didn't yet know that I had received a scholarship to the University of Denver as well as admission into the prestigious Pioneer Leadership Program. I had hidden the acceptance letter in my sock drawer. How could I move to Denver when Alfred was waiting for me in Montana? We were already planning to live together in a log cabin outside Missoula, by the Blackfoot River. College was overrated anyway, Alfred had said. Alfred had many opinions.

My parents knew everything I knew about Alfred, starting with the fact that we had met on the Internet. One of my girl-friends had found him on the then popular site hotornot.com, wherein you rate photos of people on a scale of 10 (hot) to 1 (not). Alfred's photo was most definitely a 10 in my opinion. A blue-eyed, dark-skinned boy with brown hair and a blue bandanna wrapped Rambo-style around his head, taking a break on a mountain trail so carved out and steep and snow-covered it didn't look real. I printed the photo out and tucked it away in my journal. I looked at it every day. Nothing else about the end of high school mattered, because I had this secret mountain man writing me letters and talking to me late into the night.

My mom was adamant that we should at least meet in person before I threw my future away for a stranger. He could be a serial killer, she warned. Or a fifty-year-old man. She convinced me that he should fly down to Texas the weekend before my high school graduation. In return, I'd fly back to Seattle with him and stay at his parents' house for a few days. But before any of this could happen, my mom wanted to speak to his mom on the phone. After she dialed, I hid in the hallway around the corner, heart racing.

"This is her first big crush," she said.

I was mortified. But he really was coming to Texas. In three weeks.

My palms were sweating as I walked into the baggage

claim terminal at Dallas/Fort Worth International Airport. It was May and the temperatures were soaring somewhere in the 90s, the sun whitewashing the miles of concrete that made up the airport grounds. I was so nervous I couldn't even look at the passengers coming in to claim their luggage. Instead, I turned around and looked out the window. I was wearing a red Abercrombie & Fitch polo shirt and my favorite bootcut jeans. My sister Jordan had straightened my strawberry blond hair and advised me on my makeup choices. "Don't wear lip gloss," she warned. "It looks so slimy and unnatural." My heart thrummed and I wiped my palms on my thighs. I felt a tap on my shoulder and turned around, straight into his arms. I wrapped my arms around his backpack and buried my face in his shoulder. He was trembling. Later he would say, "You were so beautiful. I never thought anyone so beautiful could love me."

Six days after graduation, I was on the road. The plan was to drive from Texas to Montana, stopping at various points along the way to stay with friends and family. Mom and Dad had a travel agent print out a road map with my route highlighted. They had me write down important contact information and addresses. I loaded my black Nissan XTerra with duffel bags of hiking clothes and gear, an ice ax wedged between the driver and passenger seats (for protection against strangers, and also for traveling across steep snowfields in Glacier National Park).

I said good-bye to the three of my seven siblings who still lived at home. Before I got in the car, Dad made me demonstrate that I could remove and then replace a tire. I had a blue bandanna wrapped Rambo-style around my head.

The route I took was indirect. It led me out of Fort Worth toward the barren desert of West Texas. With Tom Petty and the Heartbreakers blasting at full volume, I drove exactly the speed limit down a sunny, white, two-lane highway outside Jacksboro. I noticed a dark figure making its way across the road and was surprised to find it was a giant tarantula. I snacked on Oh's cereal, cheese pretzels, and animal crackers so I wouldn't have to stop at a restaurant. I felt so peaceful and free on the open road, full of intention knowing I was embarking on a journey to the frontier of my known world.

I crossed part of New Mexico, past the volcanic cone of Mt. Capulin where I was forced to pull over in a swirl of dust and sand as a dirt devil swept the highway, red taillights diving for the shoulders all around me. At the Colorado state line I was convinced a black bird with a red ribbon on its wing was following me—a sort of guardian angel. Every hour or so, the bird would dart and soar alongside my car, and I didn't feel alone. In South Fork, Colorado, I arrived at a friend's cabin on the Rio Grande. We rode horses around his family ranch and then drove to a Laundromat where I washed my laundry in a machine that wasn't my parents' for the first time in my life. I continued north to Glenhaven, Colorado, outside Estes Park, where my childhood friend Liz agreed to meet me. She and I were going to drive across desolate Wyoming together—an absolutely nonnegotiable stipulation mandated by my mother. Liz and I had met at camp when we were fourteen, drawn together by our love of horses. Now she was a firefighter who worked for the Forest Service. She had wrangled a few days off to travel with me, but then unexpectedly got sent out on a fire. I would have to drive two days across Wyoming and Montana alone. I debated if I should tell Mom. "Maybe I'll tell her after I get up there," I wrote in my journal.

Two days later, I arrived. I wrote,

The days are really flying by and already I find myself in Babb, Montana! I honestly can't believe I got myself here—HOLY SHIT! What a drive. I have finally reached a semi-permanent destination. Alfred had no idea I was going to be here today and I think he was really surprised. We just kissed and held each other for a few hours and then he had to go to work. I finally had a meal! It's been days and I was pretty damn hungry.

Also, many times, usually in cursive purple gel pen, *I Love Alfred!*

The summer wasn't anything like I expected. I had never before had a job working long hours on my feet. I had never really been on my own. I lived with Alfred in a one-room log cabin behind Two Sisters Café, where he had gotten me a job as a hostess. We had technically only known each other in person for six days, and we were living together. The electricity came on and off; his grandmother died and we drove to her funeral on the Lake Traverse reservation in South Dakota where I met Alfred's entire family; a forest fire swept through within a quarter-mile of the café and we all got evacuated while the owner, drunk and in his underwear and backlit by flames, waved a bottle of tequila in the parking lot and screamed, "I'm going down with the ship!" Alfred and I got into our car, a stray dog in his lap, and drove to the group campsite where all the employees of the restaurant would stay that night. Driving down the highway, we witnessed the hellish scene of the entire mountainside on fire. Alfred, completely devastated, began to cry. His home, his love, was being destroyed. And he could do nothing.

Everyone thought I was twenty-four years old and I never got carded in the bars, which all sat on the Blackfoot Indian reservation bordering Glacier. I watched fights break out almost nightly, and had my first sip of Black Butte Porter. It was fun pretending to be older than I was, but also I felt a yearning to be back on the road, exploring. Now that Alfred and I were finally together, I felt guilty about wanting to be alone, so I stifled my wanderlust. I had always said I'd never give up my dreams for anyone or anything. *But what about love? This love is not something I can pass up. This is it. Help me find pleasant compromises.*

We spooked grizzly bears, went out drinking, hitchhiked on the highway, and took in stray dogs. I bought huge bags of cheap kibble and fed up to ten dogs at a time from cereal bowls on the front porch of our cabin. One of them was a six-month-old pup with a thick tan, white, and black coat and amber brown eyes ringed with black eyeliner. He was unsure of himself and wary of humans, so we fell in love with him the hardest. His name, we discovered, was Maximus. Someone had given him a name and then let him wander the highway to prey on small mammals for his meals, in addition to the bacon we snuck him from the back door of the café. It took us two months of feeding him until he finally gained the courage to cross the threshold of our cabin. He lay down under a table and fell asleep. Alfred sat down on the floor beside him and slowly reached out his hand, tentatively running his fingers along the shiny, thick fur of Maximus's side. Maximus lifted his head and looked at Alfred, then laid his head back down on the floor with a sigh. Alfred looked at me, both our eyes wide with disbelief. We held our breath, trying to stay as still as possible.

"He's so soft," Alfred whispered.

We decided that day that Maximus would leave Glacier with us at the end of the summer. He was nearly feral, for sure, but also he was fragile. Even though he could face down grizzly bears, we felt he still needed our protection. And also, we were the only humans he trusted.

For the rest of the summer, in between adventures, I wrote in my journal. "I miss the solitary independence of the road." And also, "He told me the other day that he almost asked me to marry him that night with the amazing sunset. I would have said yes."

Alfred and I moved to Denver so I could attend DU for at least one year—something I had promised my parents before I left for Montana—but we couldn't tolerate city life and ended up moving back the following summer. I transferred to the University of Montana and began pursuing a degree in photojournalism.

Maximus sometimes accompanied me on walks to class. We would hike two miles from home, along the dirt trail beside the Clark Fork River, to the university. I carried a leash in my hand, but Maximus and I were working on building trust. Moving freely, he would walk beside me, watching my face, and I would hold his gaze. He would lower his ears and swish his tail, eyes on my feet and not stepping a paw ahead of me. If a squirrel ran across our path, he would be off in a flash of Tigger-style bounciness, fluffy tail sticking straight up in the air, its white tip bobbing.

"Maximus!" I would yell after him. Then, more quietly and with a low rumble in my voice, "Come here. Right. Now."

He would turn to look at me, brown eyes drooping guiltily, and walk back to me very slowly. One paw in front of the other. Maximus yearned for his independence, too.

It had taken a bit of convincing for our prospective landlords in Missoula to allow us to have a dog. I wrote a handwritten letter to the owners of our dream rental house on Walnut Street—a quaint two-room cottage with white clapboard siding and hunter green window frames that matched the shingles on the roof. It had dark, shiny hardwood floors and magnificent, leafy maple trees out front. I included a photo of Maximus—

he was irresistible. With his black eyeliner and Eeyore facial expressions, his deep brown eyes so full of love and longing. How could they possibly say no?

After a week of back and forth, the owners agreed we could all move in with a hefty pet deposit, which, of course, we never got back.

Maximus made good friends at the Bark Park and occasionally, when he got a wild hair and ran away, we could find him there. But sometimes, he would jump the fence and disappear for days. We would search for him in the woods, on trails, down by Rattlesnake Creek, and rarely find him. Once we received a phone call from a man high up on Mt. Jumbo, a mountain just outside Missoula.

"Hello, I'm calling on behalf of Maximus," he said.

Maximus had apparently taken up residence on the mountaintop, chasing the migrating elk herd, and had found this fellow and his dog to be worthy enough company that he approached them and let the guy read his name tag. Other times, Maximus would just show up back at home, reeking of carcass or covered in some kind of animal blood. He would lower his head and flatten his ears, his bushy tail swishing, knowing full-well the heartache he'd caused in his absence. His fleeing of civilization was something he just couldn't help, and despite our frustration, Alfred and I understood the impulse.

Through the rest of my college years, Maximus and I traveled hundreds of miles together on foot. We hiked every canyon in the Selway-Bitterroot Wilderness. We climbed the tallest peaks in the Bitterroot Range. We scrambled on boulders and padded over beds of Ponderosa pine needles, opening our nostrils and breathing in the wild woods. We were in the process of developing a silent language, full of body postures and eye contact, and another sense that I wouldn't be able to verbalize for many years. Once, while we sauntered up a rocky trail in the Rattlesnake Wilderness, Maximus just stopped. My body reacted to him before my mind did, and all the hairs on the back of my neck raised and my skin prickled. Maximus stood squared to something out of sight. Hackles up, he did not make a sound, but I knew he was telling me not to move. Telling me to stay back. After minutes of stillness, we turned around and scurried back down the trail from whence we had come. Later, I read about a mountain lion stalking the trails of the Rattlesnake and I felt such awe for brave Maximus and the danger he'd deterred.

The summer after I graduated from UM, I landed a summer internship in Alaska, working at the Denali National Park Sled Dog Kennels. I'd developed an insatiable love for dogs while documenting working dogs for a thesis project—a coffee table book that displayed the talents of agility dogs, search and rescue dogs, Karelian Bear Dogs, and seeing eye dogs trained by inmates at the Montana Women's Prison. When Karen, the Denali National Park Kennels manager, offered me a job, it felt like a door opening into a whole new world of dogginess.

It was 2006. I had a lot of outdoor experience but never in any place like Alaska. I had spent every summer from age twelve to seventeen at an outdoor adventure camp outside

Rocky Mountain National Park, Colorado. For weeks, I would live in a covered wagon with three other girls, breathing the outside air even as I slept. There were less than a hundred girls at camp, all middle and high school aged, and we all agreed on a code of living for the summer that we ourselves crafted. We would be honest, courageous, selfless. We treated each other like sisters. We were each other's role models, partners, and friends. And the counselors who taught us were women not too much older than we were—women in their twenties who still had plenty to learn themselves, but we looked to them as though they were the heroes of our childhoods. At camp we practiced not only how to care for and ride horses, but also how to pack them up with a week's worth of gear and lead them into the wilderness in a long, sinuous string. We not only waterproofed our hiking boots, but also we pulled each other up fourteen-thousand-foot mountains, fearless for one another. We learned how to repair backpacks and stoves, and also how to live completely self-sufficiently in the mountains for up to five days at a time. Camp made it OK for girls to have the perilous journeys. For girls to have the adventures and the camaraderie of the trail described in books we all grew up reading. Books written by men.

Most mornings at camp started with the voice of one of our counselors yelling, "It's a beautiful day in Colorado!" and ringing a bell at 7:15 a.m. Sometimes, a handful of us were awakened by our hiking counselors at 2:00 a.m. Feeling a jolt of anticipation, we put on our two layers of wool socks among a gaggle of other teenage girls lacing up their hiking boots, eating bowls of cereal in bleary-eyed silence. We were the ones who had signed up for an E.B. or "early breakfast" hike—one that required us to wake up in the middle of the night, drive to a trailhead and climb big peaks or hike long distances, and get back down below treeline by noon, when the summer storms would hit almost daily. We loaded into the big blue van in the dark, stuffing our backpacks in the back row. Then we'd travel down a dirt trail in a single file line, headlamps off, learning to feel and smell the wilderness, to let our eyes adjust. Learning to trust the girl ahead of us. We would climb Longs Peak, Mt. Merritt, or Pagoda. We would hike thirty miles and climb six peaks in one day. Later in life I would realize that all of the most badass things I had ever done required an early start, no. decipherable sleep, and the jolt of adrenaline that came with knowing I was about to do something big. And even at the age of fourteen, I knew that death was an enemy I needed to keep close. Walking on fourteen-thousand-foot ridgelines with my friends while the lightning made our necklaces buzz and lit up the clouds in every different color electrified me and made me feel closer to danger and more alive than I ever had. It became an addiction. Or rather a purifying ritual.

Before I graduated college, I returned to camp to be a backpacking counselor and pass on my knowledge to a new generation of girls. Throughout my life I would return to wilderness again and again to set myself straight. And so with a certain breathlessness, I made my way to Alaska and started my new job at the kennels.

As a kennels park ranger, I greeted hundreds of visitors each day, where I showed them the National Park Service's only working sled dog team. I told stories about the soughing of sled runners on new-fallen snow, the panting of the dogs and their frozen breath hanging in white puffs at thirty degrees below zero, the loneliness of the trail, the romance of the historic patrol cabins. That I'd never experienced any of these things firsthand did not stop me. After each talk I would hook up a small team and run them around a gravel track on a historic wooden freight sled on wheels. I enthusiastically answered people's questions using knowledge memorized from a "Frequently Asked Questions" sheet Karen had given me, but also bits and pieces I had learned from the actual dog mushers—all women, incidentally—who worked alongside me at the kennel.

My favorite musher was Jess, who became my closest friend that summer. I loved that her dog, Sesi, was a kindred spirit. They walked together every day of the summer, and on nearly every winter patrol, Sesi was on Jess's team. They even took on each other's personalities: both were sassy and loving and only willing to do precisely what they wanted, no more and no less, although Jess worked harder than Sesi did.

And yet it was a challenging summer. Alfred and I hadn't seen each other in four months, though we talked on the phone several times a week. I missed him desperately. And unlike the wildernesses of my past, Alaska took no pains to comfort me. I floundered in Denali's trailless backcountry, sinking into deep spongy tundra and spraining my ankle, trying to keep up with the backcountry rangers with whom I got to train as part of my internship. Alaska was brutal, and it seemed to either harden people or they broke against it. On nights when I couldn't sleep, I'd walk out of my cabin in employee housing and amble over to the kennels. The sky never got pitch-black, and in the strange, gray light of midnight I'd crunch down the gravel walkway alongside the dog yard and head for that very last house in the back, the one under a giant black spruce. I'd sit next to my favorite dog, Tonzona, our backs against each other, and close my eyes or cry or stare off into the woods. He would calmly lick my face or bury his heavy, square head into my shoulder. It wasn't the time for barking or hat thievery. He knew what I needed.

When my internship ended in late September, I packed up my duffel bag and loaded the car to begin the long drive south. I promised Jess that I would come back in the winter and go out on a patrol with her. In my arms was a six-week-old sled dog puppy from that summer's litter. He was one of the runts—a black and gray pup with a disappearing sliver of white going right down the middle of his face. He weighed eleven pounds, and his name was Moose. There had been nine puppies that year—a big litter for the kennels—and while four of Moose's siblings would remain at the park kennel for the rest of their working lives, five had gone to other homes. I loaded the tiny, dozing Moose into his tiny puppy kennel on the floor behind my right elbow, managing not to awaken him. I waved good-bye to my coworkers. We had been in the car for approximately one mile when Moose emerged from his nap in a panic and began to scream and howl, pawing wildly at the kennel door. His protests were deafening and desperate, and we had 2,600 miles to go.

When Moose and I pulled up at our home in Missoula, I wrapped my arms around Alfred and looked at his face, the details of which I had already begun to forget. I knelt down and got kisses from Maximus, who had done a joyous dance upon my arrival consisting of twirls and bucks and prancing. When Max met Moose, he was disgusted. After one sniff he retreated to the back of the house, curling up beneath the floor-length curtains that surrounded the sliding door and huffing his displeasure.

Moose terrorized us for the first few months of his membership in our family. After several sleepless nights I seriously considered shipping him back to the park kennel. He screamed and howled and peed and pooped. He chewed on Maximus's ears and latched on to his big, bushy tail. He only slept when the rest of us were awake, and he was *growing*. His legs were thickening, his paws were huge. He tripped on them often. His ears flopped heavily when he trotted around the Bark Park, and then one day one ear popped up and stayed there, like a flag. A week later, the other ear followed.

"He's gonna be a hundred pounds," the vet said when she gave him his rabies shot.

It took a few months for Maximus to change his mind about Moose, but he grew to accept him and even love him. They chewed on each other's faces and sprinted around the yard. They went on hikes and backpacking trips with us and curled up against each other at night. When one got in trouble, the other commiserated. Alfred loved them both, giving them each voices. Mostly it was Maximus, who often had a running social commentary on our lives.

"Hey rady, give me a berry rub," Alfred would say as Maximus rolled over. Or, "Mom alrays makes Dad do da dishes."

In April, I flew up to visit Jess for a week. She picked me up at the Fairbanks airport, and we got into her car, the northern lights swirling in the night sky. When I checked the thermometer, it was –20°F.

Jess had promised to take me out on a patrol. It took us a day to get prepared. I was nervous—it would be just the two of us sharing one dogsled and a team of dogs on a twenty-mile journey—but it was thrilling to see all the dogs again, this time in their thick winter coats. They had been working all winter and were brawny and muscular and so full of energy, nothing like the animals I'd bonded with the past summer.

The trip was absolutely hellish. The sled was heavy and unruly, and I couldn't keep it on the narrow dog trail. I crawled on my hands and knees across slick, shining glare ice when I fell out of the sled, awkwardly unable to stand upright. I pushed the sled through two feet of snow while the dogs panted and lurched and stopped to watch as Jess snowshoed ahead of the team, putting in a trail. When we finally got to the patrol cabin on the Savage River, I could barely lift my legs to walk. Jess set up a cable dropline for the dogs that was strung taut around the spruce trees surrounding the cabin. She had me take off all their harnesses and walk each dog over to the dropline where they would bed down for the night. Meanwhile, she fired up the woodstove in the cabin and placed big metal pots of snow atop the woodstove. It took five gallons of snow to make one gallon of water, and we needed about ten gallons to feed the dogs that night and the following morning. While the snow melted, we unpacked the sled and brought in our sleeping bags and gear to get warm by the stove. We chopped firewood and continually swept snow out of the cabin that we had tracked in with our boots, ensuring it wouldn't melt into water puddles on the floor. It had taken hours of work to even arrive at the cabin, and now that we were there it would be a few more before we could even eat our dinner. Dogs always ate first.

Finally the water was hot enough to thaw the dogs' dinner, and we let it soak in a five-gallon bucket. When we went outside and ladled the hot broth, meat, and kibble into their bowls, steam rose while the dogs lunged into their meals. I was jealous of them. Back inside the cabin, we soaked the dogs' breakfast in cold water overnight and then, finally, began cooking human food. It smelled good—Thanksgiving stuffing from a box and instant mashed potatoes—but I could barely appreciate it. Nothing seemed more important than sleep. My eyelids drooped lower and lower. My body hunched forward and my head yearned for a resting place.

It was the hardest thing I had ever done. I wasn't enjoying myself. I was surprised that even the company of the dogs, with all their buoyant energy, their love of snow and winter, was no match for my all-consuming exhaustion. At the end of our two-day journey, I was more than ready to get back to Montana and to the relatively easy life of two pups, a day job, and a home we could heat with the press of a button. I didn't yet understand that hard-earned accomplishments have a way of getting under your skin and enticing you to go back and try them again. I never could have guessed that the taxing experience would come to me at unexpected moments, and beckon.

The next summer, Alfred and I were married in a stand of cottonwood trees in Polebridge, Montana. It was June 23, 2007, and our friends and family had flown all the way to Montana and then driven thirty miles down the most dusty, potholed, lonesome road in the state to attend our wedding outside Glacier National Park. It was a hot, sunny day and the headwall of the Livingston Range loomed large and imposing where it rose up steeply behind the North Fork of the Flathead River. Daisies strung from fishing line dangled like pearl necklaces from tree branches. Family and friends gathered in the shade of the giant, friendly cottonwoods, sitting on cut stumps or standing with their hands clasped. Maximus had on a collar with a red-orange rose corsage. (Moose was at a nearby boarding facility, not to be trusted in a large, well-dressed crowd. By then he was already as tall as my waist and could rest his head easily on countertops and high tables.) Alfred and

I stepped inside the circumference of a ring of painted rocks and read our handwritten vows to one another.

For two years we were itinerants, wandering from one dream job to the next. Since my internship at the kennels ended, I had been working as the outdoors reporter for the local newspaper in Montana. Then, the winter after our wedding, we loaded up everything we owned in a U-Haul and drove the snow-covered road back to Polebridge where we had decided to run a saloon. We'd been romanced by the wildness of the North Fork, and the fact that Polebridge had only a dozen year-round residents and no electricity seemed like the right kind of adventure for us. We lived on a homestead with propane lanterns and a barrel woodstove. Moose and Maximus ran wild through the snowy woods and down the one road into "town," a collection of old buildings hand hewn with broadaxes. We hauled ice cold water from a nearby creek and heated it up on the woodstove. We took outdoor showers at −20°F. It was the first time I had ever smelled steam, or knew it had its own particular scent when mixed with the odd chemistry of extreme cold—powerful and almost sweet, like lavender. We got up early every day and worked at the saloon late into the night. Alfred cooked whatever he fancied, whipping up honey and lavender chicken breasts, and puffy, hot calzones, and grilled mahi mahi.

We lost ten thousand dollars that winter. On the last night the saloon was open, a brother and sister duo played old bluegrass tunes until the early morning hours. Their haunting harmonies took all the air out of the saloon. The generator turned off every night at 9:00 p.m., and in the back I stood over a big metal sink full of hot dishwater, washing dishes by headlamp. Tears slid down my cheeks and splashed into the soapy water. Alfred leaned against me and I could feel the weight of his sadness. We were giving up on our dream.

We decided to move to Seattle and start our lives over somewhere civilized. Immediately, Alfred got a part-time job as a chef in a fine dining restaurant. I scoured the Classifieds and every online job search site I could find. I spotted a job posting for the executive editor of an outdoors magazine and my heart raced. It was the only position I had seen in weeks that came close to matching my previous journalism experience. I applied and was called for an interview, which took place at the local library in Ballard. I took a deep breath, looked at myself in the rearview mirror, and exited the car. In my hand, I had a copy of the latest issue of *Sea Kayaker* magazine.

I entered the library conference room and sat down at a large table across from the editor in chief and the publisher of *Sea Kayaker*. Chris, the editor, was tan and windblown, with dark hair and shining brown eyes. He was in his forties and had a skeptical squint, but it could have been from spending years on the sea. Joan, the publisher, was a smiling, gray-haired woman with sea blue eyes who looked like she could have stepped out of a Patagonia catalog. They seemed friendly and enthusiastic, but my hands were shaking nonetheless.

Chris took out the sample article I edited for the job application.

"Of all the people who applied for this job, you were the only one who struck out the modifier for *unique*," he said.

I sat up a little straighter.

"It's one of the first things we learned in editing class at J-School," I said, relaxing. "*Unique* can't be modified."

We talked for a whole hour, the conversation meandering between all my past jobs—the newspaper in Montana, the dogs in Alaska—when finally the interview was coming to an end.

"One last thing," I said.

I took out the issue of *Sea Kayaker* I had brought in and slid it across the table.

"I went through this and . . . well . . . I made some edits," I said.

Chris's eyes grew wide. He took the magazine and flipped through, stopping to inspect the marks I had made with my red pen.

"I don't know if I should say 'I've never had anyone do this *for* me' or 'I've never had anyone do this *to* me,'" he said, laughing.

"Well, it was nice to meet you," I said, shaking their hands.

The next day, Chris called to offer me the job. I screamed on the phone.

"I'm so sorry," I said, "that was so unprofessional."

My office had a big silver iMac and a view of Shilshole Bay. Dark, stormy waters with pure white sailboats tethered in rows. Rain splattering on the windows. My coworkers were friendly, but they were a lot older than my twenty-four years. I got to make big decisions about the magazine, editing every article, designing every page, crafting a commemorative cover for the twenty-fifth-anniversary edition. I felt respected, but even though I worked full-time, I barely brought home enough money to pay the bills. When I asked for a raise, Joan said she would have to cut everyone's Christmas bonuses. And Alfred refused to get a second job in addition to his part-time gig at the restaurant. Every day, I would bike or walk home from work, saying "hello" to everyone on the sidewalk and cringing as they passed me by without a word. And when I got to my front door, I'd open it to find Alfred sitting on the futon, watching TV. Moose and Max would fall all over themselves, sprinting to greet me, yearning to go on a walk. In the kitchen, dirty dishes would be piled high.

Alfred and I had Christmas dinner in the neighborhood bar. We missed Montana desperately. A year went by and I decided I couldn't sit behind a desk anymore. I quit my job at *Sea Kayaker* and applied for entrance into a mountain instructor course with the National Outdoor Leadership School. We moved back to Montana and I immediately departed for Wyoming's rugged Wind River Range for a thirty-five-day expedition wherein I earned my NOLS Mountain Instructor certificate. The economy was bad that year—it was June 2009—but we both got jobs with the U.S. Forest Service. We were on opposite schedules and passed each other like ships in the night. Alfred grew distant, though I hardly noticed. We had, after all, fallen in love over the telephone line, a thousand miles apart.

It was August, and my hands were sore and calloused from trail work. Since June I had hunched over a pick or a Pulaski or a shovel all the way from Montana's Bitterroot Divide to Idaho's Salmon River, building trails. I was part of a four-person crew that hiked into the wilderness carrying crosscut saws, axes, and picks. We spent eight days at a time cutting, digging, sweating, or hiking. A long train of pack mules helped bring our camp in and then back out of the backcountry. As far as I was concerned, there was no better job in the world. It was one of the first jobs I'd held where the fruits of my labor were witnessed and appreciated every day. Progress was visible and tangible and propelled by my own two hands and the strength of my body.

On my days off, I'd load up Moose and Maximus and travel south to see Alfred. He was a river ranger on the Salmon River in eastern Idaho. There, the Ponderosa and Douglas-fir forests glided down from the resting place of ancient glaciers. Now, baked in the simmering hundred-degree heat, the area was always at threat for forest fires. The vanilla smell of Ponderosa bark permeated the hot air, and underfoot the pine needles crunched dryly. In perfectly spaced formation, as though they held each other at arm's length, the mighty trees descended downslope into the desert-like Salmon River basin.

That day in August it was 108°F and sweltering inside the M-T Saddle Saloon—a run-down bar a couple miles from my husband's ranger station. The saloon was a lumpy wooden structure with a western-style façade, its name sloppily painted onto a piece of driftwood. Through the swinging wooden saloon doors, patrons could admire thousands of knickknacks tacked onto the walls and ceilings. Hats, clocks, tools, antler mounts, even a boat steering wheel adorned the yellowing walls of the somewhat infamous establishment. Behind the stained wooden bar, the drunken bartender stood swaying. I'd asked him how my husband had been faring over the summer and, more pointedly, why he wasn't presently seated by my side.

"You're not going to like it," he slurred. But his eyes were sober and sad. My heartbeat quickened and pounded in my ears. "He should be the one to tell you."

I hadn't seen Alfred in weeks. We each worked eight days on and six days off, leaving for work before the other came home all summer. Many Montanans relied on seasonal jobs to make it through the year, and we had spent a few summers apart in this fashion. The scheduling worked out great for dog care at first, but soon Alfred said he didn't want to be tied down to the dogs on his days off. He wanted to travel around the state and go backpacking with his new coworker, but not with the burden of taking Moose and Max along. So on his six days off he boarded them at a nearby kennel. It took almost my whole paycheck to afford it. Alfred had always loved the dogs, and his sudden change of heart about them hurt. He was different, and it was clear he had new people, the denizens of the M-T Saddle Saloon. Apparently they knew him better than I did. I sat alone on a bar stool, his wife of two years and his partner of seven, come all this way to visit him.

He had excused himself a half hour earlier, saying his co-worker was going through a rough time and needed a shoulder to cry on.

I cut through the crowd of weathered miners and tan,

egotistical river guides and Forest Service employees like my husband and sat in the dry, pointed pine needles at the top of a bluff. Two hundred feet below, the waters of the Salmon flowed ceaselessly, undulating and swirling. A chocolate lab with a red collar and a jingly name tag approached me with a pinecone in his mouth, and we played fetch for half an hour. Behind us people yelled and talked and played some kind of outdoor game akin to horseshoes. And it was then that Alfred approached. His awkward, hulking figure. He could have been sweaty, and brown with sun or red with heat or white with fear. I don't remember anything except his words and the swirl of confusion and panic and heartbreak that surrounded them.

He walked me past the people playing drinking games who waved at him from atop outdoor picnic tables. Past the screen door of the saloon to a big boulder near the parking lot. We were within sight of everyone and within hearing distance of most when he said, "I'm just not as in love with you as I used to be."

The tears streamed down my face pathetically as Alfred drove us back to the station along the potholed dirt road with the windows down. The curly-haired girl coworker he would later marry sat wordless in the backseat, witnessing my collapse.

Back at my own ranger station on the West Fork Ranger District outside of Darby, Montana, I dutifully loaded my gear in the storeroom. I packed eight days of food into my Forest Service–issued bear-proof cooler and prepared tools to be loaded onto the mules. I grabbed my favorite crosscut saw— the one with the worn wooden handles painted cherry red— and unrolled a canvas cover fashioned from a fire hose over its spindly, serrated teeth. During the fourteen-mile hike into camp, I had plenty of time to think about how I'd break the news to my crew—a tight-knit, burly bunch who swore a lot, worked hard, and took good care of each other. I had earned my kinship with them, coming on to the crew late in the season when a fellow forester had taken another job. I'd had to prove that I could take the man's place, since our four-person crew was responsible for 5,600 miles of trail. Once I had shown myself to be "capable of swingin' a tool" and not prone to complaining, I was welcomed as though I was family. That trip we dug boulders out of hillsides and wrestled them into trenches, creating water bars that would direct rainwater into a ditch and keep it from eroding the trail. The others would stop to catch their breath, graciously looking the other way while tears flowed in dirt-lined runnels down my cheeks.

Dan, a six-and-a-half-foot-tall lumberjack, had rough, dirty hands and a soft voice with which he told wildly inappropriate jokes. He ate beets and carrots he had harvested from his own backyard and didn't care to wipe the dirt from them. He offered some to me on our half-hour lunch break, asking how it was going. When I told him all that had transpired over the weekend, he sat next to me on a giant, downed Douglas fir and cupped his hand around my shoulder. He usually only turned serious when he was figuring out the angle of a saw cut or working a tool so hard it broke—never on lunch breaks. He fixed his light brown eyes on me and said earnestly, "Nobody deserves to be treated like that, Kristin."

Danielle was the other woman on our crew. She had long, dark dreadlocks that hung down her back and sparkling blue eyes and an endearing constellation of freckles across her nose and cheeks. She swung an ax like a madwoman and sang while chopping roots out of the rocky dirt. In her experience, women like us needed "real men" to take care of their needs. And in her opinion, Alfred sounded like a bona fide adolescent. As the story of the M-T Saddle Saloon unraveled on our way back to camp, she shook her head and walked faster down the trail ahead of me, boots pounding on powdery dirt, setting off little clouds. When she turned her head to the side I could see her cheeks flushed in anger.

Mark, our crew boss, had been with the Forest Service for twenty-five years. Even though he was in his fifties, he had the body of a twentysomething from all those years of trail work. His skin was smooth and taut over muscular arms, shoulders, and back. He was the one who taught me how to work a two-person crosscut saw—where to place it on the face of the tree, how to set the razor-sharp teeth of the sawblade gently against the bark, how to guide the blade with one hand at first, until it bit into the wood and made a place for itself there. Most important, he taught me how to work with my partner. How I should always pull the saw toward me and never push it back toward the other person. After a few trees, we had a smooth, easy relationship going between the two of us and the saw. The metal would sing as it crossed through the wood.

Even though he said I'd picked up the work fast, at the end of the season it felt like I was disappointing him, and I told him that I was sorry my head wasn't one hundred percent on the tasks at hand.

"No!" he said, grabbing my shoulders. "Oh no. I am so impressed how you keep coming to work after all you've been through. You work so hard."

I looked at his face, tanned and worn as leather from decades of working in the sun, eyes full of tears. His white tank top was smeared with dust and oil from the tools. I heard the words, but my body was ringing, like it had been zapped with electricity. When was the last time someone had touched me like that? Had grabbed me with anything close to urgency or passion? I counted back time, mentally paging through the last four, five, six months...had it been more than a year?

My eight-day hitch came to an end and I decided to drive the handful of hours back to talk some sense into Alfred. We had been together for seven years. I was sure I could convince him he was making a mistake.

The road to the Corn Creek Ranger Station in Idaho where Alfred was working was narrow, gravelly, and dangerous. It wound along the bottom of a deep canyon, edging closely to the raging rapids of the Salmon River without shoulders or guardrails. You were supposed to roll down your windows in case you slid across the gravel and into the river on accident. I cruised past the milk shake shop in Shoup, then beyond the confluence of the Middle Fork, where its crystal-clear waters emptied into the brown, roiling Big Salmon. I bumped past one campground after another to the end of the road in Corn Creek. In the car I had convinced myself I could fix this. I smiled and laughed and sang along to those songs that built my confidence. Over and over, I rehearsed the conversation I was going to have to save my marriage.

That night after a semblance of a reconciliation, we were in bed and Alfred looked so miserable that I faked an orgasm so it would end. He walked outside and, just before his trailer door slammed shut, I watched him spit on the ground. I felt hollowness in the pit of my stomach. Less than worthless. Dirty and shamed. I needed comfort, but who was there to hold me and tell me everything would be all right? Moose and Max were just outside, each sprawled under his respective Ponderosa pine, legs stretched out in the cool dirt. I walked just past them, not wanting to disturb their rest, and lay down on the concrete boat ramp as the Big Salmon whirled and eddied past. I watched satellites spin among the stars. I traced all the constellations I knew, remembering how I paid money to have a star named after Alfred when I was eighteen. It was the first birthday present I ever gave him. He looked so shocked and touched. I glanced back at the ranger cabin and saw two cigarettes glowing in the dark.

He agreed we could go to marriage counseling. I could set up an appointment for his next days off. From the corner, the curly-haired girl watched. She was always there with a cigarette—a new thing he needed—whenever he needed it.

A week later, the sun warmed the grassy pasture outside the marriage counselor's house, and cats and dogs and horses roamed at their leisure. The counselor met me in her greenhouse, where two white chairs turned toward each other as if in conversation. Two glasses of ice water sweated on a tea table between them. Perspiration bloomed at my armpits. She held her notebook professionally, and her shiny, dark hair mirrored her shiny, dark eyes. She was compassionate, and said nothing as a cat claimed the empty chair beside mine. We talked about my biological father's death when I was little. About the "assumption of love" and "magical thinking." About how I launched myself into adventures to make sure I'd lead an exciting life in case I also died unexpectedly, like my father did.

After the appointment I called the ranger station at Corn Creek to ask if everything was OK.

"We had some extra work come up and Alfred volunteered to take it," his boss said.

The next day, his birthday, he showed up at our house. The wraparound porch was flooded with late August sunshine, and all the windows were open to the breeze that circulated high on Echo Mountain's arid shoulders. The empty corrals around the property slouched, revealing fences I'd mended poorly because I didn't know how. Inside, the clapboard floors were worn and splintering, unhidden by rugs or furniture. Outside, the paint was peeling, berated by weather. The view was magnificent, however, and every canyon in the Bitterroot opened its mouth to the east and sunlight poured through at sunset.

Despite him not showing up for the appointment, I was happy to see him. And when he told me he just didn't want to be married anymore, he couldn't do it, all of the air went out of my lungs. My anger was desperate.

"You're losing *everything!*" I screamed.

Alfred watched in stunned silence as I lunged for my car keys and called Moose and Max. He mumbled something about having to pull over on the way here to vomit. I couldn't look at him.

Moose and Maximus eyed me warily as I hurriedly shuttled them into the car. Gravel crunched under the tires as I let out a scream that had some huge part of my spirit fleeing my body. I pulled over at the top of the steep, winding hill into town and dialed my parents.

"Dad," I said. Sobs racked my lungs and I gulped for air over and over. "Dad" was all I could say.

I drove back home to find that in the fifteen minutes I gave Alfred to pack up his belongings and get out of the house, he took to Facebook to announce what he had done to the world. On his status update he wrote, "Alfred pushed the big red button and feels terrible."

My next hitch with the trail crew took us out to Witter Ridge and Eakin Ridge in the Frank Church Wilderness, which straddles the border of Montana and Idaho. We drove for hours along a winding, one-lane dirt road, unloaded our packs and tools, and hiked thirteen miles into a meadowy hole of a campsite. In that remote and hot country, thunderstorms would build up, blow in, and start fires. Down in our camp we were safe from the lightning, but up on those ridges was a different story. On our way into the camp, Mark, Danielle, and I traveled together while up ahead, Dan helped the mule packer, Dave, with the mule train. A thunderstorm flared up and struck at us, blindsiding us on top of a ridge. Mark, Danielle, and I huddled stupidly under a big tree, counting the seconds between flash and bang, while Dan and Dave watched in awe as a tree got struck by lightning and went up like a torch. They and the mules weathered horizontal rain while the tools buzzed in the packsaddles. The mules jumped with every roar and vibration of thunder.

By the time we set up camp, the sky was darkening and the wind had another storm on its breath. All through the night, a procession of three storms ripped through the dry, rough country of the Frank Church. The rain came down so hard and so copiously it was a wonder my tent poles didn't break. But I slept peacefully and comfortably that night. I allowed all my rage and sadness to join that tumultuous sky. I counted lightning flashes and their counterparts with a smile on my face. That night Mother Nature was just as pissed as I was— she took that fury of mine and manifested it into glorious, violent action. She blew down trees and lit them on fire. She caused all of the earth's creatures to cower in her presence. She held up her fist and pounded it into the ground.

"Are you going to divorce me?" I asked. I wanted to hear him say it. I wanted to make him own his decision. I repeated it again, slowly. "Are... you... going to divorce me?"

We were sitting on a curb outside a friend's house in Missoula in the hot summer sun. Alfred had his head in his hands. He had buzzed stripes into the side of his hair to be ironic, to be funny, and he looked like a little boy. Finally he looked up. "Yes," he said.

I gave him a week to get everything of his out of the house. I lovingly told him I thought he had made a mistake. I sobbed while I told him I thought we had had what my grandparents had. I thought we'd be together until we were old. My tears and snot got all over his shirt as he held me, which felt wrong. I pulled myself together, and in a measured way I told him I would be fine.

"Yeah, you'll land on your feet," he said with an exhale of relief. He was washing his hands of it right then; I could feel it. He didn't have to pity me for what he'd done now. "You always do."

42

PART 2

Driving North

The mint green Forest Service truck had a topper over its long bed, covering bags of tools shoved to one side and a foldout cot on the other. I had crawled in back to sleep for a few hours while my seventy-two-year-old partner stayed awake in the front seat, making sure nobody tried to drive back up the evacuated, closed road. A few miles up the road, the entire mountainside was on fire. We were getting paid overtime to stay up all night and make sure nobody endangered themselves by driving into the inferno.

It smelled like an old, musty cellar in the back of the truck, but better than the air outside. There the smoke burned deep into my lungs. Earlier I had stood out in it with a pair of binoculars and watched trees go up in bright torches of flame. I saw the forest fire as moving, roaring, living. I wondered what it sounded like up close as I watched embers shoot singularly heavenward from the shapeless beast. I wanted to stand there in front of it, feel the wind it must be creating, be consumed by it.

Back home later that night, it felt like the wind would have torn down the house if it had been allowed to rage on like that. It whistled through all the screens, slamming the gate on the porch, shoving the chairs into the railing. The wind chimes banged into each other like calamity. Two forest fires on either side of the Bitterroot Valley plumed and rose into the air like thunderheads. Thankfully, at midnight, a cold front moved in and the wind sputtered to a halt. Rain started falling, the first rain in months, collecting in fallen yellow leaves. A gentle, graceful rain, quelling the flames and smoke.

Weeks had passed since Alfred had left me, and now, instead

of anger, I felt defeat and humiliation. I started to think of myself as one of those big, decaying trees in the forest. A three-hundred-year-old Ponderosa that had been blown down by wind, slowly rotted through, lain on the duff with its body flayed wide open, its heart exposed and crumbling. Eventually it would decompose and return to the earth and wildflowers would grow from its rot.

A week later it snowed at our house, high up on Echo Mountain Road. The rest of the valley remained verdant, patchworked farmland. But up there in the hills the snow caked onto the sagebrush and street signs in lumps—big, wet flakes that fell in earnest like winter was there to stay. The view from the wrap-around porch was astonishing. I never knew it could be more beautiful than that summer light raking across the Sapphires, shining straight out of the Bitterroots and into my face as it set behind their granite peaks. But the day after the blizzard, a fog crept in and forced me to focus in close. It hid so much of the landscape, making it intimate and mysterious at the same time. The veils of fog eating up the familiar lights of Hamilton. I loved the outside winter world from the inside of that cozy house, candles glowing warmly on the dinner table and reflecting softly against the windows. Maximus approached me with a slow tail wag, sniffing my hand for a piece of cheese.

"Hey, rady, can I have some of that prease?" he asked.

Alfred was always the one who spoiled the dogs with human

food, but who would do that now? I held my hand out to Miz and he licked it clean.

I wondered if Alfred would ever return, and thought of my parents' advice to me after I had mentioned getting a legal separation instead of a divorce. I had divulged the embarrassing truth to them that I still held out hope for Alfred and me. Maybe after six months he'd come around and realize he made a mistake, I had argued.

"Best to make it a clean break," Mom had said as Dad nodded emphatically beside her. They had both been divorced before and knew the pitfalls of dragging the process out for longer than necessary. They agreed that the only way to truly move on was to cut all ties and be rid of Alfred once and for all.

"Krissy, I know you're going through a tough time, and I have an idea." It was Jess, my best friend from Alaska. "There's a guy up here who needs someone to watch his cabin and sled dogs for the winter."

My experiences in Alaska had not been fun, but they had stuck with me. *Cold and unfamiliar and strange and thrilling. I want to go back.* Over the years, that winter trip had found a way of sneaking into my mind. I had broached the subject of returning to Alaska with Alfred several times—he had family in Sitka—and he had no interest. But now Jess was on the phone, and it seemed the North was calling to me once again.

I told her I'd be there in a month.

Dad's head nodded for emphasis but he didn't say anything, he just stared at me through glasses that reflected the fluorescent lights of his Fort Worth, Texas, dental office. I had answered all his questions, without crying, and proven it was a sound idea, at least financially, to go to Alaska for the winter. I would take care of a cabin and eight sled dogs in exchange for free rent. It would only be for five months.

My dad's unwavering pragmatism always drew tears from his three headstrong, fanciful daughters. He had married my mom when she was a single mother of five and was, by all accounts, a verifiable saint for doing so. When he first came into our lives, he laid stern ground rules. Nobody was allowed to say the word "hate" or take God's name in vain. Cussing was strictly prohibited. When he and Mom got married, I was four years old, Kalin was three, and the twins, Jared and Jordan, were two. Our biological father, Daddy Keith, had died unexpectedly while Mom was pregnant with the twins. Ryan, the only child from my mother's first marriage, was sixteen years old. Both my parents were getting married for the third time. I remember when Dad officially adopted the four of us young ones and we all took his last name. It was days before I started kindergarten and he hadn't wanted me to have to change my name part-way through the school year, for fear I would get embarrassed. Mom said the courtroom judge had made us wait there all day, taking everyone else's cases before ours. By the time we finally got to approach the bench, it was the end of the day.

"All I deal with, all day long, is bad news. I wanted to end my day with something good," he had said.

The judge made it official—we were all Knights now—and since I was the oldest, I got to bang the wooden gavel on the judge's mighty desk.

During those early years, Dad endured pastel-colored bows and barrettes in his beard. He weathered the hailstorms of "you're not my real dad" and, especially when we got into big trouble, "I wish Daddy Keith was still alive." As we grew up, he and Mom coached all of our sports teams, from tee ball all the way up to select softball in high school. They helped us with our homework—Mom with English and Dad with math. They also worked full-time jobs. My mother was an attorney and he was a dentist. Dad was used to precise, tedious work, so he was the one who painted our nails before dances and put the ointment on our newly pierced ears when they inevitably got infected. Mom held us when we cried and came sprinting up the stairs when we called out in our nightmares. She wore bow ties and suits and cussed a lot—the world of pharmaceutical lawsuits and million-dollar trademark violations required it—so we cussed a lot, too. The stern ground rules were eroded and finally left for dead by the time the twins entered high school. But one thing remained constant: Dad was the one who said no. Mom was tougher than hell, but she could still be bribed to go along with any of our bright ideas with the help of a convincing and thoughtful hand-written letter. Dad, on the other hand, rarely fell for any heartfelt rhetoric or backed any of our million flights of fancy.

Yet there I was, twenty-six years old and feeling like an

overgrown child, sitting in his office and pleading my case. Unlike those high school days, this time I had kept my cool. And this time, even if he disagreed with me, he couldn't stop me from going anywhere. He gave me one last look, picked up his phone, and said, "Dana, clear my calendar for the first week of November."

"I'm going with you," he said.

We left the Bitterroot Valley at two in the afternoon. Coming down Echo Mountain for the last time, the valley seemed to present us with a special send-off. The Bitterroot Mountains were alternately shadowed and sunny. Small cloudbursts of rain hid some peaks while others were shot with stark sunlight. Because of this, rainbows appeared at random intervals over the entire mountain range. The intensity of their light and colors was blinding, and they followed us throughout the rest of Montana until sundown. Leaves were swept up by a dramatic swirl of wind, appearing like confetti and ribbons thrown at a parade. It was the first of November and the pastels of wintertime sunset appeared painted into the sky as we crossed the border into Canada.

By the time we reached Edmonton, Alberta, it was full-on winter. Our maximum driving speed was forty-five miles per hour, and I was grateful for the studded tires I had just installed on my SUV. In the backseat were Moose, Maximus, two duffel bags, a banjo, and a computer. The dog bed around which I had packed everything else was now in a trash can at some roadside gas station a few hundred miles back—the result of the first of many Maximus blowouts. The times Dad and I were pulled over on the ice-covered Al-Can (Alaska-Canada Highway) with paper towels and a spray bottle of cleaner, scrubbing dog shit out of the crevices of the SUV floor, were too numerous to count. Eventually, it became hilarious. Maximus would let out a yelp and Moose would start whimpering, "He's gonna do it, Mama!" Whoever was driving would slam on the brakes and pull over while the other was already halfway out the passenger door with a leash, sprinting toward the back of the SUV to get Maximus out before he shat all over the car. We never made it in time.

There was a thing that happened to me every time I hit the road for a new adventure, and this time was no different. It was as if a spider's silk had attached itself to me at one end, and the last familiar place on the other. I would start to drive away from that last place, and that little spinarette in my gut would tug more and more as I got farther away. "Go back!" urged this voice in my head. And then, somewhere along the way, the silk strand would break. Seamlessly, suddenly, I'd be singing out loud in the car. The tension would release and I'd float freely to the other end. My thoughts reaching forward instead of back. Now they reached ahead to the Alaskan Interior and my little cabin and the dog-friends I would make. They ran along the Al-Can, to the heart of Denali National Park, up to the deep snow where I would surely flail and suffer a little bit. But nothing that wouldn't add more character, that wouldn't make me better. I felt my head full of possibilities, and my heart ready to accept them.

I was reading *The Animal Dialogues* by Craig Childs, and one night on the road when feeling especially lonely, I reached the chapter on coyotes. Their territory spans the United States from the East Coast to the West. A third of their population travels in packs, a third in pairs, and a third alone. While Childs is traversing a remote section of Arizona, he spots a lone coyote tramping the sands. The coyote barks, then listens. Barks again, then listens. Nothing answers him. He curls up and tucks his nose to his tail for a nap, becoming nothing more than a big rock in a desert landscape. He lays like that for an hour, stands, and becomes a coyote again. He throws his head back and uses his whole body to exert a howl out into the desert, tail in an arc between his legs. No answer. This doesn't stop the coyote. He lets loose another howl, which is soon answered by a faint howl so far away, on the wind. That howl is answered by another shock of howls erupting from the west. Then the east. Then in all directions a cacophony of coyotes howling and yipping, filling a great emptiness.

Dad tolerated my daily crying episodes well, though his mind had been made up about Alfred from the day he first laid eyes on him. I remember my dad laughing in the kitchen as they shook hands, right after I picked him up from the airport. At the time I thought he was laughing at how nervous Alfred was. But I was beginning to realize it was at how undeserving Alfred was of his daughter. It had been less of a laugh and more of a scoff. How had this tattooed, jobless twentysomething won the heart of his teenage daughter, her whole future ahead of her, untarnished and full of promise? As we sat in a motel diner, it was evident that for Dad, this whole deal was good riddance to bad rubbish.

I missed my mother-in-law Karin's loving lack of even one iota of judgment toward us, feeding bananas and eggs to the dogs, making the first steamed mussels and butter and wine sauce I had ever tasted; father-in-law Wally's contagious, toothy laugh and his bolo ties and gorgeous Sioux jewelry, teaching me how to play cribbage on a finely carved piece of whalebone, making me believe the most ridiculous stories, stringing me along for minutes and then erupting into laughter. I knew I'd never see them again. Tears slid down my cheeks and onto my French toast. We returned to our room to find that Maximus had barfed on the floor and Moose decided he should probably pee there, too.

Maximus glowered at us from the corner of the room.

"Rhat?" he said, lacking any sympathy for us at all at this point. "You guys are de asshose."

"He did it, Mama," Moose said.

We cleaned up the carpet, loaded the dogs back in the car, and hit the road.

Late one night we descended down the highway toward a large suspension bridge. Cars were stopped in a line ahead of us. In the headlights, a moose's chest rose and fell. His crystallized breath ascended skyward in backlit steam as he lay on his side, taking up the entire lane with his massive body. The car that struck him shone on his final moments, the breaths deep and slow and peaceful, just outside Peace River.

Dad and I pulled carefully around him, then crossed a bridge over the wide river and continued west and north to the Interior. The highway cut through one monochromatic winter scene after another, giving us glimpses of lonely places. Our drive was lit more by moonlight than sun, and the green glow over the snow burned brighter than any daylight we ever saw. The cold had veiled the stars, and they twinkled muted as though through wax paper. As though their breath had crystallized around them in radiating circles.

We listened to Guy Clark and Lyle Lovett, songs that made us think of Texas and summertime and childhood road trips. I had already driven this road once with Mom, on the way to my summer internship at the Denali National Park Sled Dog Kennels. In the three years since I had made that trek, I'd already forgotten the long, lonesome stretches of road and how you had to time your days to hit gas stations before they closed so you wouldn't get stranded.

All the touristy places that were open in the summer were closed, and when we got to Liard Hot Springs at the corner of

British Columbia and the Yukon Territory one early morning, we were the only ones there. We dug our bathing suits out of our bags and closed the back door of the car, the –20°F air freezing our nose hairs, causing them to stab the insides of our nostrils. We plodded down the long wooden boardwalk that snaked through a wetland cast in frost. Silvery crystals covered every board. In half a mile we arrived at the hot springs. Close in to the clear, hot water were large, protective trees. We eyed the changing room, noting the NO ALCOHOLIC BEVERAGES sign. Dad looked at the bottle of Bailey's in his hand and we both laughed and shrugged. In the adjacent changing area I screamed as my bare feet touched the frozen decking. We emerged and sunk ourselves into the steaming pool as quickly as we could, our hair freezing in mangled, white twists as we swam around, taking shots of Bailey's. We could have stayed in the hot spring all day, but we forced ourselves to get out and change back into our frozen clothes. By the time we arrived back at the car our bathing suits were as stiff as cardboard.

That night, we arrived in Whitehorse, Yukon Territory. We took pictures of the full yellow moon hanging serenely above a frozen landscape, reflecting in the near-still waters of the wide and sluggish Yukon River. Dad and I had two more days of driving before we would reach Healy, Alaska—a small mining town outside Denali National Park with about a thousand year-round residents. There, near the end of some frozen gravel road, was a one-room cabin I would soon call home.

It had become dark. Solstice, the shortest day of the year, was a month and a half away. On that day, only four hours of daylight would shine upon the frozen Alaskan Interior. Our headlights formed two tunnels in a navy blue–black world. We turned right onto Stampede Road and passed streets whose names referenced little-known stars. Antares. Arcturus. Menkent. Until we came to Denebola. I learned later that Denebola meant "tail of the lion" and is the third-brightest star in the constellation Leo. We turned left and drove slowly down the narrow, snow-packed road. I could sense an openness beyond the car headlights—a huge expanse. An unknown. My heart pounded. Then I saw it, the cabin whose photo I had memorized. It seemed to tower above the snow-ensconced tundra. It was built on tall pylons several feet above the ground, and a half-loft bedroom upstairs added more height to the small living space. We pulled into the driveway and shut off the car, staring. A soft light emanated from the multisize windows, glowing almost, landing on the snow in rectangular shapes. We opened the car doors and let Moose and Maximus out, and the four of us crunched through the snow to the back porch. We climbed up the steep steps, swept free of snow, and knocked on the heavy wooden door. A delicate antler was its handle. James, the newly divorced guy whose cabin I'd be occupying and whose dogs I'd be caring for, had mentioned he'd likely be next door at the neighbors' eating dinner when we arrived. When the knock remained unanswered, we pulled the door open and stepped inside.

Maximus charged straight into the sixteen-by-twenty house, trotted purposefully across the green plywood floor, and pulled himself up onto a futon placed along the back windowed wall of the cabin. Maximus had never, ever sat on furniture before, but in pictures of the interior of the cabin, many dogs chose this futon as a dog bed. Max curled into a ball, head wedged against the futon's armrest, nose pressed into his big, bushy tail, and fell asleep. He was not getting back into that car, no matter what, and he was making that very clear.

"You peopre are dead to me," he said with a harrumph.

High above his head, white twinkle lights were strung in neat lines along wooden rafters. There was a small desk with built-in bookshelves overhead nestled in the corner. In front of the desk was a tall, rectangular window facing west. Lacquered, plywood countertops formed an L shape in the front corner of the cabin, with open shelving a few feet above them. On the shelves were exactly four stacked, blue plates. Exactly four stacked, blue bowls. Coffee mugs (four, all blue) hung from nails above the kitchen sink. A small tray held a handful of assorted cutlery. In the middle of the cabin was a large, square table with a blossoming Christmas cactus, pink petals falling on top of each other, cascading over the table's edge. Adjacent to the big, square table, on the east side of the cabin was a cast-iron woodstove with a glass pane door and a rocking chair placed alongside it. A pile of cut birch wood was stacked neatly in a firewood holder beside a tall, windowed door that faced south. We opened the door onto another porch upon which sat an old, weathered couch covered in snow. Beyond that was a little trail that led into the darkness. *The sled dogs must be out that way*, I thought.

There was a knock at the door and in came James—a tall, ponytailed man maybe ten years older than me, wearing round coke bottle glasses and speaking in a soft voice.

"So you found the place," he said, excited for our arrival and not a little relieved that someone would be here to care for his beloved crew of canines for the winter. He gave us a brief tour and, noting the absence of a refrigerator, lifted up a corner of the round rug under the rocking chair and revealed a square door with a silver D-ring latched onto it. He pulled on the D-ring and up came the trap door. James sat on the floor with his legs dangling down into a five-foot-deep cellar lined with white shelves.

"This is the cold hole," he said.

He instructed us to put things we wanted refrigerated more toward the top and things we wanted to keep frozen more toward the bottom. The permanently frozen ground beneath the cabin (permafrost) plus the winter temperatures would keep everything cold no problem. "If the temperature drops to minus thirty or colder"—he nodded toward a milk crate next to the front door—"you'll want to put things you don't want frozen like milk or eggs or cheese in there." At those temperatures, the cabin floor would keep those things refrigerated just fine on its own. Additionally, if I had a big grocery haul from town and couldn't fit everything in the cold hole, the grill outside on the porch provided excellent frozen storage space, James said.

Dad and I walked back out to the car for our things and James bid us good night as he made his way back over to the neighbors' where he would stay for a few days, coming over during the day to make sure I learned "the systems." The moon was so bright on the snow that he didn't need a headlamp, and we watched his dark silhouette stride up a small hill, mountains faintly outlined in glowing moonlight green at the edge of all that blackness.

Dad and I returned to the cabin, cracked open two ice-cold Alaskan Winter Ales that had become near-frozen in the car, and slouched onto the futon and the rocking chair. The labels on the beer bottles looked exactly like the scene outside: navy blue sky pinpricked by stars, a full moon glowing onto snow-covered spruce trees. The taste of the beer made us both let out that "cold beer" sigh of contentment like people do in commercials. We laughed and looked up at the twinkle lights in the rafters. Dad petted the giant, heavy head of Moose, who had surreptitiously crawled onto the futon between Dad and Maximus, pretending he didn't weigh ninety-eight pounds and wasn't really the size of a small horse. Dad nodded as he looked around the house and his gaze eventually rested on my permanently smiling face. Without saying a word, he seemed to concede the rightness of it all. He seemed to know I had wound up just where I belonged.

The next morning we had blueberry pancakes at the neighbors' house. Chuck and Karen, who had built my little cabin as newlyweds and now lived in a three-story masterpiece of giant, hand-scribed logs (that they also built), both worked for the National Park Service. Karen was the kennels manager, and she had given me my summer internship those three years ago. She was medium height with brown hair and kind eyes and a warm laugh you wanted to draw out. She had mushed thousands of miles with dogs, and when she smiled you could see all those years of weather at the corners of her eyes. When she was building the cabin in which we stood, she'd cut her leg open with a drawknife while peeling logs. Chuck stapled her leg back together with a skin stapler used for dogs. Chuck was in charge of the trail crew. He was six-foot-five or so and had a bushy black beard and dark brown eyes. He carried his daughters around like they were little pups, with an ease only a person who lived around animals could have. There was a picture of the two of them that I loved. In it, Chuck is sitting in a chair in the cabin in which I now lived. Karen is on his lap, feet dangling, giggling like a little girl. They are so young. There are dogs everywhere. They had both been dog mushers before the birth of their two little girls, Riley and Viola, who presently joined us at the table, hands and faces smeared purple with blueberries.

"We picked these this fall, right out there," Riley said, squirming and hanging off the table like a little monkey. Riley was a baby when I worked for Karen in 2006. Now she was four years old and loved being read to and had her own drawing easel and fearlessly climbed up the cabin logs as though climbing up a tree. Viola was a quiet toddler with round cheeks. She looked like a Cabbage Patch doll with big, searching eyes.

The sense of family in their warm, cozy house that smelled like pancakes put Dad immediately at ease. I'd be on my own out here, but I wouldn't be *alone*. Chuck would show me how to winterize my car. Karen would teach me how to look at the dogs' paws for cracks or cuts and tell me when to change the straw in their houses. They'd put in the mushing trail for me, if I wanted to run dogs. They'd warn me when winds were coming that would blow snow across Denebola and make it impassable. "Happens at least once every winter," Chuck said. Then they reminisced about times they'd walked down the road in howling blizzards, unsure of which direction they were going, sinking into chest-deep drifts. They laughed, eyes gleaming, sharing a bond of camaraderie. Hardships like these were what made Alaskans who they were. It's what brought them together and gave them epic stories to tell around the fire years later. Maybe someday, I would have stories like that. Maybe someday, I could be filled with that knowing.

After breakfast, we headed back home and James introduced us to the dogs. The dog yard was a hundred feet from the cabin. Inside its fenced-off perimeter were eight doghouses and a pen. The pen was for Shadow, the resident escape artist whose head was too small for her collar. Shadow was twelve years old and had retired from the Denali National Park Sled Dog Kennels. Back when she was at the kennel, she liked to steal the rings off the fingers of old ladies who petted her in the summertime when the kennels were flooded with visitors. If you looked in the patrol logs at any of the remote backcountry cabins in Denali, you'd see that Shadow had been to all of them. She had traveled at least a thousand miles a winter for nine years. Now, Shadow liked to lay inside on the dog beds or the futon. Her blue eyes would search yours, she'd sniff your hands intently for food, then she would plop back down in a warm place— usually a rectangle of sunshine on the rug.

She shared the honor of being a retired park service dog with Wrangell, who was fourteen years old. Wrangell basically lived inside as well. His hips and his back end weren't so sure of themselves these days, and when he stood on the plywood floor of the cabin his legs would slide apart slowly until he was splayed out like a puppy. He pooped in his sleep. His eyes were clouded over, but if you looked at pictures of him in his heyday, he and his twin brother Elias were big, beefy dogs with luxurious tan, black, and white fur and piercing blue eyes. Wrangell had a deep, throaty bark that was reserved for dinnertime and also for the demons that lurked around in his old mind.

Wrangell's intangible demons were nothing compared to whatever was going on in Otter's head. He was positively possessed. He never ran in harness, but instead jogged loose next to the team whenever James took them out for a spin. He was loopy, like his brain had been scrambled by aliens that time he was abducted (Otter really would have said things like that, convincingly). He slobbered a lot, and mostly wandered loose among his teammates. One time he killed a raven and piled its black feathers neatly in front of his house. It's not entirely out of the question he was making a ritualistic sacrifice of some sort.

I found out because all the other dogs were running around in circles, barking.

"Look what he did!" they said.

From inside his house, Otter stared out maniacally, drooling and smiling like a psychopath.

Otter's neighbor, Williwaw, was a white little witch. Similar to an arctic fox, she had thick fur and black shiny eyes and a pointy little black nose. Williwaw was the leader of this team. She was about ten years old and slowing down a little, but ten years old is still pretty young for a seasoned sled dog. Sled dogs in the neighborhood usually lived till they were fifteen or sixteen years old. They were in the best shape and had spent a lifetime with the best possible nutrition, care, and exercise regimen.

Williwaw was always in lead with Eave, an adorable, floppy-eared snaggletooth who loved eating shit. She would steal frozen shit out of the circles of the other dogs, or snatch it from the poop sled as I dragged it past her house every morning. She had a long body with black and tan fur, and every time you scratched her head she would curl up her lip on one side, exposing a single canine tooth. Her eyes were marbled brown and blue and she never lost a staring contest, but only in a loving way.

Her brother Gable looked like a big teddy bear. He had the same nose as Eave and the same color fur, but his coat puffed out like that of a raggedy stuffed animal. A lion's mane. He only ran in wheel—the position closest to the sled and hence the least able to cause trouble—because he liked to chase baby moose.

Koko also liked to chase wild animals, and he and Gable were the best of friends who always ran side by side. His soft brown eyes looked so much like Max's, and he was roughly the same size. Koko was the resident guard dog, and he would always let you know if an intruder was nearby, the neighbor's loose horses beware.

Then there was Maggie. She was the youngest dog at two years old. She was big and tall, with a lustrous black coat and tan eyebrows. Immediately, she and Moose were in love. They were one year apart and had the same energy level, equally willing to chase one another tirelessly through snow-covered tussocks.

Moose and Maximus were adopted into the circle of friendship by the other dogs in no time. Moose didn't realize his size could be intimidating, and he would run at the other dogs *roo roo roo*ing with his giant ears pinned to his head, tail held low, wanting to play. If nobody else wanted to play with him, he could always count on Maggie. Even when Maximus would raise his hackles, pee on someone's house, and then kick the snow with his back paws to show territorial dominance, nobody was really interested in taking him up on the challenge. Despite the sled dogs' congeniality toward him, Maximus suggested, "Maybe rhen dat tall guy is gone, Mom, you could take some of dose sred dogs to da pound."

"Maximus, I'm not gonna do that, buddy," I told him,

stroking the black line that ran from the circle on his nose up between his eyes like a mask. "These guys are our family now."

Maximus's brown eyes peered up from under my hand.

"He rouldn't even know, Mom."

James hooked up the dog team and took them for a short run before leaving us at the cabin and driving the five hours south back to Anchorage—the place he lived since he got promoted to the regional office of the National Park Service where he worked as a botanist. His wife had left him for a helicopter pilot earlier in the year. The cozy life they had built together, in this cabin and surrounded by their dogs, had caved in and you could feel the sadness of it when you looked in his eyes. I was empathetic, but also self-conscious. Did I look that sad, too? Dad and I stood outside the dog yard and watched the chaos and pandemonium that broke out when James emerged from the cabin with harnesses in hand. Each harness had a name written on it in Sharpie, and each dog eagerly pushed his or her head through the neck opening. Each dog lifted his or her paws and stepped through the body of the harness, lunging and jumping at James, howling with excitement. Shadow and Wrangell were inside the warm cabin and barely lifted their heads at all the ruckus. They had been there, done that. Moose and Maximus, on the other hand, had never witnessed such a spectacle. They jumped up on the windowsills, barking hysterically, smudging the windowpanes with their wet noses as James attached five dogs to the gangline that protruded from his tied-off dogsled. Williwaw and Eave were in lead, holding the line taut, mouths open and screaming; then Maggie by herself in swing (the position behind the leaders) leaping up and down; finally Gable and Koko in wheel right in front of the sled, lunging forward over and over again. Otter was loose, of course, and with the pull of a rope the frantic barking, screaming, and howling ended instantly. They soughed off through the snow, utterly silent, and disappeared around a band of spruce trees that hid the sprawling openness to the west. Dad and I turned back toward the cabin.

The next day, I drove him to Fairbanks and said good-bye at the airport. I didn't cry like I usually did when I said good-bye to my parents. I hugged him and got in the car and drove to the grocery store. I got enough supplies to last me a month. Then I drove 120 miles south on the icy highway, back to the cabin, to begin my new life.

PART 3

Lessons in Being Alaskan

I returned to the cabin in the dark. Shining my headlamp on the snow-covered path before me, I walked up porch steps that creaked in the cold. I pulled the thin wooden trail marker out from a crack in front of the door (to keep the wind from blowing it open and the dogs from escaping) and stepped inside.

There was a slight chill—I was instructed never to put the Toyo heater above 66 degrees—and I appraised the cabin with a sense of ownership. The polished, lacquered wood, sawed and structured by loving hands a decade ago; the tall, multi-sized windows and their thick, clear panes; the cast-iron pans hanging from the ceiling. All the built-in nooks and crannies that utilized every inch of the cabin's small space. When they built this house, Chuck and Karen saw to it that it would have everything a couple and twenty dogs could need.

Since the cabin had changed hands and become James's, I knew it had seen its fair share of pain over the past couple years. Surely it had witnessed the fights, the misery, the loneliness of breaking up just as my cabin back in Montana had. Surely, for James, it had become difficult to step inside that house and see all the memories harbored there, good and bad. He must have felt the jolt of emotion slam into the bottom of his stomach like a rock, just as I did when I'd set foot over the threshold of my old house on Echo Mountain Road. For James, the cabin wasn't fit to be lived in anymore.

But when I stepped inside that house, it was a breath of fresh air. The snow that fell outside that house fell for me. The dogs that howled out in the yard howled for me. The birds that alighted on birdhouses strung along the eaves were for my eyes only, and I savored all of it because I had never lived alone before. That house was wanted, appreciated, loved by me. I knew that cabin and the Alaskan winter that surrounded it would hold untold surprises for me, but I was there, ready to accept them. I had to believe that one day I would be wanted, appreciated, and loved by someone ready to accept the untold twists and adventures of my life. Someone strong and steady and able to turn my pain-filled past into something beautiful and new again.

In my little cabin, everything slowed down. If I wanted to eat cookies, I had to make them from scratch. To simply mix the cookie dough, I had to warm the butter in my pocket or set it in a pan atop the woodstove. Every step I took was intentional.

After Alfred left I hadn't known what I liked. From food to music, I was lost. I cooked eggs every way you could have them and found I preferred scrambled and over medium. I learned how to make coffee in a stovetop percolator. I made homemade pizza and all kinds of bread from a Nigella Lawson cookbook called *How to Be a Domestic Goddess*. The first few tries, the bread came out hard as a rock, with a gooey, uncooked dough balled inside. But eventually, I learned how to coax the bread into being. I learned the exact temperature of the water that would best feed the yeast and get it to rise.

How long to let it rest before punching the air out of it with my fist. How to knead the dough with my hands, spreading and rolling. How to fold it into the shape of an envelope. And finally, how to put the dough into a piping-hot Dutch oven inside a piping-hot real oven with a cookie sheet full of ice cubes on the rack below it to create convection. Eventually I could make bread without the use of a recipe at all. Winging it often had the best results.

The town of Healy sat eleven miles north of the entrance to Denali National Park, in a region known as the Alaskan Interior. Healy was a five-hour drive north from Anchorage or a two-hour drive south from Fairbanks (two of Alaska's largest cities). When people in Healy said they were "going to town," it meant they were driving to either city for groceries and supplies. The closest grocery store, veterinarian, hospital, movie theater, airport...all were in Fairbanks. There were two gas stations in Healy that carried limited provisions (milk, eggs, bread, frozen pizzas) and also a Carquest that doubled as a Polaris dealership (four-wheelers or ATVs in the summer, snowmachines in the winter). People in Healy learned how to fix things themselves out of necessity. Town was often too far away, and Alaskans seemed to pride themselves, however humbly, on their hard-earned self-reliance. But even though they possessed a storied kind of independence, they also relied a lot on their neighbors. Alaskans tried hard to figure something out on their own, but they also weren't afraid to ask for help in order to get a job done right the first time. Time counted, especially when winter was coming or some treacherous blizzard was blowing in or a deep freeze—40 below or colder—was in the forecast.

Shortly after my arrival in Healy, I had seen the forecast heralding temperatures in the -30 to -40°F range and was startled that this came with zero fanfare. No crazy warnings flashed across my computer screen; there was nothing in the newspapers. These conditions were just business as usual. I hopped down from the high back porch of the cabin and walked underneath, pulling the corners of a blue tarp out from under a giant wood pile. James had stacked several cords of dried birch underneath the house and assured me it would be enough to get through the winter. I rolled out a few rounds of the beautiful, fragrant wood. The white bark peeled away like paper. One by one, I stacked each round on a big, flat stump and brought the heavy, sharpened splitting maul down over and over again. The dried wood split with a satisfying crack. Even though it was ten degrees below zero, I began working up a sweat. I peeled off my puffy red coat and continued the repetitive, fruitful work—roll, stack, split, repeat—until the sun went down. Now I had ample firewood for the cold snap, which was due to last three days. I hauled some of it into the cabin and stacked the rest just outside the back door on the porch. I was getting ready, preparing, being competent. It felt good.

The next task was to haul water. Like most cabins in Interior Alaska, mine had no running water and no indoor plumbing.

Chuck and Karen, down the street, had generously offered me their shower and laundry facilities whenever I needed them, and I had showered there once a week and did laundry every three or four. At James's cabin, my cabin, I had a 300-gallon holding tank upstairs, adjacent to my bed. There was an empty water tank in the shed outside that held 150 gallons. James had told me that about once a month I would need to get water, and we had done one trial run when I'd first arrived a few weeks ago. We'd driven to the well house two miles down the road with the empty 150-gallon tank and a hose in the back of my SUV. In the dark (there were only about four hours of daylight per day in early winter), we had donned our headlamps, shuffled across a polished sheet of ice into the well house, and screwed the short hose into a metal faucet. We'd bungeed the other end of the hose onto the opening at the top of the 150-gallon tank. I had slip-slided back across the ice and flipped on a switch that turned on the electric water pump, waited two or three seconds, and then listened for the water to come up the pipe and shoot hard into the bottom of the empty water tank in my car.

On this particular December evening, I arrived at the well house, attached the hose to the pump, bungeed the hose onto the opening of the tank, and flipped the pump on, ready to zone out for fifteen minutes or so while the tank filled with water. The instant the water began flowing through the hose, it wriggled its way free from the bungee cord and flailed like a headless Hydra, spewing water all over the inside of my vehicle that froze instantly on the windows, floor, and seats.

"Fuck!" I screamed. "Fuck, fuck, fuck!!"

Instead of shutting off the pump, I dove after the hose that now had a complete life of its own, ricocheting off every surface and spewing water at ten gallons a minute all over my car and now, all over my face and body. My clothes were absolutely soaking wet, and a white layer of frost formed instantly over my coat, pants, shoes, gloves, and hair. I felt the cold cut into me in a way that instilled fear. My fingers became stiff, incapable of fine motor function. But also, I was embarrassed. Even something as simple as hauling water for my household had become a fight against frostbite in a single, complacent moment.

I resecured the hose with the bungee and jumped into the front seat of my SUV, turning the heat on full blast. My hands hovered over the vents as I eyed the untrustworthy hose in my rearview mirror. When the water level reached almost to the top, I got out and shut off the pump. I detached the hose and threw it into the back of the car with disgust.

"Fuckin' asshole," I muttered to it, under my breath.

After driving home, the next step in the water process was to hook a small water pump to the full water tank inside my car, attach two conjoined hoses to said pump, and run them through the open upstairs window into the three-hundred-gallon tank beside my bed. The tank was upstairs so that gravity could work in my favor and carry water down the series of white plastic PVC pipes that ran from the upstairs tank to the downstairs kitchen sink and into my waiting pile of dishes (or five-gallon bucket of dog food) with no mechanical effort. I ensured all hoses were secure before heading downstairs, going back outside, and walking out to the car to start up the gasoline-powered pump. My clothes had barely thawed from the car heater, and now they were frozen again in a white, frosty sheen. I primed the pump, pull-started the engine, and set it to a medium pumping speed. Water began spewing out of the part that connected the pump to the tank. A vital piece had been cracked.

A day earlier than it was supposed to, the temperature began dropping. I thought I had been smart to begin preparations for the cold snap a day before it was scheduled to arrive, but I learned that night (and would learn again many, many times) that the forecast in Alaska is always wrong, at least partially. By the time I realized what needed to be done, the temperature had dropped to –40°F. Everything breaks at –40. And there I was, rapidly approaching midnight, with 150 gallons of water beginning to freeze inside my car. The little water that had made it through the hoses had frozen almost instantly without the force of the pump to push it through. I grabbed a section of hose and squeezed it, grimacing as it crackled in my hand. No matter when or if I got the pump fixed, I would still need those hoses to get the water into the house. I detached the now stiff hoses and brought them inside, hanging them from the rafters near the heater. I felt it would be impossible to fix the pump myself, but I knew I couldn't let that sense of failure slow my progress. That giant tank of water in my car was a problem that was just going to keep getting worse. So I decided to do what you were supposed to do when you were in trouble—call a neighbor.

But Chuck and Karen had young children and I didn't even know what day of the week it was. Maybe they had to get up and go to work in the morning. I thought through the very limited catalog of friends and acquaintances I had in Alaska. Jess was out on a patrol with the park service dog team, and so was Anna. But Carmen, the assistant kennels manager at the park, had some days off and was the kind of hardy Healyite who knew how to fix everything. I very hesitantly texted her that my pump had broken while I was pumping water and that I, kinda, sorta, needed help. She immediately responded and had me text her a picture of the broken pump. I sat on the tailgate of my SUV in the dark, wearing every coat I had, and shined my headlamp on the black plastic piece that had been cracked in half. I took off my glove to snap a photo and quickly put the glove back on. As I waited for her reply, I took a good look at the small Honda pump. It was duct-taped together in a few places, and I now realized maybe those were critical places. Places that, if they broke, would render the pump useless and would thus render me incapable of hauling water into the house. I started to get pissed at James. That was back before I knew that almost everything Alaskans had, especially in the Interior, was jerry-rigged beyond belief. Many years later, an Alaskan lifer named Claude would tell me how to make the engine light go away on my snowmachine. "Put a piece of duct tape over it," he'd say, "and ride that fucker into the ground."

Carmen was a long time in texting me back because she'd driven over to her dad's garage to look for a similar part. When she couldn't find anything, she told me to drive down there and meet her. Carmen's dad's garage looked like a typical mechanic's shop, complete with naked lady posters hanging on the wall. (Carmen was quick to say how much she didn't appreciate them and hated to be in there, but this was an emergency.) Her dad shook my hand, took a look at the pump, and quickly began crafting his own version of the broken piece. He found a big metal block with the same kind of fitting as the outlet on the tank and, using sealant and a hose clamp, rendered the problem solved in a matter of twenty minutes. Carmen and I hopped back in our cars and drove up Stampede Road, bound for my cabin. We walked inside to find the floor soaking wet. The hoses had thawed out, dripping water all over the floor, and I had neglected to put towels underneath them.

Wordlessly, we sopped up the water with old dish towels. It was one in the morning and waves of cold vapor rolled onto the floor of the cabin whenever we opened the door.

After the hoses were connected to the pump via the new homemade fitting, we pull-started the pump and watched, hopeful but uncertain about whether this device would actually work. Carmen ran upstairs to see if the water was indeed completing its perilous journey up the thin hoses and into the empty tank in the bedroom. I stood next to my SUV and waited, listening for her to call out the window.

"It's working!" she yelled.

It would take about twenty minutes for all the water to pump out of the SUV and into the house, so we sat on the floor of the bedroom upstairs, backs against the wall, trying not to fall asleep. We looked at each other and shook our heads.

"Fuck," we said, exhaling in relief.

It was, I would learn, a common exchange between friends in Alaska. Some understated recognition that you both had barely escaped disaster, but were too tired to discuss it. Rehashing the details, relishing victories, and laughing hysterically about defeats…all that would have to be saved for later. Usually accompanied by beer and a bonfire and a ring of glowing, knowing faces nodding in the dark.

A few days after the cold snap, I woke to a faint light on the hills to the northeast. The sky was clear. The moon was like a fingernail clipping stuck to a smooth, blue countertop. I had been up all night drinking wine and watching *Sex and the City*, trying to fill in all the quiet space around my loneliness. I was so tired, but the dogs had to be fed. No matter the weather or the temperature or the lightness or the darkness, the dogs had to be fed. No matter how hungover I was, being bare-assed in the outhouse first thing in the morning was a surefire way to wake up. And the dogs still had to be fed.

As tempting as it was to feed them in my pajamas and go back to bed, it wasn't a good idea. First, it was −0.8°F that morning. Second, dogs get excited about food. They like to jump and hit you with their paws, and pajamas simply aren't enough protection against sharp nails and cold noses. So after heating water and soaking their food, I got fully dressed in long underwear, insulated Carhartts, fleece, down jacket, hat, gloves, wool socks, and boots. I stepped out onto the porch and pushed the wooden door firmly shut behind me. I set the five-gallon bucket of food, fat, and warm water down, jumped off the porch and picked it back up again, headed intently toward the dog yard.

Koko saw me first. He sounded the alarm that "food is coming!" with a resonant *roo roo rooooooo* and the rest of the dogs joined in. That was the exact greeting I received every morning, whether it was 28°F degrees and the wind was howling or it was -20 and the world was frozen solid to itself. And just yesterday I'd awakened to the sound of the stovepipe creaking against its buttresses on the roof. I had looked out my southern window where the spruce were bowing down low, struggling to stand back up. Magpies and gray jays were buffeted by the gusts, their tiny weight thrown into branches or down toward the snowy tundra. The needles on the trees were blown right off and stamped into the windswept drifts of snow surrounding my little cabin. I felt the whole house rock slowly back and forth, a ship tethered to the dock as the wakes rolled in.

I had worried about the dogs out there in that wind. *As soon as day breaks*, I thought to myself, *I'm going to go out there and find their coats firmly packed with snow. Their ears will be quivering in the cold and the straw from their houses will be blown about the dog yard, like the aftermath of a tornado in a hay field.* Instead, I found them happy and barking, tails wagging, eager to be fed their breakfast. Upon inspection of their houses, the straw was still in place, all of their cozy little nests in order as if the calmest winter night had reached its end. *This is just another day for them*, I thought.

As soon as everyone had a full bowl of the warm broth, all was silent again. Tails wagged lazily as breakfast was slurped down. Then the crew—my crew—of warm, happy dogs sat atop their houses facing southwest, eyes half-closed as they soaked in the sun that highlighted their fur in gold against the white snow. I sat down on the ragged porch-couch and sighed. All I wanted to do was sleep, but the dogs always needed something. For all their buoyant energy, they were still a burden— my burden to bear, alone.

That night I dreamed I was skating down a frozen creek in my slippers. The ice was crystal blue and solid and slick. Before I knew it, I was going so fast, but it was OK. I had it under control and was actually having fun. The ice became crunchy and broken and I could see a roaring river ahead of me as the creek melted into a deep turquoise. I leaped off the ice and onto the bank, only to realize it was a mud so thick and dark and brown that it sucked me down. I grabbed on to alder branches and began pulling myself out. Every heave only got me an inch out of the mud, but I was getting out. In the dream it took a week for me to pull myself only a few feet. It was slow and agonizing, but I never panicked. Nobody ever came to rescue me, even though in the back of my conscious mind I wanted someone to. Instead I watched as the dream wore on. I watched myself, strong and able and alone, struggling. I watched me rescue myself.

The first time I drove to town to resupply was in December. It was –20°F, and the trees on the roadside were crusted in flaky hoar frost. I clutched the steering wheel, not going more than forty-five miles per hour, and was terrified when a figure emerged from the woods on the side of the highway halfway between Healy and Fairbanks. It was a man, I thought. I rubbed my eyes and did a double take with my mouth hanging open. Yes. It was indeed a man, who was wearing a leaf green parka and a faded orange backpack and whose beard and eyelashes and eyebrows were solid white frost, as though his face had been carved from the snow. I slowed down to see if he would stick out his thumb for a ride, but he resolutely continued forward. His gait was clunky, like his feet were the heaviest part of him, but he plugged on with his head down. I learned later that the man was Midnight Mike, a legend in these parts. He lived somewhere in the woods off Stampede Road, and he didn't have a car. He walked everywhere, even to Fairbanks, 110 miles away, with his empty exterior-frame rucksack, to resupply. He sometimes pulled a cart behind him full of trees and brush, and he'd haul it into the woods from the community brush pile. He picked up trash on the highway, arms ballooning with plastic bags flapping in the wind. One time, years later, I saw him in the post office. Up close. His skin was weathered and papery, ingrained with dirt. His long, gray hair was divided into two braids. His eyes never looked up. Every time I saw him, my heart would begin racing. I fantasized about pulling over and asking him to get in the truck with me and tell me his life story. Here I was thinking I was brave for living alone in Alaska, but at least I could get in my car and drive to the grocery store. This dude, this sixty-something-year-old dude, was out here *walking* to the fucking grocery store in twenty below. And it was clear that Midnight Mike wanted his life to be exactly the way it was. He was a hermit. A true old sourdough. And he turned my mind to a time not terribly long ago when this highway was only a trail. The Parks Highway, which links Anchorage to Fairbanks, wasn't even completed until 1971. Alaska was still raw, and its modern developments were relatively recent. Just a few days ago I had seen two red foxes with gorgeous, crimson coats running after each other and fighting and rolling and snarling, right in the middle of this empty highway. This was a place where the wild and the civilized shared a blurry boundary, and the dramas of primeval survival spilled out into the streets.

Over a month had passed since I had arrived at James's cabin, and I sat at the desk in the corner and watched the wind pull apart the clouds and push them around the sky like a child pushing food around a plate. It had been blowing gale force all day, the snow moving like an army of specters through the trees, betraying last night's calm and glittering snowfall. On my porch the new flakes were a sparkling white constellation spread across a matte white sky. I looked at the tiny starlike crystals, no two alike, and accepted the little gift of peace and beauty they offered me. It had been full-blown daylight at 3:00 a.m. Trees' shadows stretched long across the snow. Wispy clouds swirled in the air above, a glowing moon shining through them and onto me. I basked in the moonlight as though it had real warmth and felt it resonate in my soul like rays of sunlight on my skin.

Now, sitting in front of my window and watching the wind, I was thinking about how someone I loved once, and who once loved me, could believe the worst about me. Could believe I was a bad person. My friend Stacey, back in Montana, had called me and told me that Alfred had lost all of our mutual friends. And that he had blamed it on me. He swore I had told them all he was cheating on me, and that's why they'd turned on him. I thought of all the other things Alfred had said when he'd listed his reasons for leaving me back in August. He had said that I'd held him back. That I'd stifled entire parts of his personality. I had thought we had a loving partnership, and that we had enabled each other to grow. I let his narrative consume me for a while, even though there was nothing I could do now to change his mind. I saw the fast-moving clouds out my window and wished I were up there with them, blowing over one landscape and onto another. Blowing over this valley of heartache and into the great, wide tundra, where any insignificant human emotion would surely be swallowed in its grandeur.

I'd come to know nature as a place with no definite coordinates. It was nowhere in particular because there were no limits; it was unending. It was cyclical. It created life and destroyed it. It left me breathless in the best and worst ways. I realized all of the beauty and all of the pain I saw in nature had nothing to do with me. Nature never gave me a sunny day because it knew I saw value in it.

Things that were unthinkable to humans happened every day in nature, and it didn't cause the landscape to crumble. Something we'd classify as ugly, like a wolf taking down a sick caribou calf or a male coastal brown bear eating his own cub, didn't cause the rivers to stop running. Didn't cease the howling of the wind. Didn't turn the rain off like a faucet. It was just survival. It was just life. And maybe there was more to my life than loving Alfred. Maybe there was always meant to be more to my life than that.

I realized the world would not end because of my pain. This was a scintilla of time in the grand scope of my life. The force behind the life I was born to live was humming, churning, flowing like a great river. Blowing like clouds over the mountaintops. Depositing pain in raindrops over the range and feeding flowers that would one day bloom vibrantly. It was a wilderness vast and timeless. It was so much greater than this moment.

It was nearly winter solstice—the shortest day of the year. Those days the sun didn't crest the hills to my south anymore, but hung below them as it made its daily swing from east to west. This extreme angle meant the only light of day was at sunrise or sunset, painting the wind-shaped lenticular clouds magenta and purple on one end of the sky and peached gold on the other. The sun produced a different light altogether from those brilliant rays that once warmed the cabin. Subtle and romantic and decidedly wintry.

The dogs and I wandered the snow-blanketed tundra every day. We started out on the trail along Panguingue Creek, frozen and hidden in shadow below the cabin, and always came out somewhere different from the last time. After feeding the dogs, I'd go back in the cabin to warm up and eat breakfast, then put on my big coat and hat and gloves, walk out into the yard, and let everyone loose. Traveling in a rambunctious pack, we liked to follow what appeared to be trails through the willows and tussocks, out onto a windswept ridge that over-looked a landscape swallowed by mountains and overcome by planar foothills that slanted up into the heavens. Out toward a place where, according to my human eye and its limitations, the world ended. Dropped right off into atmosphere and dust. There was nothing out there.

Sometimes we decided to go off the trail we'd already broken. We'd make our own tracks alongside those of lynx, moose, and snowshoe hare. We'd plunge deep into snowdrifts and get tired. We'd emerge from trees and stumble out onto a blank white plain as far as the eye could see, turn around and figure out where we were, and then go back. It was a little scary to leave the trail, taking those brave steps in a different direction onto untrampled snow. But we couldn't get lost. We could follow our own footprints right back to where we came from.

During that time I had been figuring out who I was while I was alone. I had never been truly on my own until then. I often thought of Neko Case's lyrics on the song "Middle Cyclone":

Can't give up acting tough
It's all that I'm made of
Can't scrape together quite enough
To ride the bus to the outskirts of the fact that I need love.

I curled up in the rocking chair beside the crackling woodstove at the end of each day and stared out the window until the sky went black. Until the only thing I could see was a reflection of myself, blurry and wrapped in a robe and drinking wine with a journal on my lap.

I've found this present melancholy to be as beautiful as the lingering sunset, backlighting black spruce trees, causing every little needle to be perfectly outlined. It has caused me to carefully examine myself. To test myself. To get to know myself. It has exposed hidden parts of me while bringing dead parts back to life. As scared as I thought I'd be to love again, I want it. I'm ready for the sun to come out from behind those hills and light my heart on fire. Till then I will continue to explore the untracked snow. No matter where I end up, all trails lead back to me, under a mouthwatering purple sky.

One night in December the dogs barked sounds of alarm. I walked out to the dog yard in the dark, headlamp lit. The dogs' reflective irises peered back at me from atop their houses while the stars winked at me from the sky. A black field of glowing dots. And then, two more sets of glowing dots peered out at me from the road. I shined my headlamp at them, expecting to see a moose cow and calf. But two horses snorted and stared back at me, unfazed by the din of barking dogs.

"Where the hell did you guys come from?" I asked them. They just stared.

I walked back inside and called Chuck and Karen.

"There's…horses…out here," I said.

"Oh, they probably belong to Coke Wallace," Chuck said.

"There's somebody named Coke?" I asked.

"Yeah, I think his number's in the phone book," he said.

"Coke?" I asked again. "Like C-O-K-E?"

I took out the Healy phone book that James had left underneath the cordless landline phone and flipped through the white pages to the Ws.

WALLACE, COKE and JOANN.

No shit, I thought to myself. I dialed the number.

"Hello!" answered a man's voice.

"Hi, yes, is this…Coke?" I asked.

"How'd you know I was here!" he said.

"Uh…" I stammered. I found out later that he spent much

of the year out in the bush, guiding hunting trips. "Well, I think I have your horses here. Outside my dog yard. I'm down on Denebola."

"You know what? Just throw some snowballs at them and they'll come home," he said.

I laughed.

"OK," I said. "I'll try that."

I went back outside and tried to pack a snowball, but the snow was powdery and dry. I looked at the horses.

"You guys get outta here!" I yelled at them.

They flicked up their snouts and their manes fluttered. I felt like I had betrayed them a little bit, by suddenly being mean. I took a couple fast steps toward them, stomping my boots on the packed snow of the road, and they ran off. I watched them go in the beam of my headlamp, until the sound of their muted clip-clopping on the snow could no longer be heard.

The dogs settled back down in their houses, sighing in the straw. I turned my headlamp off and looked at the cabin, shedding light out its windows and onto the snow. Its brightness couldn't dim the clarity of the stars above. They were like baby's breath, broken and sprinkled on black paper. Cream spilled across them in the form of the Milky Way, the arm of an entire galaxy extending into the cosmos.

I didn't follow astrology. I didn't know what moon was in what house at any given time. All I knew was that I'd lain on my back and watched the exact same sky at vastly different points in my life and each time the sky had given me something memorable. A spectacularly starry night in the Rocky

Mountains in Colorado forged one of the longest friendships I've known. On the other side of the world I watched Orion sink into the sea, lower on the horizon than I had ever seen him. On the Salmon River I witnessed stars connect the dots with other stars and race off in opposite directions. I'd seen glinting stars reflected on the water of a hot spring while steam caressed my face and froze my hair. In all instances the heavens were fascinating, captivating, brilliant, and clear. Their mind-boggling network dwarfed me, rendering me insignificant.

But that December night, what I saw in the sky drew me up tall. Lifted me off the ground. Stole my heart from my chest and sent it aflutter like a bird trying to escape its cage. The aurora borealis drew three big arcs of light from one end of the sky to the other. Slowly they brightened from pale green to brilliant white. They undulated, and angular curtains stabbed out from rounded streams that moved delicately, then frantically. Luminous fingertips drumming along the windowpane of night. Green, then white, then purple.

Meteors burned trails into the heavens like rockets. They fell everywhere. They fell constantly. They streaked right into the aurora, light cut with light. It was overwhelming. It made my heart pound hard. Held my jaw agape in wonderment. Caused me to hold my breath. Caused me to draw it in quickly. I stood in the dark out on the snow-covered tundra, but a spotlight might as well have been shining down on me. This is for you, the sky seemed to say. From the beginning of time you were always supposed to end up right here, right now, on this most wondrous of evenings. Here is a gift for you, a sign for you, to let you know you are in the right place. A place full of magic and serendipity that exceeds even your colorful, romantic imagination. A place where you are beckoned to bravely allow love back into your heart and given the strength to hold it there with all your might. From my spot on the tundra I stared, clear-eyed, straight into my future—a place more full of opportunity than any I had ever seen, but only if I had the guts to disappear into it.

Breathlessly, I turned and walked down the road in the dark. I wanted to see if the horses had found their way back home.

It was a week till Christmas and there was plenty of snow on the ground, and I was bored. Looking for distraction, I remembered the one time I had been on a real dogsled, back in 2007 with Jess, pushing that heavy sled through feet of dense snow on the Savage River in Denali National Park. During my summer internship at the park kennels in 2006, I had also hooked up a small team dozens of times during demonstrations with the same dogs, showing tourists the excitement and willingness of the only working sled dog kennel in the National Park Service. The summer kennels staff used historic leather harnesses and an old wooden freight sled on wheels, zooming around a short gravel track and ending the tiny loop in front of a grandstand where we then answered questions about the sled dogs' coats and feet and diet.

Now's as good a time as any, I thought to myself as I took the labeled harnesses off their nail on the log cabin wall. I strode out to the dog yard with the gear I thought I needed: a little waterproof bag with snacks, handwarmers, a warm fleece balaclava to cover my face, and an extra set of gloves. James had left me some humongous overmitts that hung off a lanyard that went around the back of my neck. He had also left me an oversize parka that would fit over all my existing layers if I needed to really get warm. On my feet I wore a pair of bunny boots—white, rubbery moon boots made for military parajumpers that kept your feet warm and waterproofed at the expense of the leg muscles that had to lift the heavy things.

When the dogs saw I was carrying the harnesses, they went berserk. I had been living with them for nearly two months and all we had done until that point was go on walks. I pushed the light little sled out from the corner of the dog yard— James's dogsled was essentially four sticks nailed together atop a smooth plastic sheet—and tied it to a fence post, hoping I remembered how to properly assemble a quick-release knot. I unraveled the gangline, a long cable covered by nylon onto which each dog is attached, and made sure the tug lines and necklines were untangled. Tug lines attached to the back of each dog's harness allowed them to pull the sled, while neck-lines clipped to the dogs' collars made sure they didn't turn around and get tangled with the dog behind them. The gang-line went right down the middle of the dog team, emanating straight from the dogsled, and a pair of dogs was attached to it, one on each side, with the neck and tug lines.

Once I had the sled set up, I began harnessing each dog.

I walked to Williwaw first, putting the harness over her head. She dutifully stepped through the leg openings of the harness while screeching hysterically into my ear. I unclipped her from her tether and she ran to the front of the gangline, knowing she would be put in the lead position. I snapped the tug line in place on her harness and she stood at the front of the empty gangline, leaning forward, holding it taut. I repeated the process with Eave (my other lead dog), then Maggie, Koko, and Gable. I put Moose next to Maggie and he looked extremely out of place, towering incomparably above all the other dogs. Moose was so excited he began grabbing the section of gangline in front of him, hauling back on it and letting it go. Eave and Williwaw were being yanked backward and released, over and over again, but never turned around to see why.

The whole team screamed and lunged and barked and launched themselves into the air. My heart was about to explode and my hands were shaking. There was so much power in front of me, and the little empty sled lurched and swiveled against the rope that held it. Why had I done this? There wasn't even a trail out there! This was a really bad idea, but it's too late now. With both feet on the brake, I crouched down and pulled the quick-release knot (it worked!) and was yanked violently forward into the unknown.

It took me a minute to catch my breath, grasping white-knuckled onto the handlebar. All of my focus was in front of me, on the dogs, on the invisible trail. We were going somewhere, fast, but only the dogs knew where. I felt each bump and fold of the landscape, and quickly we were far beyond anywhere we had ever walked. I knew the commands you were supposed to give your lead dogs—"gee" for "right" and "haw" for "left" and "on by" when you passed another dog team or a loose dog or moose on the trail—but I didn't say any of them. What did I know about where the hell we were going? The dogs were hauling ass and nobody looked back, not even Moose, who had only run in a dog team one time before, in a sled dog race back in Montana. They panted and the sled runners made a *shhhhh* sound as they glided through a foot of unbroken snow and the wind flowed over and around my insulated ears, and those were the only sounds. Except my heart was thrumming and that was the loudest thing. I was sure the dogs could hear it.

It was –15°F, a perfect temperature for mushing. The world was huge and we were small and directionless. Before long, we crested a low hill and the view spread out before me of a wide, white expanse. Along its edge were the angular shapes of rooftops in the trees. One of them belonged to my cabin. The dogs picked up speed and I rode the sled with one foot on the runner and one on the track brake. I was gliding forward, closer and closer to home, feeling an immense trust in the dogs getting me there.

It wasn't until we pulled back into the dog yard that I realized I had been holding my breath. I knew never to let go of the sled and my whole body had been clenched, my entire existence revolving around that one vital credo. But in the hour that we had been gone, the dogs had taken me on a tour of their backyard. At places where surely there had been a trail intersection, they cocked their ears back toward me awaiting a command and then made their own decisions in response to my silence. They had taken me out on an adventure and returned me safely home, all without a word. It was a wonder to feel so vulnerable and so electrically alive. I let the dogs loose in the yard and they took turns licking the frost from my eyelashes. Panting, they rolled around in the snow to cool off and then dutifully jumped back onto their houses, waiting to be tethered. I trudged back into the house, carrying the pile of gear and harnesses, and pulled off my hat in the warmth of the cabin. Maximus glared at me from the futon, betrayed, but I couldn't even pretend to feel guilty. My cheeks were rosy and my hair was in a greasy swirl, and I most certainly had dog shit under my fingernails, but my heart glowed. I had found it.

Over the past few months I thought I could fix anything, solve anything, make anything work. But that day, I learned to let go and trust that things would work out the way they should. I allowed myself to be pulled into the unknown to figure out exactly where I was. It turned out the middle of nowhere was actually the middle of somewhere amazing, and I was a little dot on the map that described it.

That night as I sat in my rocking chair, the words flowed out through the pen in my hand.

From the runners the world is pure, undiluted. Raw energy hums along the gangline and into my hands and feet. I can feel the dogs' excitement or fatigue in the speed of their gait. I ride the runners and let the wind whip through my frozen hair, my caked, white eyelashes. Or I run alongside the sled and push, push, push. Give the dogs some help when they need it.

From the runners I gaze upon a landscape untrammeled by man. Scenes unfold before me that clean out any other thought in my head. I am wholly in the present, faced with so much beauty I can hardly breathe. The sun sinking low in the early afternoon, casting a brilliant orange glow on a frozen lake, silhouetting my dog team as Denali's slopes rise indomitable and massive in the great blue distance. Neon pink alpenglow sharply contrasted with deep shadows on clefted, windswept peaks. A large crescent moon slowly rising in a navy sky, so perfectly drawn apart from its surroundings I feel I could reach out and pick it from the atmosphere.

I stand on the runners and forget about everything. I have no past, no history. I am this very moment, I am excitement, I am intuition, I am love between a woman and her dogs. I am pure and undiluted. I am the world that surrounds me.

PART 4

Tor's Tooth

When my neighbors, Chuck and Karen, built their house, they had twenty sled dogs out in the yard. Karen was the kennels manager for Denali National Park for nine years and they lived for the dogs. Their life was mushing and all that went along with it.

Now, I walked down the street from my house to theirs and looked out over what used to be the dog yard. Old doghouses squatted there with their maws empty, covered in snow. Other things occupied that space now, like piles of treated two-by-fours covered with tarps and a woodshed that sheltered stacks of split birch. The only dogs to be heard were my own, calling after me as I walked up Chuck and Karen's driveway.

Inside their house, it was clear that life revolved around children now, not dogs. Wooden toys and little kid chairs and tables, a chalkboard that doubled as a painting easel, a box of dress-up clothes—everything two adorable little girls could want or need. Almost all evidence of Chuck and Karen's past life was gone, and it wasn't because they didn't look upon it fondly or perhaps even wistfully at times. Something more important had captured their hearts—their two little girls. All the care and energy they gave the dozens and dozens of pups who had loped through their lives at one point or another was eclipsed by all that was needed by Riley and Viola, and one by one they found new homes for all the dogs in their dog yard. Karen retired from what most would agree is the coolest job on the face of the earth. And on the weekends Chuck juggled home improvement projects with wrangling two daughters who had an absolute hold on his heart and attention.

Though my life had taken a decided turn for the better, my past life was in my everyday thoughts. I still had pictures on my computer that I would stumble upon and then delete. Alfred's name still showed up in my mail. Alfred's handwriting appeared on my cardboard moving boxes. Memories of when our life was good and the nightmare of when it turned bad hadn't stopped stirring in my mind. The thought of it still hurt my heart. But watching Chuck and Karen gave me hope.

I thought, *One day all of this pain will transform from a stumbling block into the foundation for a new life. This winter will make way for a sunny day in May during which the spring cleaning of my soul and mind will take place. Then those new, dustless shelves will be so welcoming to the bigger and better love coming to occupy my heart.*

The holidays were imminent, and some acquaintances from the park invited me to "Stitch n' Bitch" night at the community center in McKinley Village, a half hour south of Healy. I was hesitant about going. I didn't really know anybody except for the girls at the kennels, all of whom were out on the trail with the dogs, and my social skills were beginning to deteriorate. But that night I found myself among a handful of women who sat in a circle, knitting Christmas gifts for their friends and loved ones. I was terrible at knitting, but one of the ladies there started talking to me about sourdough baking. She ended up giving me a Xeroxed chapter of a rare Alaskan cookbook called

From Cache & Cupboard. It was chapter 12, "All about Sour-dough." Whoever wrote the cookbook—I didn't know, I only had chapter 12—called sourdough starter "a living critter," saying things like "sourdoughs don't get sick very often, but sometimes they become a little tired." There were six different recipes for sourdough starters—a slow-developing yeast with a distinctive sour flavor. And the starters thrived when you fed them. "Each time it 'eats,' it likes to have six or eight hours in a nice cozy spot to digest its food before you ask it to raise any doughs."

And beyond the starters were pages and pages of mouthwatering recipes for sourdough hot cakes and waffles, breads, doughnuts, and muffins. In the side margins were little tips like this:

Tin snips and a pair of pliers are all you need to make a good cookie sheet from a 5-gallon gas can. A little more ingenuity is required but you can make pie pans and cake tins, too.
—Former Wasilla homesteader

Back at home that night, I followed the directions for "Otto's Sourdough Starter." In the morning I made the recipe for "Honest-to-Goodness Sourdough Bread" ("Your arm should be sore from trying to stir!") and patiently let the dough rise for four hours ("Let it take its time"). After placing my pan of rising sourdough on a shelf near the stovepipe, I cozied up in my rocking chair by the woodstove and did some reading.

There were all kinds of interesting old books you could check out from the kennels library—a dusty bookshelf behind the kennel manager's desk at the park—and I had been reading about Grant Pearson, one of Denali's first park rangers and superintendents. I came upon a black-and-white photograph of a woman in a wool dress with puffy sleeves and a thick, bonnet-style hat. She had a staff in her hand and trudged through ankle-deep snow, leading a string of seven massive dogs all carrying packs of supplies. Beneath the photo was the following passage:

When Grant Pearson first met Fannie Quigley in 1926, she was 55 years old and had been mining and living in the Kantishna Hills for 21 years. He described her as "up and at 'em. She was a dog musher, prospector, trapper, hunter, woodcutter, gardener, and one of the best sourdough cooks I have ever run across.

"At a Christmas dinner once, Fannie served black bear roast, gravy, mashed potatoes, fresh cabbage, hot rolls, currant jelly, cranberry sauce, and fresh blueberry shortcake.

"Only the flour and sugar had been freighted in. The rest was from the country."

I became fascinated by Fannie Quigley, and inspired by her, too. I wanted to learn more. I jumped on my computer. In the hours it took the sourdough to rise, I devoured one article after another.

"Like the men around her, Quigley drank, swore, and shot

bears—but unlike those men, she used her bear lard to create the legendarily flaky crusts of the rhubarb pies she served to her backcountry guests," wrote one biographer.

The tales of Fannie's hardy exploits were riveting. She had come to the remote Kantishna Hills on the west side of what is now Denali National Park to mine for her fortune. She showed up, along with hundreds of other hopeful prospectors, in 1905 carrying a portable stove and food supplies. She opened a business to feed the other miners and built a life for herself, marrying a fellow miner with whom she eventually parted ways. But farther down in one story came a letter she had written to her friend Charles Sheldon, a sheep hunter and conservationist who first proposed the idea of Denali National Park and was integral in its founding. She wrote, "I went to Fairbanks last fall. that was my first trip to town in seven years. I didn't see woman for three years. I tell you, I got lonsome…"

On Christmas Eve Day, I received a big envelope in the mail. I sat in the post office parking lot and opened it. Divorce papers. I sighed and set the packet in my lap. I flipped through the pages that recounted how we had nothing to split up between us. We had no assets together. We had no house. We had no children.

Somewhere in the middle of the last page, we had to certify *This marriage is irretrievably broken.* Signed, Alfred Robertson. Your signature here.

I put my face in my hands and cried. I was gutted. But it was the only way to start over.

The next day I attended an ugly sweater party at C-Camp, the seasonal employee housing area at Denali. I tried to do the theme justice by drawing a fifth-grade-level Santa Claus on a paper bag, gluing cotton balls to his beard and taping the bag on the front of a green cable-knit sweater. When I left the party, a light snow had fallen, making the road down from park housing more slippery than usual. While rounding a turn, I lost control of my SUV, slid off the road, and skidded to a halt in a bank of deep snow. My heart was in my throat. I took a deep breath, put on my headlamp, and walked around the car to survey the damage. Nothing. Phew! I got back in the car and put it into reverse, making an attempt to back out of the snowbank, but the wheels spun and spun on the ice. I rooted around in the back of the car, looking for anything I could use to dig myself out. I pulled out a windshield ice scraper—A + for preparation—and began "shoveling" snow out from underneath the car, attempting to make a pathway for the tires. When I realized this was going to take maybe literally forever, I called my friends back at the party up on the hill. Minutes later, they arrived with shovels, transported by a stranger working the late shift at the park dispatch office. Four of us shoveled the car out of the snowbank, and I gave my friends Alonzo and Anna a grateful hug. I turned to the stranger and, in the light of our headlamps, only the lower half of his face was revealed. He had a blond beard, curved lines at the corners of his mouth, and a strong nose. At the nape of his neck, curls of thick hair protruded from underneath a winter hat. I thanked him and hugged him, too. I thought to myself, *He's hot. At least the bottom half of his face. Maybe I'll see him again someday.* I got back in the car and made my way home to Healy, eleven miles north.

It was the first of February. I had been running James's dogs nearly every day and volunteering at the Denali Kennels with Jess whenever she needed me. A group of acquaintances who worked at the park invited me to drive up to Fairbanks with them to see the start of the Yukon Quest 1,000-Mile International Sled Dog Race. This year, the race began in Fairbanks, Alaska, and ended in Whitehorse, Yukon Territory, but the race switched start locations between the two towns each year.

I was mesmerized as I stood atop the Cushman Street Bridge overlooking the frozen Chena River. Beneath my feet passed long strings of paired dogs, each team adding up to fourteen, with a lone musher on the back of the sled. The mushers were tall, because their boots were made up of inches of insulation. They all wore headlamps on their heads even though it was daylight. They were draped in humongous parkas that hung down to their knees, with wolf or wolverine fur ruffs protecting their faces from the biting wind. They were serious or joyous or relaxed or petrified, depending on how many times they'd departed on this journey. I had never seen anything like it. There were more than three hundred dogs barking, lunging, leaping, howling. The energy was transcendent as each team was walked beneath the Cushman Street Bridge to the starting line by a bevy of volunteers. The volunteers each had a leash clipped into the gangline, and some of them fell down and got dragged across the ice by the excited, powerful dogs. Every musher stood firmly on the metal claw brake, the *crrrrr* sound of the brake biting into the ice drowned out by crowds cheering and dogs screaming frantically.

And then, one by one, each team was released to thunderous applause. The dogs undulated, tug lines taut, as the musher was trailed by a rooster tail of ice and snow shooting out from behind the sled brake. They were facing forward, focused, and they were going to go *one thousand miles*. I studied their disappearing forms and my imagination went with them. I wanted to be one of them, almost desperately. I yearned for it with my whole being.

One morning in late February I got a call from a satellite phone. It was Jess, on patrol with the park dogs. She was at East Fork Cabin, forty-three miles into Denali National Park, and she had a dog who'd been in a fight.

"Tor's canine tooth is dangling from his upper jaw, and he needs to go to the vet," she said.

She asked if I could meet the team at the park entrance and drive Tor to Fairbanks, and I agreed. Arrangements were made through the park for a government vehicle and a hotel in town, but then an ice storm hit and the highways were deemed "hazardous" by the Department of Transportation. The park decided to assign a paid employee to drive Tor and me to the vet. I arrived at our designated meeting place, overnight bag in hand, when a government rig pulled into the parking lot. I slid open the door and took note of Tor in a kennel in the back. I told him hello and he recognized my voice and thumped his tail against the hard plastic crate. I sat in the backseat so I could be close to him. When I looked forward into the rearview mirror, I saw a pair of dreamy blue eyes looking back into mine. The beard and long hair had been shorn, but the parenthetical lines around the corners of his mouth were immediately recognizable. It was the handsome stranger who dug me out from the side of the road more than a month ago. He introduced himself as Andy. His voice was so quiet I leaned forward to hear him better. He was so beautiful I could barely look at him.

When we arrived at the veterinarian's office, they were just about to close. The vet had agreed to stay on late to do Tor's surgery, so Andy and I sat in the waiting room as the staff began closing up shop. We were deep in conversation—talking with him was easy—and we barely broke eye contact as we lifted up our feet for the vacuum cleaner to pass under our chairs. We talked about music we loved—Wilco, Ryan Adams—and I asked him how he got to Alaska. He hesitated, then said, "I just always wanted to come here, ever since I was a kid. So when my fiancée of seven years and I broke up, I got in the car and drove here last winter with my dog, Willa. All the way to the end of the road."

My eyes widened. I just stared at him with a look of total disbelief. He laughed.

"What?"

I shook my head. "Nothing," I said.

"Tell me," he said.

I shrugged and laughed. "Well…it's just that, I did the exact same thing."

He raised an eyebrow.

"My ex-husband and I were together for seven years and when it ended, I drove up here with my dogs," I said, looking down. "To start over, I guess."

I lifted my eyes back up and he was looking straight at me. He didn't look away, just held my gaze right there. There was a magnetism to it. A yearning to find out more. But also, I felt, an understanding. Like he knew the pain of the past year without me saying a word.

After that night with Tor and me, Andy began volunteering at the park kennels. He was strong and athletic, able to lift heavy lengths of timber and load them into the dogsled. He ran in front of the team and helped break trail. He laughed with abandon, his cheeks rosy. He knelt beside the dogs and let them lick his mouth and nose. When he talked to Pingo, one of the leaders, he called her "friend." I would go home from an afternoon volunteering and Andy would stay with me all day in my thoughts.

There was, of course, a roadblock. In January I had had a one-night-stand-turned-one-week-stand with a young hunting guide who worked on Kodiak Island. He was in Denali visiting my friend Anna—they had gone to school together in upstate New York. He was tall and manly, with dark hair and cobalt blue eyes. He smoked cigarettes. He walked around with a rifle slung across his back, just in case he saw a fox. He wanted to make me a fox fur hat that would match my red hair. He had a thing for redheads.

I'd been craving bodily contact. So when Bill came over to go out on a dogsled ride with me, I saw an opportunity. After a day out on the trail, he stayed for a grilled cheese sandwich and soup. Then for a movie. Then for making out. He was hot and I never thought I'd see him again. What the hell, I figured. I need this.

What I really needed, though, was to fill the void left by Alfred. And so in the week that Bill's flight to Kodiak got delayed again and again, I convinced him to love me. I didn't lie to him, but I did everything he wanted. I said everything he wanted.

"Would you put your hair up?" he'd say. Or, "You'd look so beautiful with makeup on."

Finally, he told me he loved me. I knew it was coming— I had engineered the moment perfectly. First with a northern lights viewing, then a delicious meal, a bottle of wine. It was his last night there before a guiding stint. As soon as he said it, I felt instantly satisfied and not satisfied at all. Getting things the easy way felt cheap. Like cheating. The gutted-out feeling that Alfred had left me with was a permanent scar. It felt futile to have this person try to fill it one drop at a time. He wasn't the right person and I knew it. But I wanted to feel filled so badly.

Though he had left for that trip to Kodiak more than a month before, Bill had vowed to return. Shortly after Andy, Tor, and I returned to the park, I drove south to Anchorage to pick Bill up from the airport. He would be staying at my house for two weeks before going back for the spring and summer, when I would leave to return to Montana for my summer Forest Service job.

"I'm just gonna tell myself Andy has a tiny dick," I said to Stacey over the phone.

"Kristin, you cannot do that," Stacey said with a laugh. "You are allowed to see more than one person at a time. You know that, right?"

I sat on the phone silently.

"Right, Kristin?"

"I don't know, Stacey, Bill fuckin' told me he loved me. And I wanted him to!" I said.

"Just because all you've ever done is be in a monogamous relationship, doesn't mean you're supposed to marry every guy you meet, Kristin," she said sternly. "Andy sounds amazing and I think you should give him a chance."

Right, but how do I give him a chance with this other guy staying at my house? I wondered.

A bigger, looming question remained, too. How do I give him a chance if I'm moving back to Montana in two months?

With Bill asleep in my bed, I tiptoed down the steep wooden staircase and watched the northern lights out a downstairs window. They wound in a green, orbital swirl, then faded. I texted Andy and told him to look out his window, too.

He wrote, There's a Rilke line that goes, "Beauty is nothing but the beginning of terror." And I think of that line every time I see the northern lights.

I smiled. Who the fuck writes a text message like that? I had learned at the vet's office that Andy had all but finished his PhD in lyric poetry and phenomenology. He had taught creative writing at Brown while he was a grad student, then went on to the University of Denver for a PhD but never wrote his dissertation. He and his fiancée had been breaking up and getting back together and moving all over the country working odd jobs before finally going their separate ways.

Throughout the week I'd sneak a peek at my phone to see if he had written anything. Sometimes, we'd text each other at the exact same time. We were always on each other's minds, it seemed. But I couldn't say that to Bill.

On March 13, my friend Angela invited me to her birthday party at a nice restaurant down in McKinley Village, about forty-five minutes south of Healy. Bill wasn't feeling well, so he stayed at home. I knew Andy lived nearby, so I shot him a text and told him about Angela's party.

I'll save you a seat, I offered.

When he walked into the restaurant, I blushed. He wore a nearly threadbare plaid western shirt with pearl snap buttons, and the deep blue in the plaid perfectly matched his eyes. I waved him over and he sat by my side, right where two tables had been pushed together. Later, when he got up to go to the bathroom, Angela grabbed my hand and excitedly chirped, "He's cute!"

After dinner, we all went back to a neighboring house where everyone but Andy and I did mushrooms and smoked continuous bowls. People whirled around and laughed and played games in a blur, while we were in our own sharply outlined world. We weren't afraid to stare at each other. I stared at him because I didn't quite believe he was real. There was something familiar about him, but I couldn't pin it down.

By the time we decided to leave the party, it was 1:00 a.m. Even though I was sober, I texted Bill that I had had too much to drink and was going to spend the night at Angela's. I drove Andy home and he invited me in.

We walked inside and the house was dark. Not just because it was nighttime in March, but because blue foam board covered all the windows.

"Don't you want to see outside?" I asked him.

He mumbled something about the foam being good insulation, keeping in the heat. Looking around the house, my heart felt heavy. Not only were there about two pieces of furniture, but also every window was covered up. He was hiding in here.

I sat down on a shabby blue love seat while Andy got us two glasses of water. I didn't know if it was because of the late hour or because I felt sad or maybe because I didn't want him to feel alone in his sadness, but my throat tightened and tears filled my eyes.

"Andy, I was..." I struggled to finish the sentence, and wasn't sure I should have started it. "I was...left."

I sank into the cushions. I wasn't afraid to be ashamed and broken in front of him. The truth was, the person who had known me better than anyone in the world had already left me.

"I'm so sorry, Kristin," he said, coming to my side and setting down a glass of water for me on the table. He very gently put his arm around me.

"I'm sorry," I said. "I'm still kind of a mess because of all of it."

He put clean sheets on his bed and told me I could have it. He would sleep in the loft on the other side of the house.

"You don't have to," I said. "It'd be nice to have some company, if you want."

He gave me a T-shirt and some baggy Thai-style pants his hippie, yoga-instructor ex-fiancée had gotten him.

"I don't even know how to put these on," I said, laughing.

He very carefully wrapped the waist of the pants around my torso and held out the drawstrings for me to tie. He did it all without touching me.

We got in bed and sat talking, shoulder to shoulder, for a

long time. I told him about Alfred. I told him about Bill. By now it was four in the morning, and we were both struggling to stay awake. He let me rest my head in the crook of his arm as I faced him. Very slowly and very gently, I touched his arm with my fingertips. I ran them over his skin in slow, sweeping motions. It was smooth and white and freckled. I ran my fingertips up to his neck and down to his heart. I could feel his heart beating. I wanted to touch him, but I didn't want to touch him. He was fragile. But I needed to know he was real. He was the most beautiful man I had ever seen, and I couldn't believe he wanted anything to do with me.

He reached out and stroked my cheek with his hand. He traced the curve of my neck. I couldn't see his face, but I could feel how he was holding his breath. I could feel the heat emanating from both of our bodies. I knew it was getting close to 5:30 a.m., when he would have to get ready for work. I began to sit up, but he leaned in toward me.

"I don't want to make life more complicated for you, Kristin," he said, looking right into my eyes.

Those eyes were crystal blue. Deep as a pool of cerulean water, with a flicker of light in them.

"I don't think I'll be able to stop thinking about you," I said.

He pulled me to him with surprising strength. He held me tight and lowered me down, palm pushing into my lower back, cradling me. He pressed his lips to my lips and held them there so sweetly, like this kiss was a careful gift. My eyes had been closed, but I opened them in that moment, just to make sure this was truly happening. A fringe of long eyelashes fluttered, like they wanted to open but he willed them shut. I closed my eyes and held him tight. His body was leonine—muscle and sinew—under pearly smooth skin.

We went downstairs to eat some breakfast before he left for work. He made egg sandwiches and couldn't finish a single bite—something I would later learn was exceedingly rare for Andy with his monstrous appetite. My entire body wouldn't stop shaking, and I crossed my arms around myself to try to make it stop. Inside, my soul was on fire, flaring at the sight of him. It felt as though we were long lost partners, lovers reincarnate, finding each other again.

That day I went home and told Bill he had to leave. He cried. He was twenty-three years old and had a hundred dollars to his name and had just traveled all this way to be with me, the woman he thought he loved. I felt like an asshole. But my relief as he walked out the door was immediate. I could stop pretending now. I could make a choice about who to love and how to love carefully and honestly and without desperation. I could build a foundation ever so slowly. And this time, I wouldn't let my mind lie to my heart.

Andy and I took turns staying at my house and going over to his house. I took all the foam board off the windows and brilliant March sunshine lit up the floor in neat rectangles that Moose, Max, and Willa laid in. Andy bought furniture from a coworker and Willa claimed the throne-like recliner while

Moose and Max slept tail to tail on the massive green couch. We held one another and stared into each other's eyes for literal hours. It seemed like we were absorbing each other's histories. Like we didn't have to speak at all if we didn't want to.

Andy fell in love with Moose, Maximus, Maggie, Otter, Williwaw, Eave, Gable, Koko, Shadow, and Wrangell. He put his arms around them and let them lick his nose, eyes, and cheeks. I taught him how to mush and he fell for that, too. He radiated sincerity.

Andy's voice for Moose was so spot-on that I knew he understood Moose's sense of humor right away. Most people were intimidated by Moose because of his unbelievable size. Or they found him aloof. Even stupid (those people were immediately crossed off my friend list, not to be trusted). But Andy understood Moose's intense curiosity. His frank assessment of his own size. That perfect Moose voice could be described as a cross between Scottie Pippen and Cleveland from *Family Guy*.

"Hey, man!" he would say when anyone entered the house.

"I'm just this tall, Maw-ma," he would explain when his chin rested on the countertop, sniffing our dinners.

"Maw-ma? Brother-Dog says he doesn't like Girl-Dog," he would claim, translating for Maximus in reference to Willa.

"My brother-dog is going to kill that bird, Maw-ma."

The spring days began to lengthen and stretch, erasing the darkness six minutes at a time as we headed toward the equinox. Andy and I hooked up the team and took turns driving and sitting in the sled. The dogs trotted forward into the landscape and we never spoke or looked at each other.

Occasionally one of us would point something out, like a distant herd of caribou or Denali's looming silhouette, and the other would smile and nod or give a thumbs-up. But we understood the rules of mushing. The silence was a gift. The focus was always on the dogs.

Toward the beginning of April, the snow began to rot. We put the dogsled away and brought the harnesses inside to dry out before storing them for the summer. Andy had just spent an entire day hiking around on the tundra looking for Maximus, who had run away when the wind blew the cabin door open. After eight hours, Andy had called me at the park where I was volunteering, a little panicked. I told him to just wait him out. Maximus always came back, even if it was days later. When Maximus finally returned home, exhausted from chasing a herd of caribou for twenty-four hours, Andy lifted him up and carried him into the cabin. He laid him down on the futon and hand-fed him until he got all his strength back. Maximus didn't really like anyone else, and would often hide in the corner whenever other people came over. But he loved Andy after that, and would often crawl up onto the couch and nuzzle his head into Andy's lap. He wasn't the only one falling in love.

A few nights later Andy and I stumbled outside into a solar storm whose invisible winds whipped light across the earth's atmosphere. It was a show beyond compare. Light moved like snow blowing across the road in a blizzard. Thousands of miles per hour. Pulsing at the whim of some invisible hand, from one horizon to another. To and from all four directions. White, green, red, purple. Xylophonic. Keyboarding. Curtains, swirls, stabbing blades, flashes on and off. And we two below it, necks outstretched, mouths open, billowing guffaws and gasping in disbelief. The energy burned images into our eyelids, infusing us with some untold thing.

I always had an urge to downplay my pain, to belittle my hardships, to think they were nothing in the grand scope of horrible possibilities this world harbors. But then, what had I endured to deserve this? This unparalleled magic that was my reality. So much wonder. I sat cross-legged at the foot of it all. A student of the ineffable world, mouth agape, feeling myself grow bigger so I could take it all in.

In mid-April, my phone rang and a Montana number flashed on the screen. It was my trail crew boss calling to see if I was returning to work this summer. I thought about how amazing that job was. How satisfying it was to see my progress at the end of a hard day's work. About the remote trail, the wolves, my loyal crewmates, and what they did for me after Alfred left. The whole experience was magical and healing.

But I felt with sudden urgency that I didn't want to leave Alaska. The second sentence out of my mouth upon my arrival in November had been: "How could I ever leave this place?"

My face upturned, lit by twinkle lights as I marveled at the big crossbeams of my precious cabin. That wall of tall windows before me. Nearly half a year had gone by since I set foot over the threshold. Since I decided to let my grief grow up strong and fully developed, right in front of my face. Let it finish what it had started in that big empty house in Montana. Or at least give it the chance to become less of a stranger. And out of that silence came a flourish of new knowledge. I was allowed to be who I was. No emotion ever had a reason to be stifled. The grief or any of the others. All of them were living side by side, within me, in this place.

Earlier that afternoon my boots had broken through a thin layer of snow, the warm wind had rain on its breath. It was too warm to mush now, and the ten dogs and I hiked uphill on a trail of our own making, one that was rapidly disappearing with the melting snow. Up there in the sunlight, the sweet scent of water and burgeoning pussywillows blossomed in my lungs. The snowshoe hares were marbled with brown now, and new birds flocked to the ground around my back porch every day. And I was this fledgling, perched at the edge of a small but paramount period of time spent growing and learning. Each day devoted to nothing but those sad, intimate, nurturing, lonesome lessons.

I looked wistfully at my bunny boots and refused to put away the harnesses that hung on the wooden drying hook. For me the Alaskan winter was not something to live through, but to live for. The big white cold. So bleak and purifying. The dogs' rhythmic panting and the sough of the sled through powdery snow. All winter long, I had stood solitary on those runners and watched my relaxed shadow twist and glide and grow long to the north, touching on willow branches packed with crystals, on frozen riffles of lake water.

I didn't want to leave Alaska because I didn't want to let go of someone. I didn't want to let go of Andy, but also I didn't want to let go of me. I was still fleshing out the details, but right there in that place I had found the root of myself. A seed had grown from the pit of my stomach and out through the rest of me. Branches sprouted from my ears and head and chest. Roots drove down deep into the dirt through the soles of my feet. To uproot would surely feel like tearing out my own heart.

I called my boss back and told him no, I would not be returning. It was painful, because I loved the friends I'd made so much. And I loved that smoky, rugged country. But that same day I got a summer job offer from Denali National Park to be a backcountry ranger. The job entailed patrolling the trailless wilderness of Denali for days at a time, and issuing camping permits to visitors. It felt like the universe was in cahoots with my heart. I accepted. They needed me to start right away.

Eleanor was a platinum blonde who wore leather pants and drove a motorcycle, and also she was my more experienced patrol partner—it was her second season as a backcountry ranger. In June, she and I were on a ten-day backcountry patrol that had us crossing the Alaska Range and then floating down the West Fork Chulitna River back to the Parks Highway. We'd start the trip by trekking through the most popular backcountry areas in Denali, making sure people were following the rules of their backcountry permits. Then, we'd venture into some of the more remote sections of the park—places backcountry rangers hadn't patrolled in years.

As the two of us climbed higher and deeper into the trailless Denali wilderness, we made some mistakes. We went a few miles in the wrong direction, then gave ourselves the nicknames of S.B. (Stupid Bitch) and D.B. (Dumb Bitch), laughing as we made our course correction and got back on track. In a headwind full of stinging ice crystals, we lugged our heavy packs up and over Anderson Pass, where massive, unnamed glaciers tumbled down to meet us.

"I'm naming that one Cuntface Glacier," Eleanor said.

Not many rangers had come this way in recent years, so we were traveling in the blind, so to speak, when we made a bad decision about where to go on the West Fork Glacier.

"Well, this is stupid," Eleanor said as she leaped across a turquoise gorge of rushing water over the glacier ice.

One false step and she could have been swept down into a crevasse—a bottomless crack in a glacier—never to be seen again.

After safely crossing the gorge, we looked out ahead of us. The glacier's belly emerged, here and there, like a greasy, black slug from piles upon piles of graveled glacial moraine as far as the eye could see. Over thousands of years, this receding glacier had chewed up rocks and churned up the surrounding landscape. Over the next eleven miles, it would send us easily, invitingly, in one direction only to show us cavernous sinkholes or turquoise ponds filled with icebergs or moulins where water poured over the ice and disappeared forever. We struggled, finally setting up camp at midnight and falling asleep without eating our dinner.

The next morning, we inflated our pack rafts and put in on the West Fork Chulitna River, which gushed forth in a powerful gray spray from the toe of the West Fork Glacier. I flipped my boat and lost all my gear. The raging torrent carried me for a quarter mile, bouncing me off rocks and sucking me under rapids. I gulped for air loudly and uncontrollably, like my body was trying to keep itself alive without my brain. I was surprised by the desperate noises coming from my throat. I realized that nobody was going to rescue me from the current, nobody could, except for me. I planted my feet—something you are never supposed to do because your foot can get stuck in river-bottom boulders—and launched myself out of the water. I landed on my chest on a large boulder and clung to it while the current pulled at my legs and feet. From there, I pulled myself up onto the rocks, panting. I was alive, and I had rescued myself.

Miles later, Eleanor and I were reunited. We gave each other a hug, then got down to the business of setting up camp with only half our gear—my pack had disappeared around a bend in the river along with my raft. We had no tent, no cookstove. We ad-libbed. We used a trekking pole to hold up the rain fly and staked it out with river boulders. We mixed dehydrated soup in a gallon ziplock bag, then cut the corner of the bag and squeezed the cold soup into our mouths. We sat on the banks of the West Fork, our backs to the sinking sun, and brushed our wet hair and laughed. The only things missing were lounge chairs and cocktails. We felt ready, in an easy way, for anything. Barefoot on the high riverbank, we knew that river would look no different whether we had pulled ourselves from its waters hours earlier or not. It would have been the same ashy current, the same misty clouds shoring up against the high passes, the same summer sunlight without our breath in it. But here was a place to witness simple, raw beauty. To see how earth was shaped. To see where rivers were made. And to walk on and in those forces made us feel at home. In the heart of a wilderness so big as to render us insignificant, we were a force, too.

That summer I told Andy I loved him. I did it for myself.

I said, "Everyone in my life who I love knows it, except for you."

I told him that I needed him to know before I took off on some long backcountry patrol and faced all the dangerous things out there, and that if anything happened to me I would have regretted not telling him how I felt.

He panicked. He said he wasn't ready for the responsibility of love.

"I will be careful with your heart," he said.

Months later, in early August, Andy and I were on a

three-day backcountry patrol together. After we set up camp, I sunk into the fragrant green tundra and faced upward, wind swirling my hair into a mess. The sky was decorated by a lazy painter, roller of white pressed not quite hard enough onto a ceiling of blue.

I sat up and the light parceled out every inch of surface in my vision, individuating each strand of my hair, each blade of tiny tundra flora. It was impossible not to feel all the particles of energy I inhaled. Impossible not to turn all my attention, unaffected, to that very moment. In the backcountry, I tuned in to breathing, to stepping on surfaces, to feeling cold water in my boots, to inhaling the scent of wet summer grasses in the sunlight.

Something bothered the corner of my view and I snapped to noticing them: dozens of caribou filing by, their dainty hooves clattering against the gravel but the wind making a silent movie of it all. Thick shining coats the color of coffee, velvety antlers, their peaceful countenance and doglike way of checking in. What a kinship we felt with them, those graceful wild animals. Allowing us a blessed stay on their ground for a few nights.

The next day a prism of color arced over that great, green swath—double rainbows of distant rain colliding with sunshine. Our backs pressed against a giant rock blocking the wind as we peered onto a river bar with our binoculars and watched a pack of eight wolves weaving and loping in intricate formations. And then the peaks, the polychromatic mountainsides, embroidering the world in a jagged circle from one horizon to the other. My heart and mind were a single, unwavering line warmed by the sun—a pure agreement reached by them only in this setting. And then Andy's voice in my ear.

"I think now is a good time for me to tell you that I love you," he said.

I measured time in seasons now, rather than the days composing them. Instead of feeling rushed along by the new season's approach or anxious for winter, I greeted the fall with a gratefulness slow and full. It was the time of year when we all could take a deep breath and stop running around crazy to fulfill the needs of park visitors. We could see each other's faces around the fire again. Pick blueberries until the sun set and see the moon's glimmer in a shroud of evening clouds.

Andy had taught me the beauty of slowly built foundations. What gorgeous decoration time and thought and patience could add to my own architecture. And what I found was not my frustration at things not happening right away, but instead the gratefulness and happiness that overwhelmed me suddenly for the smallest things. I saw now how every trial rooted itself underground, under my ground, and how they had spent last winter deciding how they would push through the earth and grace my days. All those bulbs with roots fed by heartache and hurt and loneliness. To look at them now, how they flowered up slow and graceful but full of vigor and full of color. Not to be ignored or forgotten, but rather incorporated into my life and welcomed and tended. What a surprise and a relief to see their petals float to the ground one by one. To see the soil in which they now go to rest as a composition of nurture and gentleness and love. Not as the entrance into a finality, but as an entrance all its own. The first step into something.

September was a smash of color, blinding even with the sun already set. The pointilism of fluttering golden leaves set against black spruce. The never-ending carpet of red, sweeping for miles and then creeping up mountainsides to dissipate in white powdery peaks. "This is our home," we said, still not quite believing. "This is where we live."

And in the simple wonderments of foliage and light we continued to find ourselves awestruck. To have traveled all this way alone, empty. Knowing only one thing, and that one thing was North. Reconstituting our insides down into their simplest ingredients and holding fervently to them. And then we were called out of the dark to stand in the light and be recognized. You, we said. I know you.

PART 5

A Winter in the Wilderness

From my upstairs window the doghouses were perfect white squares in the twilight. The first dusting of the year found the flatter surfaces and settled there and on rooftops and in spruce boughs. The curtains were off the windows in the cabin and the moonless night's appearance was unchanged whether my eyes were open or shut. It was the time of year to burrow, to hibernate, to bed down.

Yet I awoke earlier than ever, donning my headlamp and warm clothes. The bucket clanked on the porch as I set it down, and before I'd turned to close the door, the dogs cried out in expectation of a warm breakfast. I fed them, drove to work on the dark, icy highway, pulled in to the park service kennels, and warmed up water. I finally had the job of my dreams, working as one of the real dog mushers at the park, just like Jess had done. In winter, the park service dogs helped accomplish all kinds of projects in designated wilderness, where no motorized vehicles were allowed. They hauled building materials to remote backcountry cabins for repairs. They carried researchers out to monitoring stations scattered throughout the park, along with solar panels, batteries, and other equipment. They also maintained a winter trail system from park headquarters out to McGonagall Pass, at the base of Denali.

I quickly fell for the park service dogs. They were huge— up to one hundred pounds, with shining, thick coats and an air of troublemaking about them. We communicated like dogs did. With nuzzles and growls and howls. With touch and eye contact and also another sense that existed only between human and dog. A heart sense, I think. Where they could feel what was in my heart, could sense the good in it or the fear in it, and knew how to fill it up in ways nothing else could. My back hurt, but my heart grew big and bigger still for those dogs.

Most of my days in the backcountry with the dogs were full of hard work. In a typical day, I mushed twenty miles in temperatures as low as -40°F, breaking trail for ten of those miles, running alongside the sled and pushing it through three feet of snow or walking ahead of my team on snowshoes when it got deeper. I got up in the dark. I got to the next place in the dark. Throughout the day I'd eat a handful of food and drink from my thermos when it wasn't frozen shut. When I arrived at a park service cabin exhausted, I'd unharness my team, stake them on the cable dropline, put away my sled, and get out an ax. I'd walk down to the river with a pull-behind sled and three buckets, hack away at the dense river ice until water splashed all over the front of my bibs and into my face, freezing in lacy patterns on my clothes. I filled up the buckets with water, hauled them back to the cabin, and began heating water for the dogs' dinner. By the time I ate I was ready for sleep, but there was always a minute when I lay down in my sleeping bag and wished for those loving arms around me. Wished for Andy to be there, smiling, touching my cheek, telling me he loved me. More than electricity or running water or three square meals, that was what I missed every day on the trail. For days and days and days.

Back home, at James's cabin, I didn't have an endless litany of chores to do in exhausted silence. Andy always stayed there while I was on patrol, so all the dogs were fed and cared for. At precisely 6:30 p.m., Moose and Max would unfurl themselves from their beds and Willa would run down the stairs and the three of them would stand and watch the door with bated breath. They'd hear the boots knock against the porch steps and the door would open and Andy would crouch down to let them kiss his face. After several minutes of romping dog rodeo—complete with Maximus skipping sideways, Moose *roo*ing with ears laid back, and Willa rearing on hind legs— Andy would stand up. "Hi, human," we'd say to each other with a smile. The dogs would retire to their cozy beds, curling up by the woodstove. And outside the window was the purple sky and the red glow on the mountains and the shimmering, silver moon.

At the kennels, I learned a dozen different knots for a dozen different uses. I always tried to tie a bowline—the strongest knot. When tied correctly, it was a beautiful thing—the sinuous loop like a bow in a river with a line to something important emanating straight out of it. It was the knot used by climbers to create an anchor. It was a knot on which to rest the certainty of your existence. I loved it so much that I often tied it at the wrong time. Once, in the fall, I accidentally used it as a quick-release knot, and when I tried to pull it loose, the ATV bucked and almost flipped, attached to a tree while twelve dogs were trying to pull it forward with all their might. Another time was when I was hauling materials out to a backcountry cabin by myself, doing a project alone for the first time.

It was −10°F and everything I wore was soaked in sweat. I was hauling a hundred-pound sledge behind my dogsled and it was loaded with firewood and three new mattresses. As I separated the sledge from my dogsled to pull it down the narrow, quarter-mile-long walking path to the cabin, a swell of nervousness enveloped me. While I had made sure the leaders were tied off to a tree and the sled was tied securely to a road sign, I knew it would take me nearly half an hour to haul the sledge on my own power while breaking trail to the Savage Cabin, where I would switch out the old mattresses for the new. We were fifteen miles into the park, and if the dogs somehow broke free while I was gone, I would be stuck out there.

As rapidly as I could, I unloaded the sledge, switched out the mattresses, wrapped the old ones in a tarp, and secured the load onto the sledge with ratchet straps. As I finished, I stood and listened. Nothing. I hauled the old mattresses back down the trail, visualizing the worst-case scenarios. I could see each and every one of them as vividly as real life. This was Arc's first full season in harness, and she was still a youngster with bad habits. What if she chewed the gangline and set the rest of the team free? Yakone was old-school, nearly ten years old, but he had been leading teams down these trails his whole life. What if he thought I was making a mistake and decided to turn the team around and now they're all tangled?

I turned the corner back onto the main trail and saw seven sets of pointy ears and seven wagging tails off in the distance.

I sighed with relief. *OK, first crisis averted*, I thought. I still needed to untie the team, turn them around without causing a fight or tangle, reattach the sledge with the old mattresses on it, and travel fifteen miles back to the kennels. It was about 3:00 p.m. One hour of daylight left.

After one moderately tangle-free turnaround, I attached the big sledge. The dogs were going crazy. I had made them wait long enough, and now we were finally going home. I got on the runners and took a deep breath. It seemed like I was actually going to pull off this operation singlehandedly, and mentally I celebrated. I imagined mushing back into the dog yard and the kennels manager patting me on the back, saying, "See? I knew you could do it." I crouched down and found the tail of the knot I had tied, and while yanking the end of it I yelled, "OK, guys! Ready?" The dogs barked and leaped forward into their harnesses like they were running into a brick wall. The sled wouldn't budge. I looked behind me, back at the post to which I had tied the team, and eyed the knot. It was a bowline. That knot was not coming undone, no matter what. I looked down at the rope, then back to the post, then down at the rope again. Should I cut it with my knife? If I do that, I won't have any rope at all for the whole run home. What if I ran into a moose and needed to tie off my team to a tree? I couldn't risk having no way to secure the dogs. I looked forward at the dogs who were by now becoming unhinged. The tug lines were violently pulled taut as they slammed into their harnesses over and over. I decided I should cut the rope halfway between the post, which was about fifteen feet away, and my sled. That way I would at least have enough rope for an emergency. I walked behind my sled as nonchalantly as I could and took out my knife.

"Just take a break, guys," I said to the dogs. "Calm down."

The dogs were panting, looking back at me. They were quiet.

"Good dogs," I said as I very slowly began cutting the rope with my knife. "That's it, nothing to see here. Just taking a break."

My knife blade gnawed through the last fiber of the rope and I dove for my sled just as the dogs took off at a dead run. I grabbed on to the frayed tail end of the rope and held on for dear life. Two metal snow hooks clanked on the trail underneath me, having failed at their job of anchoring the sled. The golden rule of mushing was so ingrained in me by that point that it was more of a natural instinct: never let go. I closed my eyes as my shoulders dragged against the packed snow, feeling my grip loosen. I held on for a hundred more feet and was overcome with a sense of dread as the end of the rope slipped through my hands. I stood up in a panic, watching my team fly down the trail back toward the park headquarters. My clothes and pockets were packed with snow. The dog team got smaller and smaller. And then, to my complete surprise, they made a miraculous left turn onto a grown-over trail we didn't use anymore—an old habit from winter patrols past.

"Woah, guys!" I yelled as I sprinted toward the team. "Woah, woah, stay right there!"

I was not calm. My heart was exploding out of my chest and my hands were shaking with despair, excitement, and relief all at once. I got within arm's length of the sled and dove on top of it. The sled and the dogs were ensnared in spruce trees, but nobody was growling yet.

"Good boy, Yakkers!" I said to Yakone, grateful for his old habits. "What a good dog."

Once I steered the team back onto the main trail, darkness crept in at the edges of the sky. The forested world was encased in a crystalline frost, and a dense fog began to cloak the lower elevations. A subarctic sunset at its shoulders, Denali emerged from the back of the Alaska Range, eighty miles away, and towered over its much nearer counterparts. True cold was setting in, and the dogs developed a hoary halo around their fur as my eyelashes and hair and face mask froze solid. The flat light made the snow harder to decipher, but it didn't matter. I trusted those dogs now. We had been through a trial together, no matter how stupidly the trial came to be. And in the coming season, we would go through so many more of them.

With every patrol I learned how to be a better musher. Jen, the kennels manager, had run the Yukon Quest the winter before she was hired to replace Karen. She taught me how to think calmly in stressful situations, and to take charge and make decisions. Even in the chaos that was dog mushing through gnarled willows on a creek while the ice collapsed beneath the dogs' feet, she said if you see someone go in the river, you run your team around them and keep moving forward so that their dogs will follow you and pull the sinking sled out of the water. She had faith enough to put me in charge of multiple patrols, to allow me the chance to lead. My confidence grew.

My last patrol of the season was going to be epic. My

patrol partner, Toubman (one of many Jesses in Denali who went by her last name), and I would be out for three weeks, breaking trail along the north boundary of the park to Wonder Lake ninety miles away and stopping along the route to do maintenance on a research station.

The trip began in complete silence in a thick, cottony blizzard. Then, after three feet of snow fell, the wind came. It blared like a jet engine as it blasted us from the west, and nothing was out there to stop it. The tundra was endless. The wind swirled in sheets like a ghostly aurora, turning distant trees to black smudges, blanching the dark fur of the dogs, blurring even the closest ones to the sled from our sight. *In case you needed a reminder, you are insignificant*, the wind seemed to say.

Once the wind finally stopped, we saw that it had cast all the footprints out on the trail in bas relief. Anywhere the snow had been packed down by something—a dog paw, a fox paw, a ptarmigan foot, a dogsled runner here and there—it was now raised up, the wind having whittled away all the loose snow around it. Bits and pieces of the trail were visible, but most was left to the imagination. We looked to the dogs to put in the trail, but instead of facing forward and taking up the gangline, they simply looked back at us. The blank white space can be terrifying and confusing to dogs who are used to traveling through varied topography, with trees and mountains providing reliable landmarks. And out there on the north boundary of the park after the storm cleared, it was blinding white tundra, searing late-February sunshine, and faded blue sky. No landmarks. Toubman and I realized it was our turn to lead. She was a GPS guru and loved trail-finding, and I was much more comfortable mushing dogs than she was, so she strapped on a pair of snowshoes while I tied our two dog teams together and mushed nineteen dogs at once. I held the giant team while she marched ahead, GPS in hand, finding the right route.

It took us eight days to reach the research station whose maintenance we were scheduled to complete on day three of our patrol. If the dogs didn't break trail, we broke it on foot. A second storm came in, and even if we walked into the wind and broke trail out as far as we could, by the time we turned around to go back to a patrol cabin it would already be wiped free. Those days, the dogs led us home by their noses. We took turns following each other. We took turns knowing the way. Between two girls and nineteen dogs, a trust was woven tighter with each passing mile. The care we took of each other was the only controllable thing. And then we fell into the river.

With Toubman in front of the sled on snowshoes and me on the runners, we struck out on the Clearwater River early in the morning. The second storm had ended, and the snow was deep and sparkling. Pyro, an energetic two-year-old leader with a lustrous black coat and testosterone-fueled confidence, led my team onto the frozen waterway covered in three feet of new snow. The dogs kicked up a fine, sunlit powder as they pranced, picking up their paws high. It could not have been a more beautiful day, one we felt we'd earned after more than a week of hardship.

First, Pyro disappeared. "What the hell?" I said, stopping the team. "Toubman!"

The dogs froze. I stomped in a hook while Toubman hurried back to the dogsled. I made my way to the front of the team and saw Pyro dangling down into a ten-foot-deep fissure in the shelf ice, water flowing below. His partner, Cassin, curled up into a ball on the ledge of the crack, making sure we wouldn't move forward. We pulled Pyro up by the harness and hauled the team way over onto the shoreline of the river. Toubman and I looked at each other, terrified.

"The whole rest of the river is going to be like this," she said. "There's so much snow, we can't know what's underneath."

We didn't know what to do. We were running out of food and needed to get to the next patrol cabin. But we were paralyzed.

"It's times like this I just think, what would Jess O'Connor do?" Toubman said.

I thought of Jessie, my best friend in Alaska for so many years now. Jess was small and hardy and smart and practical. She had the sense of humor required of Alaskan wilderness travelers. Toubman and I decided that in this situation, Jess would say, "Oops, I fucked up!" and then she would keep going.

I remembered once during a summer dog demo how Karen had told the park visitors that she let her most trusted leader loose to run ahead of the team and lead the way when breaking trail over rivers. The dogs had a much better sense of the thickness of the ice and the location of ice bridges under the snow than we humans ever could. Toubman and I let three trusted dogs loose. She followed them on her snowshoes, tamping down a trail. I stood on the brake and held back the dog team until she gave me the signal to follow her. We made it up the river without falling through the ice again.

It was hard not to be scared every day of the trip after that. But it wouldn't get us anywhere. We had to be practical. We had to break down these overwhelming situations into one step we could accomplish at a time. So at the end of the trip, Toubman and I returned to the kennels with a stunned sense of relief and accomplishment. We quietly put all the dogs back in their houses. Nobody was there to greet us. We heated up water and fed the dogs a meal. It was so strange to come back after such an epic, transformative time away, to no applause. No fanfare.

While I was on that patrol, Andy had moved my two duffel bags of things from James's cabin over to his place. We had decided to move in together, and his house had running water and more than one room, so it made the most sense. I drove to Andy's house and walked inside. Moose, Max, and Willa jumped all over me, sniffing my clothes intently. Andy wouldn't be home for a couple more hours. I rounded the corner and walked into the living room, and strung across the room from wall to wall was a giant homemade banner in the shape of a ribbon blowing in the wind. *Welcome Home!* it said in Andy's handwritten cursive. I laughed. I looked down and found a typewritten note with a date from two weeks ago, folded in triplicate on the coffee table.

```
Five  days  now,  &  I've  been  picturing
you  in  your  various  backcountry  mushing
```

dispositions—on the runners with your hat bundled tight against the cold, or in the makeshift yard feeding, or under a wool blanket in a cabin with the woodstove piping & the ice crystallizing on the windowpanes. I thought of you as I stood outside under the blood red moon, that strange & sudden darkness over the white tundra. Or while I curled up with the dogs on the futon, or ran them out to Fish Creek. I thought about you while I cooked dinner, or listened to music, or slept, or awakened. I thought about you while I breathed.

I've not committed to writing yet my gratitude for your presence in my life.

I walked into the bathroom with a smile still on my face and looked in the mirror. Last year I was embarrassed by the wrinkles in my face, the creases of heartbreak and hardship burrowing and furrowing. And now there were more of them, but their character was different. They came from squinting as I mushed into the sun. They came from laughing till the muscles burned in my ribs. They came from surprise after surprise after unexpected surprise. And disbelief. And awe. And from loving somebody that much. I thought they were beautiful.

I finished off my season as a musher for the park service by volunteering at the 2011 Iditarod Trail 1,000-Mile Sled Dog Race. I was flown out to the remote checkpoint of Nikolai, a tiny village on a bend in the Kuskokwim River on the north side of the Alaska Range, on the outskirts of Denali National Park. My job was twofold: represent the park service kennels by doing some outreach and education, and work with veterinarians caring for "dropped dogs"—dogs mushers had decided to leave with the veterinary team for reasons ranging from strategic (it takes a lot less time to put booties on ten dogs than it does twelve) to injuries (sore wrists, tweaked shoulders).

I worked for a day to help get the checkpoint ready for the mushers, dragging bags of each mushers' supplies out to the packed-down dog lot and lining them up in alphabetical order by last name. I couldn't fathom the amount of work it must have taken for the mushers to plan out every bit of food and gear they would need for a thousand miles well before the race and ship it out to themselves at these remote checkpoints.

Out of nowhere I heard someone yell "dog team!" with great enthusiasm. I stopped to watch as people from the village emptied out of their houses. We stood there on the edge of the Kuskokwim River in total silence as the sun was coming up. Then we heard jingling—the tags on the dogs' collars. Around the corner came a perfect sixteen-dog team belonging to Martin Buser. They trotted uniformly on frozen white water, each with an identical gait. It took my breath away. I had never seen dogs move like that, with such grace and efficiency.

They weren't very big like the park dogs—more like forty to sixty pounds—but their coats were thick and their legs were long, and they were cohesive, of a piece. They had just traveled more than two hundred miles in two days, and now here they were. I tried to wrap my mind around that. At the kennels, we mushed forty or fifty miles in two days, and I thought that was covering quite a bit of country. But these dogs had run four times that distance in the same amount of time, and they were all wagging their tails and giving kisses to Martin Buser.

I watched him in awe. In less than five minutes, he had taken all sixty-four booties off his dogs, fed them a hot meal, and bedded them down in straw. He was bubbly, ecstatic to be leading the race, and he answered questions from the press with a high-pitched Swiss accent. His eyes were striking blue in contrast to his wrinkled, weathered face and his red-and-black-checkered trapper hat. I knew that between Nikolai and the last checkpoint, Rohn, was some of the craziest, most rugged trail in the race, but nobody asked Martin Buser about the adventures he must have had. That's because Martin had run the Iditarod thirty-one times and had won it four. But you could tell just by watching that it was still a thrill for him, decades after his rookie run. He unfurled a blue sleeping bag and laid it in the straw beside his dogs.

"I sleep here for maybe an hour," he said with his thick accent.

Then he crawled inside the sleeping bag and was sound asleep in under a minute. It blew my mind that he would be getting up in one hour to do this all over again. And that he would do it for seven hundred more miles.

More and more teams began to arrive at the checkpoint and I watched the dogs in disbelief. They were barking, screaming, wolfing down food. I had never seen athletes of that caliber. I watched the mushers, too, and made assessments. Some of them, like Martin, were searingly efficient, getting their dogs hydration and nutrition and rest in mere minutes. And some of the more novice mushers would stand and talk to the race officials and to the press in a daze, looking around at the dog lot, distracted. They would begin a sentence, then trail off, while their dogs remained standing on their bootied feet.

"Those dogs could have been sleeping for the past ten minutes," another musher would mutter.

I took it all in. I thought about what I had been through with the park dogs. Everything in me welled up—the years, the miles, the lessons. All the things I had overcome to stand right here. I knew without a doubt the purpose that would drive me now—to embark on a great journey, perhaps the greatest one there was, with a dog team of my very own. I watched the next musher leave Nikolai and disappear around a bend in the river. I longed to know what they would see out there. To experience it the way that they would. My imagination forged ahead, up into the wild distance, and I vowed that someday soon, it would be me on the runners. *By 2015*, I thought. *It will be me by 2015.*

PART 6

Learning from the Champ

W ell, aren't you just a regular Fannie Quigley," Jeff King said to me as we stood outside Andy's cabin. He had just bought the place from Andy's landlord, and I was filling him in on the plumbing issues and how we "fixed" things when they broke, sugarcoating nothing.

"It gets pretty fucked under here," I said, squatting to point under the house where the gray water was expelled from a white PVC pipe. "A little mini ice-climber would have a great time under here in the winter. We usually just pour boiling water down the drain to break it all up."

After giving Jeff the tour of the house's issues, I sat beside him in the late August sunshine on the porch. Not only did he own a lot of real estate in these parts, but he was also the winningest musher of all time, with four Iditarod championships, one Yukon Quest championship, and literally dozens of mid-distance race wins. He had made over a million dollars by winning sled dog races alone, and that didn't include his immensely successful summertime tourism operation down the street. Three times a day in the summer, busloads of tourists would arrive to get a tour of his beautiful kennel, Husky Homestead. They would sit in a grandstand and watch the dogs run in team around a short loop, then hear stories from the trail. Jeff had been mushing dogs since 1976—he had a *lot* of stories. Last year, though, he had gone through a divorce and retired from racing, selling all but twenty-two of his most promising young dogs.

"I went through a divorce, too," I said.

He squinted and cocked his head. "Huh," he said.

I could tell he wasn't interested in sharing any kind of intimate, personal sob story with me, a practical stranger. So I told him I was a dog musher, too.

"If you're not running your dogs this winter, how about I run them?" I proposed. "I live right down the street from your kennel; I can go over there and feed and run them every day. I don't have a winter job."

Jeff had one leg crossed over the other as he leaned back on the porch chair. He looked at me in silence. Then he said, "Well, I'm thinking about running the Iditarod again."

"Oh, holy shit!" I said, surprised. "That's great!"

"I realized after not doing it last year that it was a thing that makes me truly happy, and I plan on running it every year until I can't anymore," he said.

Jeff was fifty-six years old, short-statured, and athletic, like many dog mushers. His fingers were a bit gnarled, from where he had lost sections of them to frostbite. I could tell he wasn't very trusting of people, being an Alaskan celebrity and all. But I wasn't guarded around him. I told him exactly what I wanted and exactly what I thought.

"Well, I'm going to run the Iditarod someday, too," I said. "By 2015. That's my plan."

"Oh really?" he said, raising his eyebrows and turning the corners of his mouth down in contemplation.

A few days later Jeff called and asked if I wanted to work for him as a handler and live in the handler cabin next to his dog yard. "Adam can come, too," he said.

"It's Andy," I corrected.

People had to impress Jeff first before he bothered remembering specifics like names. And Andy worked for the National Park Service. And Jeff, like many Alaskans, hated the park service. In 1980, when the Alaska National Interest Lands Conservation Act was passed, much of the country was uproarious with glee. Alaska's flourishing wildlands were a resource for all Americans, and now they would be protected forever inside the boundaries of national parks, preserves, and wildlife refuges. Alaskans viewed it differently. They saw their backyards on which they had come to rely for subsistence—food, shelter, livelihood, and general good health—being locked up. Celebrated Alaskan author Seth Kantner once famously said that the concept of designated wilderness terrified him. "What could I eat out there if I'm not allowed to shoot my dinner?" he asked.

But it didn't take long before Andy impressed the hell out of Jeff. In the middle of the night when it was colder than -60°F (that's the lowest the thermometer went and that little red arm was bottomed out, hard) the heater in the handler cabin sputtered to a stop. Andy threw on a parka over his pajamas and went outside to discover the coal hopper that fed the heating system was on fire. If he didn't do something quick, the entire thing would melt down and catch the adjacent shop on fire. Thinking fast, he jumped into Jeff's bobcat, miraculously fired up the engine, and began removing the piping-hot coals from the hopper with the shovel of the machine. He got as much as he could out of the big metal funnel, then he drilled holes in the bottom of it and poured water over the remaining coals, putting the fire out. Jeff remembered Andy's name after that.

The fire incident marked the beginning of an extremely cold winter. All the big rivers were frozen by December—something that was basically unheard of in recent memory. We celebrated when the temperature climbed to –30°F. "Finally, warm enough to run dogs!" we said.

Running dogs with Jeff was eye-opening. I had never seen twenty-two dogs hooked up at once, on the same gangline. And I certainly had never seen anyone run a dog team with a truck. Every morning, before it snowed enough to be on dogsleds, we would load up the twenty-two dogs and drive a half-hour south to the Denali Highway, a 135-mile gravel road that became an unmaintained winter trail in the off-season. Then we'd unravel the gangline, attach it to the front of Jeff's Dodge Ram (a prize from winning the 2006 Iditarod), and hook up all twenty-two dogs. They launched themselves against their harnesses, rolling the truck forward and back against the parking brake. It seemed fucking insane.

Jeff was completely calm. "Calm and assertive," he'd say to me almost every day. "When you're running dogs, you want to be calm and assertive."

Then he'd put the truck in drive and off we'd go up the highway at ten miles per hour, for longer and longer distances each time. The morning of one of those drives, signups for the first mid-distance race of the season had opened. The Sheep Mountain 150, a 150-mile qualifying race, would begin in early December. If you finished it, it counted as a qualifier for the Iditarod. You had to qualify before you could sign up by running several mid-distance races. The Sheep Mountain was a twelve-dog maximum and a ten-dog minimum, and Jeff had signed up with twelve dogs, and only one spot remained. We had ten more dogs in our team, so with palms sweaty and heart racing, I waited for about seven miles as we chugged up the Denali Highway with the dog team strung out in front of us before asking, "So...do you think I could race a ten-dog team in the Sheep Mountain?"

Andy sat beside me with his hand on my thigh, steadying me. We had practiced what I would say the night before and it definitely didn't come out how I had planned, but it was out there now. The worst he could do was say no.

Jeff laughed a big, open-mouthed guffaw, slapping his hand on the steering wheel.

"Only took her seven miles!" he said to Andy.

He agreed I could run the other ten dogs in my very first sled dog race. I could not stop smiling.

The snows came and Jeff had me run a six-dog team with a sled, just to make sure I knew what I was doing. Then he gave me eight dogs, then ten. We ran together with Jeff up front and me behind, either whipping around on winding, forested trails near the kennel or loading up all the dogs and trucking out to the Denali Highway for longer runs.

"You're gonna run forty miles today and I'm gonna run fifty, so I'll have you stop and turn your team around at Seattle Creek today," Jeff said at the trailhead, a few weeks before the race. "I'll just meet you back here at the trailer."

We hooked up our teams, with Jeff's team tied off to the front of the dog truck and my team tied off to the back of the trailer. Jeff looked back in the din of barking and gave me the thumbs-up and I gave him one in return. Off he went. I gave him a minute before pulling my safety knot, after which I clipped the side of the open trailer door and flipped my sled on its side.

The dogs were supercharged after watching Jeff's team take off, and there was barely any snow at the trailhead. I dragged behind my team as something big and white came sprinting into my view. A man dove on top of my dogsled crying out, "Woaaaaaahhhh."

It was Ramey Smyth, a well-respected musher whose father, Bud Smyth, ran the first-ever Iditarod in 1973. He'd been camped out at the trailhead and witnessed my bad start.

My team came to a stop. Together, Ramey and I righted my sled and stood on the runners.

"Thank you so much!" I said, embarrassed but grateful.

"You got it?" he asked.

"Yes," I said, nodding.

He leaped off the runners and my team zoomed forward. I put my foot down to stomp on the drag brake but there was no brake. It had flipped up when the sled tipped and now I put my foot straight down onto the ground. My feet went out from under me and I wiped out, clasping the metal bar brake as I belly-flopped.

"Woah," I said. *Calm and assertive. Calm and assertive*, I thought.

But we were picking up speed. I tried to pull myself up, using the brake as a pull-up bar, but the friction from the dogs dragging me at twenty miles per hour down a hill was too much to overcome. My grip weakened, and finally I fell off.

I stood up immediately and began running.

Two miles later I approached Jeff, straddling two dogsleds attached to two teams of impatient, barking dogs. I had my hat, gloves, and coat in my hand and was drenched in sweat. Breathlessly, I jumped onto the runners of my sled and looked at him, worried he was going to kill me or at least give me a well-deserved tongue-lashing.

Instead he smiled mischievously.

"You warm enough?" he asked.

"Fuck you!" I said, laughing. And off we went, down the trail.

We departed on our final training run before the Sheep Mountain 150 with a plan for me to learn how to camp out on the trail with the dogs, and to make sure all my systems were ready to go before race day.

Our runs were many hours long now, and we started in the daylight. First, we put booties on every single paw of every single dog. I was still slow at putting their paws in the bootie, wrapping their wrists with the elastic band, and Velcroing it securely around their wrists—not too loose and not too tight. Then, after taking off, we would go slowly for the first half hour.

"Injuring a dog in training is like"—Jeff thought for a second—"getting pregnant from recreational sex."

We watched each dog intently, looking for changes in their gaits. Jeff taught me to have an indicator dog—a dog with a smooth trot even at eleven or twelve miles per hour who I would watch and make sure never broke his pace. If that indicator dog was ever loping, we were going too fast. If a dog started limping, Jeff taught me to take the dog's booties off first and watch them again for a while. He taught me to watch for snowballs building up in the dogs' paws. There were so many little details, even if what we were doing was outwardly chaotic. That calm assertiveness was important not only to keeping the dogs confident in their driver, but also to zeroing in with laser focus on any tiny alterations in each dog—their gait, their attitude, their happiness level.

After sundown, in the gloaming before the moonrise, details were lost to a uniform shadow. The dogs picked up the pace and hunted caribou along the winding, frozen Nenana River and flushed ptarmigan from the willows alongside the trail. We were a single, smooth, and sinuous motion relentless through the snow, all of us a pack of wild things traveling together. Our eyes dilated in the dark, our senses piqued to their highest levels. Through the hours we metamorphosed from many to one, plural to singular. When the moon came up, it was just like sunrise—beginning as a faint glow on the highest ridges and then broadening to light entire mountainsides. And just as though it were midday, the light emerging from behind clouds beamed on our backs and cast shadows of our dogs and our sleds and our figures on the glowing snow. Every cleft and cliff of faraway mountains, every bit of spruce frondescence, was gilded in a way only winter knew.

At the slightest change in pressure on the brake the dogs responded, a chorus of triangular ears and hanging tongues lifting simultaneously to me, wondering why we had slowed or stopped. I told them it was for their own good. We couldn't keep up this pace for too long and now we were going to take it slow and easy all the way to camp. I looked around us and marveled. The moon made it look like we were traveling into a circle of incandescent mountains gathered around a fire.

When we arrived on the Canyon Creek bridge, Jeff already had his cooker out. He showed me how to use the contraption—essentially a five-gallon metal bucket with holes punched in it for airflow and a fuel reservoir in the bottom. He poured three bottles of Heet into the reservoir and dipped a handful of straw we had brought for the dogs into the fuel. He lit the straw with a lighter and then dropped it, flaming, into the fuel reservoir. *Whoosh.* The cooker was lit. He took a three-gallon stainless steel cookpot and walked to the edge of the trail, filling the cookpot with a small amount of snow. Then he set the cookpot in the cooker and let the snow become boiling hot water.

"A lot of people fill these cookpots all the way up with

snow," he said, "but this process goes a lot faster if you let it get to be boiling water really fast and then add more snow once it's boiling."

While the water heated up, we took all the booties off the dogs, put down straw for everyone, and unclipped all their tug lines so they could move around more freely and curl up into a ball to sleep. We dropped our own vacuum-sealed meals into the hot water. We poured the water over insulated buckets of chopped-up beef and fat, screwing down the locking lids on the buckets, and let the frozen meat thaw. Then we set out bowls and ladled out the mixture to all twenty-two dogs. Once the dogs were done with their meals, I watched Jeff put insulated coats on his team and I copied him. Then Jeff took out a big sleeping bag–like parka and put it over his head. The parka came all the way down to his feet. Wordlessly, he curled up in the straw beside his beloved leader Deets and fell asleep. I looked at him in disbelief. I had never camped out in winter without a tent before, and I had just assumed he had one in his sled. *OK,* I thought, *I got this. I can do this.* I walked over to my sled and unrolled my –40°F sleeping bag and spread it on the ground next to my favorite yearling, Solo. Solo had a ring of white around his black nose. He was gray with a cream-colored chest and searching brown eyes with light eyebrows. Solo was shy, especially of Jeff, but I coaxed him into crawling into my sleeping bag with me. With Solo's white chin resting on my chest and his body alongside mine under the insulated sleeping bag, I quickly fell into a deep sleep.

When we awakened hours later, we were covered in a

thick blanket of snow. The temperature had warmed and big, cottony flakes piled up all around us. We packed up our gear and headed back toward the truck, 50 miles away. Once we had been on the trail for an hour, the dogs hit a level of perfection I hadn't seen on regular training runs. It seemed like the second run, after a camp, was a knitting together of sorts. The dogs gelled. Their trots were perfectly synchronized. Everyone was loose and smooth and focused, as though they were one animal with one mind. *If they look this good after 50 miles,* I thought, *imagine how good they would look after 150.*

On the night before the race, all fifty mushers gathered inside Sheep Mountain Lodge, nestled in the rugged Chugach Mountains, for the prerace meeting. I don't remember a single word of it. I huddled on the floor next to Jeff and stared at everyone around me with wide eyes. I was petrified. All of these people were hardcore, and they were going to kick my ass.

"It's just a dog race," Jeff said. "It's just a couple days on a dogsled."

The race format went 50-50-50, with the first and last 50 miles being an out and back on the same trail. The middle 50 miles was a loop that came back to the Eureka Roadhouse, the lone checkpoint.

We took off and I stood hard on the brake, just like Jeff had told me.

"I don't want you to get off that brake until the last fifty miles," he said. "Then you can go as fast as you want. First, a lot of people will pass you. Then, at the end, you'll scoop them all up like an Easter egg hunt."

Jeff had given me his trusted leader Deets, who had finished the Iditarod many times, but the rest of my team was as green as they come. And Skeeter, Brennan, Brooks, Vespa, Rebel, Clipper, Solo, Barnum, and Bailey were pissed about going so slow. We went up a massive incline and Clipper began to scream. I had never seen her do that before in training, but we'd never climbed up anything this steep before. I looked behind me and thought, *Jesus, we're gonna have to come back down this*. Night fell and I fumbled for my headlamp. I put it on and then looked out ahead of my team onto the trail. No tracks. We were in second to last place. *I should be seeing a lot of dog paws and sled runners marking that trail*, I thought. I stopped the dogs and turned them around, got back on the right trail, and then my headlamp went blink-blink-blink. The batteries were dying. *Mother Fucker*. It was completely pitch-black as I pulled my extra batteries out of my parka and began to open the battery casing of the headlamp by feel. I couldn't remember how to open it and I didn't bring an extra head-lamp to shine on it so I could see. Suddenly, a light came up behind me. The last place musher. He gee'd his team around me and I yelled "Wait!" with a level of desperation I had never previously experienced. He stopped.

"I'm so sorry, this is such a total rookie mistake, but could you please shine your headlamp on me for a minute while I change these batteries?"

"OK," he said, shining his light on me.

"I'm sorry, this is my first race ever and I'm already totally fucking up," I said, my hands shaking.

The musher laughed. "This is my first race ever, too," he said with a French accent. "Some really steep hills coming up here. Big mountains. Really big."

"Uh-huh," I said as I got the new batteries in.

What was this guy talking about? Jeff hadn't told me about any big mountains. He took off and we weren't far behind him. I saw his light become smaller and smaller and finally disappear out of sight.

I turned my headlamp up to its highest setting as we angled up a steep pitch in the darkness. I looked around me and saw no trees, just white, angular slopes. The higher we climbed, the tighter I gripped my handlebar. It felt like we were on a roller coaster ratcheting up, up, up. I knew the drop was coming soon. The trail arched up and then gave way to the backside of a perilous summit. It dropped then sidehilled, dropped then sidehilled. Finally, a long narrow corridor took us back below treeline, where the twists and turns of the trail had claimed many victims. Imprints of sleds going off the trail and bodies falling. Tree branches scattered all over the place. Gouges in tree trunks.

Fuuuuck this, I thought to myself. I never let go. I never dumped the sled. I never even tipped. But it also felt like I never took a breath.

I arrived at the Eureka Roadhouse and parked my team, lit up the cooker, took off the dogs' booties, put down their straw, and fed them. I lay on my back next to Solo and turned off my headlamp.

"Well?!" Andy asked giddily. He was driving the dog truck and had been waiting for me at the checkpoint for a few hours. "What do you think? What is it like?!"

I closed my eyes and sighed.

"People who do this are missing a part of their brains," I said.

A blizzard came in and erased the trail, a handful of teams scratched, and I wanted to be one of them. But now there were only fifty miles left to run. One more run to the finish line. I could do that, I told myself. Even if I had to snowshoe out the entire trail, that was something I had done before. I told myself I was competent.

The dogs and I went over the same perilous summits as the first stretch of the race, only this time it was in the daylight. We crested a high pass in the Chugach Mountains right as the December sun went down. I didn't touch the brake and I let the dogs run as fast as they wanted. I was shocked that they wanted to run about eleven miles per hour—two miles per hour faster than Jeff had let me train these guys—the B team. We logged the sixth-fastest run to the finish line, even passing a few teams on the way. I couldn't believe it, but I was having *a lot* of fun. The dogs were hunting, sniffing the air, grabbing tree branches, and playing with them as they ran. I arrived at Sheep Mountain Lodge to a small smattering of applause. Jeff rushed to my sled and gave me a huge hug. He was effusive.

"You did it!" he said. "I'm so proud of you."

"Did you win?" I asked him.

"I did," he said.

The dogs wagged their tails and began to bark. Barnum started humping Clipper. They weren't tired at all. In fact, it appeared they wanted to keep going.

"Man," I said. "If they look this good after a hundred and fifty miles, I can't imagine how good they would look after three hundred!"

Jeff clasped his hand on my shoulder and laughed. His look told me I wouldn't have to imagine for long.

When Jeff told us he was going to sell four of the four-month-old pups out in the dog yard, Andy and I looked at each other with eyes wide.

"I'll sell them to you for a real good deal," he said. "There are lots of ways to start your own kennel, but if you have the time, starting with good puppies and training them up yourself is the cheapest way to do it. The older they get and the more experience they have, the more expensive they'll be."

That night, lying in bed, we looked into each other's eyes for less than a minute before knowing what we would do. Giddily, we texted Jeff that we would take three of the pups—one big male and two smaller females. We couldn't stop smiling. We were going to start our very own sled dog kennel.

I had a vision of Andy and me together in a small and hand-made place in the wilds, surrounded by dogs and still in love with each other a long time from now. I had a vision of our children and I thought how wonderful it could be for them to grow up with so much love and beauty and wilderness all around. I thought that maybe, I could believe in marriage again. I had always viewed marriage as the highest form of loving someone, in which case I wouldn't have any other vocabularic way of expressing to Andy how much I loved him. I didn't know what to call him. Certainly not my boyfriend. My partner? That sounded weird, too. I knew words and categories didn't matter. But I also knew that we were linked at the heart. I knew that we were family.

I never wondered if he felt the same way. We told each other how we felt about each other every day. And yet I still questioned. *Will he propose to me?* I'd dream up ways he could propose and when they didn't happen, I'd get disappointed. In this perfect life we had together, I was making up reasons to be let down. I realized that putting all the pressure on him to instigate the next phase of our life together was ridiculous.

When I stopped shaving my legs years ago because I didn't have running water—it was impractical and I didn't have time for it—I wondered, *Who came up with this? How is this even a thing?*

When I had told Andy I was never going to shave my legs again, he had smiled and said, "Well, darlin', you're a mammal."

Now I wondered, why do women have to wait for a man to propose to them? Years later I would read the wise words of Chimamanda Ngozi Adichie: "I truly wish for . . . a world in which either person can propose, in which a relationship has become so comfortable, so joy-filled, that whether or not to embark on marriage becomes a conversation, itself filled with joy." I smiled so big when I read that, because that's exactly what happened with Andy and me.

We were sitting in the handler cabin just before New Year's Eve. "We have to die at the exact same time," I said.

"OK," he said as I rested my head on his shoulder. "I'll see what I can do."

We burst into laughter at his accidental creepiness. And then we decided that when we became old enough to see the end was coming but were still able-bodied enough to have our dignity, we would hike up a mountain in a thunderstorm, stand at the top and, raising our hands in the air, get struck by lightning at the exact same time.

"I want you to be my husband," I said. Tears streamed down my cheeks.

"There's just no reason we shouldn't get married," he replied as we both grinned. "We should just be married, right now."

A week later we gathered up a handful of friends and

invited them over for chili. We told our friends Lynn and Bub (essentially Andy's version of Chuck and Karen) there was more to the party and we had asked Bub to be the one to marry us while Lynn filmed the whole thing.

"Jesus Christ, you guys," Lynn had said when we asked her to keep this huge secret from everyone—even family members— for a week. But now, everyone was at our house eating chili on a forty-below January night when Bub exited the house in his long underwear, walked out to his truck to get a suit coat, and reentered in minister-like apparel.

"Attention please, everybody," he said, walking into the middle of the cabin. "Gather 'round."

He announced that everyone in the cabin was "privileged to witness and participate in a ceremony, celebrating the public acknowledgment of love that Andy and Kristin have for each other."

Silence.

"Kristin and Andy now, in essence say, welcome to our marriage," Bub said. "Welcome to the celebration!"

Jess, Carmen, and the rest of our friends stared in shock, jaws dropping, wiping tears from their eyes. Neither of our families were there—we had only told them of our plan the day before the ceremony and they were thrilled for us.

"Bet ya didn't think this was gonna happen tonight!" Bub said.

Everyone laughed and cheered, raising beer bottles.

He turned back to Andy.

"Do you have rings?" he asked.

"I do, sorta," Andy said, as we both giggled like teenagers.

"One is a keychain," I said, laughing.

"This is fucking great!" Carmen exclaimed.

Bub read some short and sweet vows and we repeated them. They ended with, "May love dwell between you and me forever."

"What lies ahead, good or bad, you will face together," Bub said as Maximus loudly lapped up water in the background. "Life's circumstances may try you, but if you look to each other first, you will always find a friend."

Bub pronounced us husband and wife and everyone toasted and cheered. Later that night, Maximus and Moose jumped up on the counter and ate half the wedding cake Lynn had made. After everyone left, Andy and I took a walk hand in hand. The woods were lit up with moonlight, and we belonged to each other.

The Iditarod was starting in a matter of days and I lay awake early in the morning. I was excited, but also sad. The winter was coming to an end. The dogs let out a morning howl and I got myself dressed for chores. Years ago, the first time I tried howling in a dog yard to see if all thirty-five dogs would howl back plumb didn't work. At the Denali Kennels, Willow, a sweet little thirty-five-pound female with ice blue eyes, was always keen to howl. She loved my attempts because that meant she wasn't the only one trying to start a ruckus. But the way Willow did it was different. Her howls were quiet, like an intimation on the wind. It was almost as though she tried to imitate a howl from a distance—something that always made the whole dog yard howl back in concert. Most days, when Willow started a howl, it spread through the kennel like a wave.

That was in 2006. Since then, my life had become decidedly doggier by the year. I'd learned all the different things that howls meant. On patrol with sled dogs for the park service, we would get up at 5:30 every morning to start melting down snow on the woodstove in whichever cabin we inhabited for the night. As the propane lanterns ramped up their glow, and as that glow began emanating from a frosty window or two, the stirring on the dropline outside would begin. The pre-breakfast howl ensued. I think that one was more for the humans. "We know you're awake and we know what you're doing in there!" the dogs seemed to say. Then, with full bellies and a hint of sunlight brushing morning clouds, came the full dawn chorus. Usually led off by a leader of the pack, this was a feel-good chant that unified a strong group of disparate personalities. It was a thing any musher standing in its midst felt honored to witness. It was contagious. It lit up the insides.

Every now and then I witnessed the special howls reserved for calling and answering. *Are you out there?* A lonely sound in an echoing, winter wilderness. Answered by the most miraculous thing! Miraculous because, ninety miles out into Denali National Park, we thought nobody was listening. Nonetheless, packs of wild cousins throughout the years would answer "Yes! We're out here with you!" And sometimes they'd talk back and forth, the dogs and the wolves. One chorus of howls calling, another chorus of howls answering. The humans watched in wordless wonderment, having no place in a howl like that.

Out in Jeff's dog yard, the golden sun warmed us for real. As Andy and I worked through morning chores—going from dog to dog, feeding, scooping poop, and saying hi—the temperature began its ascent from -30 to 0°F. As the rising sun's light reached each row of doghouses, that row of dogs emerged from their comfy beds to soak it up. Finally, everyone was milling about the yard, happy and full, when I arrived at Bailey's house. Bailey was big and black with a shaggy coat and calm, deep brown eyes. It was a secret from Jeff that he loved to play and jump on us—he was a very serious sled dog while running in the team—and his paws were up on my chest as his mother, Skeeter, eyed me with a low tail wag, her big ears flickering up and down, ready for her turn to be loved. Andy and I had gone through the entire dog yard up to that point, stooping to rub bellies, scratch backs, caress ears, or play, depending on the dog. That was the ritual of every morning for the past six months, and I felt its culmination keenly. The Iditarod was about to start and I wouldn't see the dogs for weeks, and then it would be spring and my job here would end. I walked over to Solo's house and sat down. He crawled into my lap, stomping his paws and flicking his head up to lick my face, then back down to rest his cheek against my heart.

Instinctively I let out the howl that had lain latent in my

throat all winter. Atop a neighboring house, Merlot laid back his ears and closed his eyes, nose skyward, joining me. From there it spread like a fire across the yard. One dog to the next, illuminated breaths given to the air—little geysers of exhalation in the sunlight. A perfect chorus of dog harmonies.

PART 7

Build It Yourself

L ike many litters of sled dog puppies, the three pups we bought from Jeff were named by a theme. These pups were "the meat cuts litter": T-Bone, Kabob, and Porkchop. T-Bone was a brawny, black and brown boy with long legs and a deep chest. He had a mohawk of black fur rising up between his shoulder blades and running along the nape of his neck. He deeply loved food. His sister Kabob was black and white with black speckles on her white legs. She had a stillness about her that was preternatural. She stared calmly right into our eyes and gave very slow, sweet kisses with her pink tongue. Porkchop was the wild card. She was small, gray, and lightning fast, and her head was tiny. She rarely came when called, and instead skittishly patrolled the perimeter of the dog yard just out of our reach. We began calling her "Littlehead" as a joke, and eventually the name stuck. These three dogs would be the foundation of our sled dog kennel and their parents, Merlot and Clipper, were invaluable members of Jeff's Iditarod team. We knew they were going to be good, and we knew that they and their children and their children's children would make up our race team for many years. We were thrilled. But one thing was missing.

The connection I had with Solo was something I had never experienced with another dog. He had a direct line to my heart, just like Moose and Maximus, but he worked for me. Not like an employee. Nothing like that. More like, he loved me so much and was a phenomenal athlete who knew the pride I felt for him when he did a great job and that was his number one goal—to feel that pride. It made him happy to make me happy. And it made me happy to watch him run and do what he was born to do. We had accomplished so many firsts together. We did our first campout together. We ran our first race together. He was the first dog I ever leader-trained one on one, where I tied him to my waist and ran through the wooded trails and taught him every command he'd need to know.

"Haha, OK, buddy, I love you, too," I had said, when he kept turning around and running back to me. He had his harness on and I had attached a twenty-foot line to it, which I connected to a belt around my waist. I had gathered up about ten feet of the line in my hand, but the other ten feet were stretched out between me and Solo's tug line. Except, of course, when Solo would turn around and jump up on me, slathering my face with slobbery kisses.

"All right, go back out there now, we're working," I told him. "Line out."

Solo dutifully trotted to the end of the line and leaned forward, holding it taut.

"Good boy," I said.

He turned around to look at me, overwhelmed with the urge to come running back again, but the second he began to turn I cut him off.

"Ah-ah!" I yelled. "Line out!"

Solo faced forward.

We stood like that for ten minutes. I was teaching him patience. Lead dogs needed a lot of that.

"OK, ready?" I asked.

Then I started running down one of the dirt trails outside

the handler cabin. Solo trotted ahead, leaning into the work now, realizing that's what we were doing. His ears were turned back toward me. My strides were huge, he was pulling me so hard. We were coming up to a fork in the trail, and I wanted him to turn right.

"Gee!" I yelled to him, a few feet before the turn.

Solo turned left. I stopped.

"Gee," I said again as I lifted him up and placed him on the right fork of the trail.

He looked back at me and I held my right arm out, pointing to the right.

"Gee," I repeated.

He pulled the line tight and off we ran again. There was another fork in the trail a hundred yards or so farther along, and just before it I yelled "Gee."

Solo turned right.

"Good boy!" I yelled, exploding with happiness. "You're so smart, buddy, good boy!"

But I didn't stop. Stopping, for sled dogs, is not a reward. I ran faster.

"Yeah, Solo!" I yelled. "That's it, bud!"

Solo wagged his tail while he ran, leaping forward with happy energy.

"I'm da best dog, Mom," he said, wriggling. "I'm da very best rone."

We did this for weeks, running through the woods learning other commands like haw (left) and woah (stop) and easy (slow down) and on-by (pass by another person or team on the trail). I taught him how to jump off the trail and break a new one at my command. I taught him how to run through flowing water. I didn't think I could start a kennel without him. So I wrote Jeff a handwritten letter.

"Solo is my soulmate dog," I wrote. "I would be so honored if he could be the father of our kennel . . . I even have a special song that I sing to him . . . ," and so on, and so on.

The letter was two pages long. I poured my heart out to Jeff. I needed Solo and he needed me. He wouldn't even come to Jeff at the end of training runs. Routinely I'd get a text message from Jeff saying, I got everyone back on their house except Solo. Please come out and get him.

But Jeff wasn't swayed.

"It's very rare that a yearling is as promising and talented as Solo," he said. "Maybe we could breed his parents again for you and you could have one of the pups. But I can't let him go."

I was heartbroken. Solo and I were meant to be together. I just knew it. This was all wrong.

Weeks went by and Andy and I prepared to leave Husky Homestead. The final weeks in the handler cabin were stressful and claustrophobic, and we couldn't wait to leave. Jeff and his staff were getting ready for the upcoming summer season, and construction projects were ongoing on the property through all hours of the night. Headlights flooded our driveway at 2:00 a.m. Our cabin shared a wall with the main office, where the phone rang off the hook. We could hear every word and wondered if they could do the same. We covered up all the windows because someone was always outside. It didn't feel like a respite or even a home. We were miserable. And once Jeff found out, he felt terrible.

"I had no idea the living situation was so awful for you guys," he said in an e-mail. "What can I do to make it up to you?"

Fed up and with nothing to lose, I wrote back with one line: "How much for Solo?"

A few days later, I got a text back. It was an astronomical price for us, more than the down payment we had just put on a ten-acre plot off Stampede, but Andy said, "Kristin, Solo is *your* dog. He is priceless. We'll do whatever it takes."

I asked Jeff if I could pay for him in installments, and he said, "Of course."

We loaded up Andy's truck and my SUV with all our belongings and headed north. In the back of Andy's truck were Moose, Max, Willa, and the three pups. Riding shotgun with me was Solo. He leaned against the passenger seat, smiling a dog smile with his pink tongue hanging out of one side of his mouth, and placed one paw on my shoulder.

"Aw, bud," I said, looking into his shining brown eyes. "I can't believe you're mine."

Andy and I had found a place for sale near James's cabin on a road called Regulus (the star at the heart of the lion in the constellation Leo). It was ten acres without power, water, or road access, but it had a log cabin already built way back on the property, about an eighth of a mile from the road. We had donned our tall, rubber Xtratuf boots and walked the muddy trail back, winding through stunted spruce trees until a high, red roof came into view. To the north, we could hear Panguingue Creek rushing. We walked toward the sound and stopped when we reached a hand-carved wooden bench set at the edge of a high bluff. Dozens of spruce- and birch-covered ridgelines plunged down toward the creek, some a thousand feet higher than where we stood. We couldn't see a single roofline. We smiled.

The cabin had thick, round logs scribed together so they sat perfectly atop one another. The construction was sturdy, except for the floor. As we stepped inside, we could see that the floor bowed where the heavy, cast-iron woodstove squatted at its center. It was twenty feet across without any bracing underneath, which meant if we ever wanted to rebuild it, we'd have to jack the cabin up on bottle jacks and start all over again with the floorbox. It didn't faze us. Copper lines snaked along the edges of the cabin walls, carrying propane to three glass lanterns you could light with a match in winter. A tiny solar panel sat atop the house, and with its power you could plug in a coffeepot or a laptop. A steep ladder led upstairs to a sleeping loft, and in one of the two dormers a bed was built into the wall. It was high enough that you needed a stepping stool to get in, or at least a running start. That way, you could use the space underneath the bed as storage. Andy and I climbed up onto the bed so we could look out the window. We were stunned. Downstairs, we had been in the thick of a tightly knitted spruce forest. But from the loft, we could see the 360-degree rim of mountains that cradled the entire Nenana River valley and Stampede.

We knew we would have to spend much of the summer hauling water, building a dog yard, creating a better entry trail, and putting in power, but we didn't care. Here, with our four hands, we would build what we had dreamed. A kennel full of loving dogs. A true homestead.

That summer the dogs ran unfettered, leaping, dashing through green tundra and waving white smudges of cotton-grass. They were wild, chasing birds through watery ditches and darting just out of each other's reach. They were playful. And then that aimlessness would find a purpose—the scent of a moose or a porcupine or a squirrel—and they'd settle into their absolutely perfect gaits. Those smooth and effortless trots I'd watched for hours and days in winter, coming out almost on accident during our lazy summer wanderings. I couldn't tire of watching their movements.

We had e-mailed one of our favorite up-and-coming Iditarod mushers—an Alaska Native named Mike Williams Jr. who came in seventh place the year I volunteered. We told him how much we loved his big, leggy dogs with thick, shining coats. We asked if he would want to do a breeding with us. To our surprise, he accepted and sent Zigzag, one of his best females, sixty miles up the Kuskokwim River from his village of Akiak on a boat to Bethel. There, Zigzag was loaded onto a small plane to Anchorage, where Andy picked her up and drove her the five hours north to our place. Zigzag had a creamy white coat with golden tips. She had amber-colored eyes with black eyeliner. She looked like an Egyptian princess. We bred her to T-Bone and waited in anticipation for the first litter of puppies our kennel would ever have.

Now that we were expecting puppies, we decided we needed to legitimize our operation with a name. There were so many good kennel names out there. Our friends Paige and Cody, another husband-and-wife team who both raced the Iditarod and the Yukon Quest 1,000-mile races, had a kennel name that stood out from the rest: Squid Acres Kennel. They settled on that because, in addition to being a long-distance dog musher, Paige was also a fisheries biologist who studied squids in grad school. There was Wild and Free Mushing—musher Brent Sass's kennel named from the lyrics of a song by Alaska's official balladeer, Hobo Jim.

There's a part of me, wild and free
In my heart there's a wild wolf howling through the tall
pine trees
It's a long cold trail that I've been on, there just doesn't seem
to be an end to this way I've been going
I can see that road spreading over the land, see a young boy
standing with a suitcase in his hand
It was long ago, the boy was me, and I was running like a
wolf in the mountains, wild and free
I've got it in my mind that it must have been the times that
made me to wander away, from a
Family that I love and a warm roof above but everybody
round me did say, it was just me, being wild and free

There was Team Tsuga Siberians, named after the hemlock grove where Mike and Sue Ellis started their kennel back in New Hampshire before they moved to Alaska. There was Douglas Fir Mushing—Mandy Nauman's kennel that she named as a tribute to her dad, Doug, who had died in an accident. It seemed that every kennel had a name that told a story.

We thought back to the kernels of inspiration that were planted years ago and that grew into the current dream that we were chasing. And really, it all started back at the Denali National Park kennels. It all started with Moose.

Because we spent what amounted to hours per week yelling "Hey, Moose!!" at Moose, who wandered the tundra and pretended like he couldn't hear us despite his giant radar dish ears, we named our kennel "Hey Moose! Kennel." We made a little wooden sign with a drawing of Moose's face on it and placed it out where our trail met the road. We traded in Andy's little Tacoma for a roaring diesel flatbed with a dog box. Andy built a beautiful new house and pen for Zigzag and made a wooden sign for it that said PUPPY PALACE. We marked the calendar for sixty-three days from the breeding. Puppies were due to arrive sometime in September.

Autumn became winter in a series of panicked and joyous episodes, set in a landscape crystallized in frost, shrouded in fog. The September soundtrack was provided by migrating birds—so many thousands that the earth couldn't seem to hold them all. Under the moon at Eight Mile Lake, a few miles west of our cabin, they settled for the night. Their squawkings of welcome and farewell kept us awake until the morning revealed a crystalline world, sparkling under the sun. The sky was liquid with sandhill cranes, the alpenglow-painted mountains were set against a robin's egg canvas of cloudless sky.

The cranes' cacophonous calls continued for weeks. When a massive levitation of the huge birds broke open the sky directly overhead, it was too much for Moose to handle. One couldn't help but feel the gravity of this migration. But it was more than that for Moose. In an instant, he was gone, following the birds southeast along Panguingue Creek and taking Solo and Kabob with him. For days we searched, walking from the Panguingue Creek headwaters near Eight Mile Lake to where it poured into the mighty, near-flooding Nenana River. Our voices were ragged and our spirits were low as we put on boots and gaiters for the third day, packing wire cutters in case the dogs were caught in traps; posting fliers with their names and descriptions (Kabob—small, black. Solo—medium, gray. Moose—XXL, gray). When we heard they had been hanging out on the highway, six miles away at a construction site, my stoicism failed and I collapsed into panic. Imagining life without half our family was too much to bear. And then the call came.

"We have your dogs," a woman said. "My kids were supposed to call you yesterday and tell you, but I think they like the dogs so much they wanted to keep them."

We were ecstatic, though a little leery of the winding dirt road upon which we drove and drove. Upturned roots and fresh mud lined its sides and we turned left where they had told us, at a wooden sign painted in blood red words that told all who entered of this family's loyal service to Jehovah. How in the world had our dogs ended up here, twenty-five miles away from our house? We followed a young girl on a bicycle, thinking for sure that we were about to get murdered. We braced ourselves as we rounded the corner, wary of what kind of place we were about to see. I closed my eyes.

"Holy shit," Andy said.

I opened my eyes to see a dog yard as clean and perfect as a painting, surrounded by giant hay fields and a whitewashed farmhouse; a barn full of fresh straw, a litter of puppies, yaks let out to pasture. And there in the middle of it all were Moose, Solo, and Kabob. Wagging their tails and barking with the rest of them. The luckiest dogs in the world.

That night we collapsed into a happy and total exhaustion, a dreamless sleep that needed to be so much longer than it was. At 5:00 a.m., Andy was just about to leave for work when he ran back inside.

"Puppies!" he exclaimed. "Puppies are happening!"

A jolt of adrenaline shot me out of bed and I rushed into the dog yard in pajamas and Carhartts. It was the windiest day of the year, and Zigzag had decided she preferred the pit she'd dug in the ground to the beautiful puppy palace we had built her. First there were two. One was stillborn. I took her warm body in my hands and rubbed her with a towel, trying to bring life into her, but... nothing. The second one had a cleft palate, or some kind of deformation that didn't allow her to breathe and nurse. She came out gasping. She took two breaths and then faded away. Zigzag pushed her away and bore down to give birth again. Quickly there were three more pups. Then five more after that. She curled around them, protecting them from the wind. They grunted and screamed, pushing their way forward to nurse, even though their eyes wouldn't open for nearly two weeks.

In the competition for prime real estate on Zigzag's teats, three of the eight pups were getting pushed away and not making it back. It seemed like they weren't able to propel themselves forward, because their front legs stuck straight out ahead of them in a V. They looked kind of squashed, like starfish—nothing like Moose's litter when they were born, which were the only puppies whose birth. I had witnessed. Over and over again, we picked up the starfish puppies and put them on a teat. But over and over again, they would slide off and lose their ground to the healthier puppies. We brought Zigzag and all of the puppies inside, so that even the ones getting pushed away could stay warm and we could keep an eye on them. But Zigzag began shoving them into the corners of her whelping box. And when we woke up from a couple hours sleep, the starfish puppies were dead.

Half of our first litter of puppies had died. We were heart-broken. I called Paige sobbing, and she told me that when they had had their first litter of puppies so many years ago, she sat out in the pen during the birth and did the same thing that we had. She took any weaker pups, the ones that kept getting shoved away, and put them back on the teat. In the long run, they died, too. Sometimes within days, sometimes weeks later.

"The mom always knows best," she said, trying to comfort me.

I now saw Zigzag as this mighty mother who made decisions for the good of the whole, rational and unsentimental but oh so nurturing. I wanted to ask her what she was thinking, how she knew which puppies wouldn't make it and which ones would, but wordless she remained.

The night the pups' eyes opened, the harvest moon lit the earth while the aurora river pulsed green across the firmament. Days later, when the snows came, the crystals landed unbroken on their thick, delicate fur. Stellar dendrites, twelve-branched stars, sectored plates—all framed perfectly on the coats of sleeping puppies. As the weeks went by, their faces began to look like dog faces. With black whiskers and curious noses, teeth that bit and claws that scratched. Eyes that implored, tails that wagged, behaviors that tested. Every day they started anew, eyes and ears open to our winter world.

In October, it was time to get electricity into our cabin. Chuck and Karen had given us nearly five hundred feet of copper wire—worth thousands of dollars—for free. The only hitch was, we had to dig it up from underground, and it had been there for fifteen years. We stood exhausted in the sleet, covered in mud, staring at a broken shovel. We were shin-deep in a trench outside Chuck and Karen's house, and while we had uncovered about half of the wire, we still had a few days' worth of work left to finish the job. Once the wire was heaved out of the permafrost and coiled up, we hauled it off Chuck and Karen's property and buried it all over again at our place with the promise of flipping on a light switch someday, leaving a heater on, refrigerating our food. We wondered whether, years from now, we'd miss the flickering glow of the propane lanterns against the hand-peeled logs and thought maybe, eventually, we would laugh at the memory of all the hard work we did when we were young. One day we'd be wistful of what our bodies were capable of doing. But that also meant that maybe, someday, things would be easier. And it seemed we never did anything the easy way.

We ordered a power pole and the day it was delivered was the first real snow of the season. Everyone in our neighborhood lined up and carried the pole on their shoulders to the corner of our property. We carefully anchored the pole in the ground. Then our friend Brian, who had read lots of textbooks on electrical engineering and had wired his own house, climbed up the power pole and installed the transformer. Jon, the master electrician at the park, lived nearby, so he stopped by to inspect Brian's work before the power company came to connect us to the grid. When the power truck drove away, Jon walked down the muddy trail to the cabin with us.

"You guys ready?" he asked with a grin.

"Do it!" we said.

Jon flipped the switch on the breaker. We went inside and plugged in a lamp to one of four outlets Brian had installed in the house. Andy and I took a deep breath.

"One...two...three!" Andy said.

The lamp threw golden light onto the cabin walls.

That night we rocked in our chairs by the warm fire and drank a little whiskey with ice cubes brought by a friend a week ago, still unmelted on the porch. Outside the window, the dogs were quiet. The puppies slept like a pile of leaves drifted into a corner, overlapping. Treetops and mountain ridges climbed and descended. The spruce swayed in the breath off the mountains, their snowlit boughs a comfort from the inside of our cabin. We rocked and sipped to the tune of old country songs spinning on a dusty record player. We looked at each other and shook our heads, and I thought how almost nothing was better than a warm and well-lit place with windows to the cold outside.

Over the next two years, Zigzag, T-Bone, Kabob, Littlehead, and Solo became the backbone of our team. T-Bone and Zigzag's puppies grew up to be incredibly powerful, emotionally connected sled dogs. Solo and Kabob had a litter of eight pups. Andy and I threw everything we had into training for our qualifying races.

During those long nights on the runners, the dogs flowed along the trail under the light of the moon. They became a single unit after hundreds of miles of training together. They hardly ever heard our voices, because when we spoke it needed to mean something. And upon hearing us their ears would glance back, picking up that sparse and valuable information. A direction. A command. Some reprimand or praise. Communication was important, but so was silence.

I drove a team of dogs that consisted of big, strong, sure boys and smooth, steady, determined girls. They were exactly what we dreamed up. Thick, shimmering coats. Long, powerful legs. Friendly, but with enough of an edge to push themselves farther and further. Solo was confident enough to break out a trail he had only come to learn in the past month. The trail had disappeared in the wind, and he boldly trotted out onto a blank slate of clean, white tundra and put the trail in where it was before. Few things in my life had ever been more rewarding than working with my team. I eyed each one of them thoughtfully and tried to imagine my team years from now. The sons and daughters and grandkids of these dogs. Bits and pieces of their personalities lasting generations, emerging in a particular bark, a bear hug, a circle of white around a black nose. The payoff—of hours spent literally running by their sides, teaching them commands, working with each dog one-on-one because we had no leaders—was this: when I said *gee* our team turned right; when I said *haw* our team turned left; when I said *over* they swung to the side of the trail; and when I said nothing they strode silently and confidently forward into the unknown. Across a sparse, wild space painted in pastels and surrounded by serrated peaks. Over a moonscape, under the moon that lit our way.

In 2014, I finished the Copper Basin 300 and the Two Rivers 200, racking up 650 miles of qualifying races (including the Sheep Mountain 150 from a few years ago) so that I could finally sign up for next year's Iditarod. Andy was running his first qualifying race, the Yukon Quest 300 (run at the same time and by the same race organization as the Yukon Quest 1,000), which began in Fairbanks that year.

In 2013, when the Yukon Quest 1,000 started in White-horse, Yukon Territory (its start location alternates between Whitehorse and Fairbanks every year), Andy and I had volunteered at the Circle checkpoint, which was 700 miles into the race. We saw the mushers, stupid and exhausted, hauling their buckets in 40 below zero having just traveled 150 miles without a single checkpoint.

Fuck that, I had thought to myself. *I'm never doing this race.*

Not that any thousand-mile race was necessarily harder than the other. They were just so different, the Yukon Quest and the Iditarod. The first Iditarod Trail 1,000-Mile Sled Dog Race was run in 1973, but the idea for it came about in the 1960s when Joe Redington Sr., a dog musher and bush pilot, realized a quintessentially Alaskan way of life was disappearing. Back then, every family that lived in Alaska's remote villages had a dog team. Dogs provided transportation. They carried the mail. They delivered groceries and medicines. They brought goods like gold and furs from the villages to the towns of Fairbanks and Anchorage. But the snowmachine came along in 1960 and made all of those functions a lot easier, and soon, the sled dog all but disappeared. Redington knew that, without action, the sport of dog mushing and all the cultural trappings that went along with it could disappear, too. He and another mushing enthusiast, Dorothy Page, belonged to the Aurora Dog Mushers Association, which had put on a race several years earlier that employed part of the Iditarod Trail—a rugged route across Alaska from Seward to Nome that served as an important artery of Alaska's winter commerce amidst mining camps, trading posts, and other settlements from 1880 to 1920. In many places, the trail followed the ancient routes of Alaska Native people, who had used special winter modes of travel over it—the snowshoe and the dogsled. What better way to shed light on the spirit of the sled dog and its remarkable history in Alaska than to have a race on that same trail?

The first time the Iditarod was run, thirty-four teams ventured down the Iditarod Trail. Twenty days, forty minutes, and forty-one seconds after the race began in Anchorage, Dick Wilmarth and his lead dog Hotfoot mushed down Front Street in Nome. Wilmarth received a first place prize of $12,000. As the race matured over the years, so, too, did its popularity. It became more and more commercialized, drawing million-dollar sponsorships and a cap of one hundred mushers. TV and camera crews were all over the race trail. The winner would receive $70,000 and a brand-new Dodge Ram truck. Competition became fierce, as mushers reached Nome faster and faster. And in 1983, four mushers sitting at the Bull's Eye Saloon in Fairbanks decided maybe there should be a new race. Maybe an international race. Maybe it goes up the Yukon River. Maybe not so many cameras.

That conversation between Roger Williams, Leroy Shank, Ron Rosser, and William "Willy" Lipps became more than an idea when the Yukon Quest 1,000-Mile International Sled Dog Race was born. The race would commemorate the Yukon River, which was the historical highway of the North. It would trace the routes that prospectors followed to reach the Klondike during the 1898 Gold Rush, and from there it would plunge into the Alaskan Interior, and the start would alternate each year between Whitehorse, Yukon Territory, Canada, and Fairbanks, Alaska. The first Yukon Quest saw twenty-six teams depart Fairbanks in 1984. During the next sixteen days, twenty teams arrived in Whitehorse, with six dropping out along the way. Alaskan musher Sonny Lindner became the first Yukon Quest champion, winning the race in twelve days.

While both thousand-mile race trails followed historical routes that celebrated the history of the North and required mushers to be wholly self-sufficient (mushers got disqualified for receiving any outside help), they did diverge in a few important ways. First of all, the Iditarod took place in early March, when there were twelve hours of daylight and an average low temperature of +19°F in Anchorage. The Yukon Quest took place in early February, when Fairbanks saw seven hours of light per day and an average low temperature of −13°F. Secondly, the Iditarod had twenty-two checkpoints along its race route, while the Yukon Quest had only nine. That meant that on the Iditarod, the most mushers had to travel between checkpoints was around 77 miles, while on the Yukon Quest, mushers had to be self-supported for distances of up to 210 miles. However, the Iditarod took place on a trail that was completely off the road system. The only way someone other than a dog musher could reach any checkpoint on the Iditarod Trail was via aircraft or snowmachine. Checkpoints on the Quest trail were largely reachable by highway, save for the middle 300 miles of the race. This allowed Quest mushers the luxury of having a handler—someone who followed the race driving a dog truck. Handlers could take any dogs or gear the musher didn't want to carry forward on the trail (they still couldn't get those dogs or that gear back, however. It just meant the dogs got to go home in a truck with someone they knew, instead of on a small airplane back to Anchorage like they would on Iditarod). Handlers could give the musher a pep talk at a checkpoint, but nothing more. No outside help was allowed, except for at the halfway point in Dawson City. This was another way the two races diverged. On the Iditarod, there was a mandatory twenty-four-hour break during which the mushers still had to be wholly responsible for their dog team. On the Yukon Quest, it was a mandatory thirty-six-hour break, and during it the musher could go to a hotel room in Dawson City and sleep the whole time while their handlers cared for the dogs. The handlers weren't the ones standing on a dogsled for hours at a time, facefirst into –40°F with a forty miles-per-hour headwind on the Yukon, but they did drive 2,700 miles in a shitty, breaking-down diesel that got cold-started in those same temperatures.

So, in February 2014, Andy was about 200 miles into the

Yukon Quest 300 at the checkpoint of Central and I was handling for him, driving the dog truck. He was traveling in a mixed group of 300- and 1,000-mile mushers, including Mandy Nauman, the only woman running the full 1,000-mile Quest that year. Mandy and I had run the Copper Basin together and trained together quite a bit. She was blond, brawny, and foul-mouthed, with the loudest, most infectious laugh ever. She called everyone who didn't agree with her a pussy, and she did it with a strong Minnesota accent.

While Andy rested, I sat in the Central checkpoint with Mandy, who was relieved to be over and done with some of the most rugged terrain in the race, but she still had hundreds of miles to go. She was nervous about leaving Circle, the next checkpoint, and mushing out onto the Yukon River. It was vast and cold, with hardly any cover. And there was only one checkpoint between Circle and the halfway point of Dawson City, which meant it was the only one in 310 miles.

"That's insane," I told her. "That's why I'm running the Iditarod. I think the longest distance between checkpoints is seventy miles or something."

Mandy's face was windburned and chapped and her eyes were puffy. She was sleep-deprived and two hundred miles into a thousand-mile race, but she was drinking a beer and eating a burger at the bar.

"You don't have enough qualifying races to run Iditarod," she said.

"Yes, I do," I said combatively. "I have six hundred fifty miles."

"You need seven hundred fifty miles, you fuckin' idiot," she replied, laughing. "If you wanna run a thousand-mile race next year, it's gonna have to be the Quest."

"What?" I asked, panicking.

I went to the Iditarod website on my phone and scrolled through the race rules. There it was. A musher had to complete 750 miles of qualifying races before she could sign up. The Quest only required 500. The vision I had had of starting the Iditarod the upcoming year was completely squashed. I ordered a beer and sulked.

Sebastian Schnuelle, a German musher who had won the Yukon Quest years earlier, was sitting beside me. He had crazy gray hair that stood on end, making him look like a rugged Albert Einstein.

"The Yukon Quest is actually a much friendlier race for rookies," he said. "I always recommend mushers run it as their first thousand-mile race, then run Iditarod."

"Why?" I asked. "How is this easier? There's hardly any checkpoints! And it's a month earlier than the Iditarod, so it's that much colder and darker."

"Handlers," he replied. "And the hospitality."

That wasn't always the case. Before the early 1990s, Iditarod rules encouraged mushers to stay in the homes of people who lived in the remote villages along the trail. And rural Alaskan villages had been producing some of the most celebrated mushers in the state for decades: George Attla, the Huslia Hustler; Herbie Nayokpuk, the Shishmaref Cannonball; Emmitt Peters, the Yukon Fox. Alaska Natives won the Iditarod from 1974 to 1976. Mushing was intrinsic in Alaska Native culture along the Iditarod trail, and there were deep bonds between the villagers and the mushers running the race. Then, in 1992, a new rule banned mushers from staying in the homes of their friends in the villages. The rule required mushers to park their teams in a dog lot at a village checkpoint, and to stay in a communal sleeping area like a school gym or library. The rule was instated to promote fairness and to ensure mushers were receiving no outside help. But it also made the race less personal, keeping the mushers at a distance from the members of each remote community.

Scott Smith, an Iditarod veteran who ran his first 1,000-mile Quest in 2013, said it like this:

"If the Iditarod is fast food, the Yukon Quest is home cookin'."

As Andy rested his team in Central, I thought about my drive over Eagle Summit on the way here. Up there, the sky had tried to steal the earth. The flat light kept the edge of the road and the beginning of the clouds a secret. Even inside the car, the music playing on the radio was drowned out by the wind, swept up in drifts. Below that maelstrom, spreading out in all directions like the veins of a great eye, were drainages that became creeks that became the Yukon. And herds of caribou thousands strong, their antlers disappearing into a frozen mist, scattered away from the truck. Wild and scared and unaccustomed to humans. Somewhere beyond where I could see, the Yukon Quest trail was winding and wending a ribbon around the edges of all that I knew about Alaska. And now that I knew the Yukon Quest was the only way I would be able to run a thousand-mile race next year, I began to look at it in a different way. Instead of being just 100 percent excited for Andy to be out there now, running a part of this long trail, I began to imagine, with no shortage of fear, *me* being out there.

Of course you don't get to run the easier race, I thought to myself.

After Andy and the team took off for Circle, I packed up the dog truck and hit the road. The Circle checkpoint was housed in an old fire hall, and it didn't take long for the spare and dusty building full of strangers to feel like home. Together, we all slept on a concrete floor. Race judges, handlers, veterinarians, and mushers. The checkpoint was bustling because it was kind of the last port in the storm before the thousand-mile mushers ventured onto the vast, exposed Yukon River. It was also the turnaround point for the three-hundred-mile race. They came here and rested a good long while before turning around and mushing back to their finish line in Central. And the seemingly never-ending Birch Creek—usually the coldest spot on the Yukon Quest trail—that connected Central and Circle with a series of curlicuing oxbows would have to be run again, so none of the three-hundred-mile mushers was ever in a particular hurry to get back on the runners.

Circle was a place ruled by poverty, with 50 percent of families and 42 percent of the population living below the poverty line, according to the 2000 census. Only a hundred people resided in Circle, which was named by miners who wrongly thought they were on the Arctic Circle. It was established in 1893 when gold was discovered in Birch Creek, and it served as an unloading point for supplies shipped up the Yukon River from the Bering Sea. In 1898, Circle was the largest mining town on the Yukon, with a population of seven hundred. Now, it seemed more like a ghost town populated mostly by native Athabascans. But the people who lived in Circle made everyone feel at home. We met Margaret and Irene when they brought food to the fire hall for the mushers and volunteers. They said Grace in Gwich'in, then fed us bacon and French toast. They told us old stories in their slow, stilted way— about the Yukon River flooding right up onto their doorstep; about sharing their home with strangers who showed up in a canoe—and we learned to resist filling in the quiet parts. They gave Andy a Gwich'in name—*Andrew Cho*, "Big Andrew"— and kissed us on the cheeks when they left. They told us they loved us, and to come back in May, to watch breakup. It seemed impossible that the feet-thick ice on the Yukon would ever thaw, break up, and turn into water again.

Andy finished the Yukon Quest 300 in ninth place, which happened to be the Red Lantern, or last, because so many teams had scratched. Every musher who had already finished the race came out into the cold to cheer for him. A checkpoint volunteer made him a red lantern out of a red Solo cup, cutting out a little hole for the light of a tea candle to glow through. Solo crossed the finish line in single lead and jumped right onto my chest. Andy's mustache was covered in ice when I kissed him. I looked around and, with awe, realized that every person showering him with congratulations had been a total stranger mere days before. Standing among this community of incredible people, it became clear that some of us were just meant to travel into the unknown, and Alaska was the bright sun that brought goodness right out from under our skin. We were imbued with a happiness that perhaps had lain dormant in our previous lives, but now glowed on our faces in freckles and wrinkles. It was a wonder that, even across this much country, we discovered our own kind. We never left as strangers. We found a light at the end of the road that was ours.

With nothing but excitement and not a single reservation, I signed up for the 2015 Yukon Quest the following August. By the end of November, our dogs were running forty to fifty miles at a time. We were in the midst of a training schedule that Andy made, based on his own ultramarathon training schedule (he had finished his first ultramarathon the winter we were married). We were essentially living out of our dog truck, running dogs up and down the Denali Highway just like we had learned at Jeff's and stopping to camp every few hours. There wasn't enough snow to mush the dogs with a sled, so we were running them out in front of the truck. Often, we tried to end our runs out at Alpine Creek Lodge, sixty-eight miles down the remote highway from Cantwell. There, mushers could camp their dogs outside and come in for a warm meal, even in the middle of the night. The owners, Claude and Jen Bondy, loved dog mushers.

By the time we loaded up all our dogs in the dog truck and drove the hour and a half to Cantwell from Healy, it was usually around dinnertime. In Cantwell, we would attach twenty-three dogs to the front of the truck. We would run forty miles, which took about 4.5 to 5 hours, and then stop to camp. I know it sounds boring to roll along at ten miles per hour watching dog butts for half the day, but just watching the dogs was exhilarating. How they started a run, what they did after a snack break, how a dog might change whether he or she was in the front of the team or the back, how everyone congealed so beautifully the more hours they ran together in harness. The most gratifying part came when we stopped at the end of a run, because no matter how long it was, the dogs were *so* happy. Their eyes shined. Their tails wagged. Many of the veterans on our team were disappointed that they couldn't keep going, and wouldn't hesitate to let us know it by jumping up and down and starting a teamwide howl. When it was time to camp and the dogs were bedded down, Andy and I slept shoulder to shoulder in the front seat of the truck. In the middle of the night, the alarm would chime a cheerful wake-up call. It seemed to say:

"Remember how you chose this? *You* actually set this alarm a few hours ago! For 3:00 a.m.! You are crazy!"

Unbelievably, we were full of energy. We couldn't wait to see how the dogs would do on each run. After running three or four more hours, we would arrive at Alpine Creek Lodge. Immediately, we would serve the dogs a meal. One clank of the bucket against a thigh set T-Bone off in an instant. Then he and Zigzag's kids—Trixie, Bullock, and Hoss. Then everyone. Feed-up time was here! Quickly we spread out an array of bowls on the snow. One of us measured out supplements like probiotics and psyllium while the other ladled warm, meaty water and kibble into each bowl. We fed the loudest dogs— T-Bone and his sons Hoss and Bullock—first, since the lodge always had guests who could still be asleep this early in the morning. After their meal, we went around to each dog and rubbed them down—who doesn't like a massage after a long run? Then, we would head inside the lodge for a human meal—moose bacon with the perfect amount of crisp; eggs scrambled with caribou sausage; pancakes with blueberries picked this season; or better yet, blueberry baked oatmeal. We would sit by the fire and listen to the Bondys bicker in their endearing way. (Claude: "Woman, where's my meal?" Jen, with a thousand-watt grin: "Watch it, Jack (short for jackass).")

After a few hours, we would head back outside to begin preparations for our run back to Cantwell. On those short days, our breath would turn to smoke in the waning light and we would realize we were whispering. The alpenglow on the mountains was dazzling as the sun sank below the horizon of the broad Susitna River valley. Even with two dozen dogs there, silence prevailed. It was a sacred hour and such an earned and satisfying peacefulness to have a yard full of quiet, sleeping dogs. They dozed and dreamed while we packed up bowls and buckets. And at the first clink of a tug line snap being opened, they jumped to their feet. They were always, always ready to go.

To my surprise I was selected to be one of the subjects of a documentary about the 2015 Yukon Quest, along with Ryne Olson—a rookie like me—and Mike Ellis, a Quest veteran many times over. "I'm more scared of living a boring life and just dying without having lived, than I am of the Yukon River," I told the documentarian.

Around the same time, a *National Geographic* photographer told me she had covered stories about people forced into survival situations, those who were pushed to make life-or-death decisions by extenuating circumstances, often brutal. Why, she asked, do mushers choose to put themselves in these situations willingly? In thinking about how to answer her, I realized the answer to that question was the reason behind everything I'd done in my life.

Nearly thirty years earlier my biological father had died of a heart attack. My mom, siblings, and I called him "Daddy Keith." The one memory I had of him was surprisingly vivid: I was perched atop his shoulders and ducking under doorways, spinning on his six-foot-six frame in a yellow swirl of dandelions in the backyard. Anything else I knew of him was from my mother's stories. With his Texas drawl, he called everybody "pardner." He said things like, "The harder I work, the luckier I get." He still held all the basketball records at his high school in a small town in Texas. He was the vice president of a big corporation and also he could fart the national anthem. He was outwardly intimidating and privately hilarious.

I often wondered what happened to any of us after our last

breaths were exhaled. In my imagination, what happened was that we got to travel to all the places we never got to see. We got to experience the lives of our loved ones. We got to stand in their shoes. The wind got to blow through Daddy Keith's hair as he stood on the runners behind my dog team. He got to peer skyward in the arctic cold as the auroras rose gently from the horizon like steam off a near-frozen river. In pillars and curtains. Breathing. Or maybe there was just...darkness. Something that terrified Andy and thus me, too.

When I was four years old, I had a dream about climbing into a casket beside my mother. Everyone had gone and I had waited until nobody was looking. She was in her business suit—a charcoal gray sports coat with a matching skirt, a pressed white dress shirt with cuffs pinned together by silver cuff links, and her collar adorned with her signature maroon bow tie dotted with navy blue paisleys. I wedged myself between her body and the satin-pillowed lining of the casket and closed my eyes. She was the only parent I had left and I was going with her.

My mother, of course, was alive and well. It was Daddy Keith who was dead. But the dream encapsulated a promise I made to myself at the time. I visualized it every night when I knelt beside my bed to say my prayers. "God bless..." and then a list of everyone in our family who was alive and then a list of everyone in our family who was dead, may they rest in peace. I pictured Daddy Keith resting. A forced nap in a casket that would last for all of eternity. He wasn't allowed to ever sit up, and I thought that would be mighty uncomfortable.

To me, "rest in peace" sounded like a condemnation. If Mom were ever to die, I would go with her. I didn't want her to be uncomfortable, and I didn't want to be left alone.

At age four, I didn't yet know what it meant to be alive, but I knew with a despairing sense of finality what it meant to be dead. Daddy Keith was in a box looking at blackness forever. I never, ever wanted that to happen to me. That created a kind of morbid fearlessness in me. I thought about dying every day, but I also thought about making every day mean something, because what if it was my last day on earth?

I likely became a dog musher in my heart soon after Daddy Keith died, because that's when I began imagining the worst-case scenario and making a plan in my head for how to get out of it. I remember riding in Mom's old gray Mercedes at age five. She drove us across a bridge over a tributary of the Trinity River in Fort Worth and I imagined the car falling into the water. I imagined us landing on our side, and the green-brown creek would slowly fill up the inside of the car. Very calmly, I would roll down the window and swim out, I thought.

The fact that I thought I had any power in the face of death could only be described as purely delusional. It could also be described as "magical thinking," this according to the marriage counselor who ended up counseling me, alone, that day when Alfred was a no-show. I thought I was some sort of superhero. I still carried the beliefs of a child. In that regard, I was stunted, stalled out mentally at the age I was the moment of Daddy Keith's death. And when I looked at it from this perspective, Alfred's disappearance made a lot of sense. I thought my presence could protect the people I loved. If I had been there when Daddy Keith was playing tennis that day, maybe he wouldn't have died of a heart attack. And if I was always with Alfred, maybe he wouldn't die at all. Death would have to contend with me first. I stifled Alfred. He couldn't go anywhere without me, from poker nights out with his old buddies to big solo hiking trips through Glacier National Park. I forced him to drag me along. It shouldn't have been a surprise that the moment the opportunity presented itself, he was hitchin' the first ride to freedom.

With Andy, I had learned to let go. I practiced staying positive, nurturing the belief that he was capable and strong and didn't need me to protect him. But every so often, the old panic would arise. I would think the worst and let myself sink into the feeling of loss. I would be inconsolable.

"What if you die?" I'd ask Andy, crying. "Nothing bad is ever allowed to happen to you."

"Babe, over the last five years you've imagined me dying in every awful way possible, and the whole time I've been sitting right here, drinking a beer and scratching my balls," Andy said.

I laughed, wiping away tears.

"Please stop mourning me," he said, holding me tight. "I'm right here."

I remembered being on a break from college and sitting on the dock at my parents' lake house. Mom was never one to give me advice; more often she would just let me make my mistakes and learn from them, giving me unconditional support along the way. But I always looked to her. After Daddy Keith's death, she was this superwoman who finished 10Ks in first place, pushing the twins in a stroller, while raising five children alone. But that day on the dock, she shared with me her most hard-earned pearl of wisdom. She told me to make sure that whatever I chose to do in life, I could do it by myself. To that day she still remembered how it felt to be suddenly alone with three young children, pregnant with twins, unable to untangle the complicated web of family finances and investments that Daddy Keith had managed. Not even knowing how much money was in the bank. Unsure of the basics of survival.

"What am I supposed to do now?!" she had screamed in the halls of the hospital when the doctor had come out with bad news.

What she said stuck with me. I yearned to go back time and again and test myself and my self-sufficiency. Whatever I was doing, I needed to know that I could do it alone. And it became an addiction. Or some kind of purifying ritual. I thought so very often of life or health being taken from me as it had from every person in the history of time. A loss from which no one could escape. It could happen any second. And what had I done with my life? Didn't I want to see what I was made of? Perhaps that's the reason why running thousand-mile races called to me. I could face the longest, darkest night, and still come out on the other side.

The imprint was how we knew. How I knew, really. Who knows what dogs perceived in this situation? But the imprint of the caribou's body on the deep, soft snow was how I knew the wolves must have been successful. Their tracks were so fresh and so surprising that it appeared the pack dropped from the sky. Kabob, running in lead, slowed and turned her face, and that's when the high, lonesome howls rang out from the gnarled alders at the trail's edge. The dogs' pace quickened as snow spilled away from the runners and we plunged eastward into darkness. We had just begun a 160-mile training run on the Denali Highway, which the state of Alaska stopped maintaining after the first significant snowfall. Unlike truck training earlier in the winter, the highway was now a long, snowy trail with a bright orange sign at the start of it warning all who entered to be fully prepared for winter travel with no hope of a timely rescue. Now, the only way to travel its 135-mile length was on a snowmachine or a dogsled. We had one month to go until the start of the Yukon Quest, which would take us through some of the most lonesome country in the world, but even in training we were encountering all the wildness Alaska had to offer. The wolves' howls trailed us as we plunged into oncoming darkness.

I thought of wolves often while working with my dog team. They were so similar to these dogs, but they were wild. They gestated in their mother's belly for sixty-three days, just like the dogs. They were weaned off their mother's milk around eight weeks, just like the dogs. They had double-layer coats—a soft, downy undercoat topped with a layer of long, hollow guard hairs—just like the dogs. When I worked at the park service kennels, I read a paper by scientist Ted Greenlee titled "Temperature Adaptation in Northern Dogs." He concluded that animals with an insulating mechanism (thick double coat) coupled with a heat-releasing mechanism (panting) can maintain their body temperatures even with big changes in outside temperature. Back then I had wondered, when my hands and feet became tingly and numb and susceptible to frost injury in extreme cold, what happened with dogs in these situations. We humans are not well insulated, so our bodies, in order to protect our vital organs, will shut off blood supply to the feet and hands. For a dog in –60 or –70°F temperatures, his body will do no such thing. Wrote Greenlee, "Instead of stopping the blood supply to the extremities so the blood does not become chilled, what occurs is that the warm, oxygen-carrying arterial blood going into the limb runs right next to the cold, unoxygenated blood leaving the limb. Since they are right next to each other, the warm blood gives up its heat to the cold blood, preventing the loss of this heat as it gets down to the exposed part of the dog's foot. The oxygenated blood can get to the vital parts of the foot to maintain their nutrition, but at the same time does not allow a loss of body heat to the cold air."

And what other kinds of animals had developed such an adaptation? Wolves.

Like wolves, my dogs howled in a low, mournful chorus. And like wolves, they had a pecking order, and I often feared if given the chance, they might gang up and kill a dog they didn't like. Whenever they, as a group, saw weakness in one dog—let's say a dog was vomiting in the dog yard—they would all zero in on that dog and leap at her, high-pitched yelps in their throats. "Kill her!" they would say. Even if it was their own mother or sister. Even if it was their best friend. Though I spent all my time with these dogs, I still didn't really understand the way they operated as a pack.

As we distanced ourselves from the wolves, all the tracks from snowmachines and other teams that had come before us down the Denali Highway disappeared, and we continued; fine, sparkling powder fluffing around the dogs' legs and frosting the fur around their faces. The waning daylight muted the folds and shadows of rolling topography, and the shock of an early afternoon sunset glowed magenta beneath peeling, gray clouds. The silent purity of unbroken trail became punctuated and pocked, punched through with the weight of a thousand pounds—moose were using the trail, too. Half the moose in a six-member harem trotted north, upslope, while the three bulls loped south—their giant antlers silhouetted against the fast-slipping sun. Lavender and rose and so much white. The heart-quickening exclamation of deep, chocolate brown moving so eloquently against it all.

We ran seventy miles and took a six-hour break, then continued. Thirty miles later, snowmachine headlights appeared at the crest of a hill right as I finished untangling a tug line. I hopped on the runners and said "All right!" and the dogs lunged against their harnesses, sliding over to the side of the trail to pass the snowmachine. The engine was loud and the exhaust created a fog around the team when a woman's panicked voice pierced through all of it.

"Wait!" she yelled. "Wait! My husband is back there and I lost track of him! I can't turn this machine around and you're heading that way, so can you please make sure he's all right?"

That's when a dozen glowing, green eyes came toward me. Curious and worried about the panic in the woman's voice, Solo, who was running in lead, had folded back on his teammates, creating a mess of snarls and growls and twisted lines. The front half of the dog team was coming back toward the sled.

"No!" I screamed. "Get up there, guys!"

But it was too late. The dogs in the middle of the team who had never liked Solo much to begin with now had their chance. In moments, Solo was on his back. Five mouths tore into his belly and legs as tangled dogs took out their frustration and confusion on the nearest scapegoat. My team was like a pack of wild wolves taking down an outsider. It was hard to be calm and assertive amid the flashes of white teeth; the insane snarling; the focused intent to kill. I grabbed the leader line that connected Solo to his partner Kabob and hauled it up as hard as I could, falling over in knee-deep snow, crawling on all fours. My heart was pounding in my ears, sending every ounce of power I had to my upper body. By brute strength I unraveled the knot of angry dogs and pulled the gangline taut. Breathless, I collapsed on my knees in front of the team. Solo had a gaping hole in his groin—I could see inside his body— and a half dozen puncture wounds in his leg.

"I need a vet," I said to the snowmachiner, panting.

We were seventy trail miles from the town of Cantwell, where a veterinarian—Dr. Jayne—lived and had a clinic. Dr. Jayne was a good friend and also a dog musher. But we were only three miles from Alpine Creek Lodge.

Andy and his team caught up to me on the trail, and I told him to stay with both our teams while the woman snowmachiner gave Solo and me a ride to the lodge.

At the lodge, a space was cleared on the bunkhouse floor. Owners Claude and Jen were suited and booted and out the door in minutes, headed down the trail to help Andy with the two dog teams. Their son, Bob, and two employees, Ania and Chrissy, lay on the floor next to us. Solo's head was in my lap while strangers' hands petted him, held his legs, held first aid supplies, expertly packed his wounds with gauze soaked in sterile solution, patted my back. Solo licked the tears off my cheeks as Dr. Jayne's voice crackled through the satellite phone line.

"Kristin, he's going to be OK," she said. "Dogs are amazing."

Strangers' voices spoke kind words. Strangers brought me dinner. These strangers were guests staying at the remote lodge, and they dropped everything to help us. The woman snowmachiner, Colleen, turned out to be a nurse who may have found her calling as a vet tech. She tenderly and adroitly packed Solo's wounds. Three guests were members of a group called the Motorheads—a club of extraordinary gentlemen who rode their snowmachines all over the state and who also happened to adore *Downton Abbey*. Those three men—Bob,

Steve, and Ed—agreed to abandon their trip to haul Solo and me the sixty-eight miles down the trail to Dr. Jayne's first thing in the morning.

The next morning, a sled was filled with straw, a sleeping bag, a dry bag of clothes, an extra sterile bandage, and some dog food. Once it was attached to the back of a snowmachine, I climbed in and Solo crawled right into my lap. We were covered with a sleeping bag and off we went. The Motorheads came up with a series of hand signals for me. They stopped and checked in every ten miles. They had someone ahead and someone behind. They watched us every second to make sure we were safe and sound. They wiped the snow off Solo's face and offered me hot coffee.

We pulled into Dr. Jayne's empty parking area and got Solo inside. As the Motorheads drove away I felt my eyes well up with tears. I owed so much to them, and didn't know if I would ever see them again. I didn't even know their last names.

Jayne was returning from Palmer, Alaska, several hours away, and didn't arrive until later in the evening. She gave us a bed to sleep in and in the morning she sutured up my soulmate lead dog upon whom I would depend to lead me down the Yukon Quest trail in one month. The Bondy family provided me with a snowmachine to drive the sixty-eight miles back to the lodge, but I'd only been on a snowmachine once in my life. So Lynn and Bub, our dear friends who facilitated our wedding, drove out to the trailhead in the morning and showed me what I needed to know. They got the machine off the trailer, started it, handed me a bag of homemade sandwiches and cookies (still warm), and sent me on my way.

Two hours later I pulled into Alpine Creek Lodge, got on a dogsled, and mushed the sixty-eight miles back to Cantwell, where our truck was parked. By the time we arrived at Jayne's it was 11:00 p.m. Solo was wide awake and trying to play with Jayne's dogs despite his three drains and a new set of sutures.

It was 2:30 in the morning when our heads finally hit the pillow back home in Healy, but I couldn't sleep. My thoughts were a flurry of worry for my precious dog, stretched out on the bed between Andy and me and groaning occasionally with the pain of his bruised and stitched abdomen and leg. But they were also a flood of gratitude for the people of the North. The mushers in my life comforted me over the phone and guaranteed another dog would step up and take the lead for me if Solo couldn't heal in time for the Quest. It happened to them, too, once. On the Iditarod trail. On the Quest. On the Serum Run.

"Someone will step up and surprise you," they said. "Maybe they've been waiting to be up there in front of that team their whole life!"

Finally, it was the week of the Yukon Quest race start, and we loaded up fourteen dogs—including Solo, who had healed up beautifully—and drove sixteen hours to Whitehorse,

Yukon Territory. Over the course of a few days, the mushers had mandatory meetings that ranged from vet checks to a detailed trail report from the trailbreakers to signing hundreds of posters for race fans and sponsors. The twenty-six of us mushers sat beside each other behind a long rectangular table that separated us from hundreds of fans. The line snaked around the room and out the door. It seemed like everyone in Whitehorse came to meet the mushers of the thousand-mile race, take selfies with them, and have them sign souvenirs. The 2015 Yukon Quest saw the most competitive field in decades, with multiple former champions vying for the win, including Jeff, who hadn't run the Quest since he last won it in 1989.

I was seated between Cody Strathe—the musher who ran Squid Acres Kennel with his wife, Paige, and who also built tough, artful dogsleds, including my own—and Brent Sass of Wild and Free Mushing. In the loud room, we all talked more than we were used to, gulping down cold beer to wet our throats. We glanced at each other piteously, more than ready to be out of the spotlight and on the trail. Near the end of the night, a man in the line of fans struck up a conversation.

"I can't believe *you're* running this race," he said to me, slurring his words a bit. "Aren't you scared?"

"Uhhh, well of course I'm a little nervous, but I'm really excited, too," I said. "I've been working toward this for a long time."

I finished signing my name, then pushed the poster back toward him.

"I mean," the man continued, sneering, "I'm a *man*, and I'd never run this race."

He said it as though simply being a man better qualified *him* to run a thousand-mile sled dog race than an accomplished female musher like myself.

Cody turned to me with his eyes wide. His wife, Paige Drobny, was one of my best friends and also a veteran of both the Yukon Quest and the Iditarod. She stood behind him and laughed.

"Yeah," I said, without missing a beat for the first time in my life. "Just imagine what I could accomplish if I had a penis!"

Brent guffawed, putting his hand to his forehead.

"Uh, no, I mean…" the drunk man stuttered, "that's not…"

"Why don't you move along," Brent said, laughing. "You're just gonna dig yourself deeper."

I nodded in agreement with Brent and gave the guy a sarcastic smile that said, "Kindly fuck off."

I wish I could say that was the most surprising interaction I had with a fan, but a fifty-year-old woman said the thing that stuck with me the most.

"I'm so amazed by you three women," she said, referring to me, Ryne, and Tamra Reynolds, the only three women running the race. "I just can't imagine doing what you're doing. You three are so brave. Aren't you terrified of being out there all alone?"

She said it like we women had an additional burden to bear. Like our experience would be that much more scary and difficult because we weren't men. And also, like men didn't need to be brave to run the Yukon Quest. Like they just came that way, with bravery built in.

"Well, all of us are doing something we've trained for many years to do," I said. "Both the women and the men."

"Yeah, but you're..." she paused, raising her eyebrows and gesturing toward me. Like I was supposed to understand what she was hinting at. Like we had some kind of wordless understanding about a woman's place.

"Don't you think you should value yourself a bit more?" I asked her. "You're a woman, and I'm sure you've done some very hard, brave things."

Her grown child, a young man in his twenties, stood beside her.

"You're a mother, you've brought a kid into this world," I said. "That's not easy. And it's a thing only women can do."

She blinked at me, a little taken by surprise.

"All I'm saying is, what all twenty-six of us here are about to do is difficult and scary and it has taken us our whole lives to prepare for it," I said. "And the women are just as capable as the men, and you shouldn't believe otherwise."

I was grateful to be in a sport where there were no divisions between men and women. And out on the trail, we could hardly tell one another apart. Underneath the big parkas and frozen ruffs, we were all one thing: dog mushers. And with our well-trained teams lined out before us, panting quietly, ears picking up our commands, we were all equally in the paradise we had made for ourselves. In that yawning expanse that cared nothing for human constructs—our gender roles, our customs, our pain and suffering—we were all equals.

PART 8

The Yukon Quest

Twenty below is the temperature at which you can walk outside and, if you're not wearing exactly enough layers, the cold is in. Immediately. It's through your clothes and poking at your skin saying, "Hey, I'm dangerous." Twenty below is the perfect temperature for running dogs. You're working hard enough to stay warm, and the dogs are working hard enough to need the cold, and to feel perfect in it. To feel a balance. Twenty below is like the 60-degree, brisk fall day for a dog.

Thirty below is when it starts to get exciting. A shot of adrenaline surges through you when you see –30 on the thermometer. You prepare to do battle. You put on a *lot* of clothes. You take a breath before you head out the door and steel yourself against the cold. You actively remind yourself to warm up individual limbs every few minutes while on the sled.

Forty below and colder is just absurd. When you see –40 on the thermometer you simply have to laugh. What the hell is Mother Nature trying to prove here? Forty below is the same whether it's Fahrenheit or Celsius.

So in Whitehorse, Yukon Territory, Canada, on February 7, 2015, it was both –40°Celsius and –40°Fahrenheit and the Yukon Quest 1,000-Mile International Sled Dog Race was starting in one hour. But I was not laughing. Tears streamed down my pallid face as I held my waterproof overboots over the dashboard heater of the dog truck, dogs yanking the one-ton rig this way and that from drop chains that surrounded the vehicle like the hem of a big hoop dress. I looked out the driver-side window at Ryne Olson's dog truck, motor running, and at all the other trucks in the parking lot. Every last one was idling to keep its engine from freezing. Out the passenger-side window were Andy, my brother Jared, and my friend Mandy, the one who called everyone a pussy. She had agreed to drive the truck with Andy and Jared for the entire race. They were preparing our dogs for the extreme cold by layering them up with coats, leggings, and booties.

I thought back to that first time I'd seen the start of the Quest five years ago. Finally, it was my turn to have the volunteers walk *me* to the start line. To have *my* dogs proceed two by two by two with their hind legs outstretched and lunging into the harnesses, pulling me irrevocably forward. It was my turn to don the enormous parka, to stand tall in my big pack boots...except my boots didn't fit. I had left them out in the cold truck all night and now they were frozen solid, not giving a single millimeter. I had tried shoving my wool bootie-lined feet into the overboots and jumping up and down, jamming my toes ever forward, but it hadn't worked. The heater was my last hope. I was about to run one thousand miles with my very own dogs. It had taken me years to get here and I couldn't even get my boots on.

Panicking, I creaked open the truck door and approached every other musher in the lot (there were twenty-five besides me) and asked if they happened to have a pair of NEOS overboots one size bigger than the ones I held limply in my hands.

Ryne was sympathetic. She, like me, was having her race followed by a photographer who was documenting both of our rookie runs. We had only hung out two or three times to meet up with the photographer before the race, but we got along, even though I'd been intimidated when I first met her at sign-ups. She was confident and super athletic, with dark hair and a deep voice and sincere blue eyes. She called herself "a professional dog musher," and she knew with certainty that someday she would win a race like this. She came up under the guidance of superhero musher Aliy Zirkle, the only female ever to win the Yukon Quest. And I was sure she would give me some kind of patronizing vibe when I asked her about the overboots. But instead, she just laughed at how big my feet were and said she definitely didn't have any boots that size.

"Are you nervous?" she asked, shoulder to shoulder with me as though she were my very concerned best friend.

"Yes," I said, looking around at the gathering crowd. "Are you?"

"I'm just ready to get out of here," she said.

She wished me luck in finding new boots and I trudged over to Mike Ellis, a tall, gruff musher who was running his seventh Quest. He looked at me with grave concern and disappointment. His beard was already firred with frost.

"You didn't go one size up for the cold?" he asked.

I shook my head no.

"You always go one size up when it's this cold. The material shrinks," he said, reaching over and giving the boots a little shake.

Defeated, I walked over to Paige and Cody's truck, where Cody was preparing to run his second Quest.

"Oh, mine totally did that, too!" he said, surprisingly

happy-go-lucky considering his penchant for doomsday-style worrying. "I just stomped into them really, really hard."

"I already tried that," I said, choking back tears.

"Go into that building over there where it's warm and just stomp your feet as hard as you can," he said, pointing to the visitor center on the edge of the parking lot. "Maybe the fabric will warm up and stretch."

I scurried over to the visitor center where hundreds of tourists were readying themselves for the upcoming race start. It was a cavernous building, kind of like a train station. The ice cleats on the bottom of the overboots clacked hard onto the tile floor and echoed embarrassingly loudly as I jumped with the full force of my weight up and down. Everyone stopped what they were doing to watch. "She's one of the mushers," I heard them whisper, shocked at such a public loss of composure. Over and over again I slammed my feet down, leaping upward with high knees to get the most downward force possible. I knew there was no such thing as dying from embarrassment. I also knew I could lose my feet if I didn't get these goddamn boots on.

I wedged my feet into the overboots enough that my heel was only slightly elevated—maybe one inch or less—so that I walked as though I wore high heels. The start was in thirty minutes, and this was going to have to do. I knew all about how dangerous it was to wear shoes that were too tight in this kind of cold. My feet needed space around them to fill up with the warmth from my body, and that warmth would be insulated and protected by all these layers of boots. But I had to put that out of my mind now. In about ten minutes, I'd have to start harnessing my team. I had to focus on what I was about to do.

I tiptoed back to the dog truck with my toes scrunched and pulled out the harnesses. Solo knew that we were at a race start and overbrimmed with eagerness. It never ceased to amaze me that the same dog who loved tennis balls, belly rubs, and lap sitting was also insatiably competitive. Racing was what he loved, and he was so impatient to get his harness on that when I fumbled in the cold he gave me a hard nudge with his nose, as if to say, "Give me that thing. I'll put it on myself." He was literally vibrating with excitement.

The rest of my race team watched me harness Solo, waiting their turn. Littlehead was usually Solo's calm and tiny counterpart, except I didn't start with her in lead on race day. She was the kind of dog who stood at the front of an empty gangline and waited to be attached to it. There was no denying her place. Except when she would do this thing we called "Littleheading out," when she would just start galloping off to the side of the trail. That meant she didn't want to run in lead anymore. She translated for her sister, Kabob, who loved to chase animals and enjoyed chaos of all types. "My sissy says she's better than the rest of the dogs," Littlehead would often say, in her high-pitched whisper of a voice. "My sissy says she isn't actually a dog."

Kabob's daughter Loretta and son Buck were two phenoms that made the team as yearlings. Though they looked more like Solo, their dad, they had Kabob's unblinking stare, her sweet brown eyes, her slow and intentional face licks. Ferlin was the other yearling on my team—a long-legged powerhouse with a corkscrew tail and floppy ears. He rolled over for belly rubs every time he got booties on his feet. Belly rubs were his toll for being able to pull the hook on a run. And once we took off, Ferlin never, ever looked behind him and never let off his tug line. Brothers Ox and Iron were brawny and muscular, and they leaped on their hind legs to hug each other and play before I could put on their harnesses. Race photographers loved Ox and Iron—Ox for his white and gray face mask and Iron for his reddish coat tipped in white frost. Andy-dog was a big blonde with daddy long legs and a sharp-ended tail that stood straight up, or whipped around and around like a helicopter when he was happy to see us. Though he'd already finished the Yukon Quest before in Brent Sass's team, Andy-dog was a little nervous at the sight of all these people. He tucked his face into my legs like a shy toddler. And he was not happy about being partnered with Norton, who reared up like a great black and white orca breaching from the ocean, mouth agape, teeth gleaming. Norty was straight-up psychopathic when it came to hookup. And with the added excitement of a race, he was not to be contained.

"He will literally give you a black eye," I warned Mandy.

"Or a bloody nose," Andy added. "Just make sure you turn your face away from him."

Hoss, my eighty-pound gray and tan wheel dog, rubbed his giant head against my leg and licked my hand. He was the heaviest dog at Yukon Quest vet checks. He leaned up against me and stretched like a big cat. His brother Bullock waggled his thick black body with his thick black tail, sidling up to Hoss and *roo*ing with excitement. With these two sweet, massively athletic brothers in wheel, I knew we'd be able to get through anything. I got emotional just looking at them. I had watched Zigzag give birth to them, and now I was about to leave the start line of a thousand-mile race with them right in front of my sled. The two newest members of the team—Rowdy and Magnum—were on loan from Paige and Cody. Magnum was almost Norton's identical twin—black and white with dark brown eyes and an unquenchable desire to pull straight ahead forever. Rowdy, on the other hand, was a very sweet white and gray boy with the fluffiest of tails. He loved to play keep-away, and had taken off on us as we loaded up the truck to leave Healy a few days earlier. We lured him back into the dog yard with our neighbor's female who was in heat. Rowdy was an amazing leader, but I was taking a risk bringing along any dog who wouldn't come when called.

A race volunteer came by the truck to tell us "five minutes." Rapidly, we attached the dogs to the gangline, with Solo and Kabob in lead. I put my giant parka over my head and buckled my race bib—Number 12. I scanned the crowd through the fog of frozen exhaust and spotted my mom's electric orange parka and, beside her, my dad's blue one. I couldn't see their faces, but I waved and stepped onto the runners of my dogsled.

The dogs knocked people over on our way to the start line, but even in the din of barking I could hear Andy's gentle voice behind me. I could feel the warmth of his touch through all the layers of long underwear and fleece and two insulated knee-length parkas. In all of this chaos, he was the steady force, the safety net. And at the end of the announcer's countdown, I sped away from him with the gusto of fourteen dogs hell-bent on destruction.

The crowds were well behind us, but the dogs were still amped up as we weaved in and out of snow-covered trees and dipped down into steep-banked, frozen creeks. We came down a long hill and banged hard onto slick, glassy, glare ice, taking a ninety-degree turn and slamming into a stand of trees. I crashed so hard onto my right elbow that I saw stars, and felt absolutely positive that the bone was shattered. I remained on my side, holding on to the handlebar of my sled and saying "woah" as calmly as possible. The sled mowed down little spruce trees like a piece of heavy machinery meant for clearing land. I could see Solo was taking it all in stride, head down, trotting steadily. But Kabob, in lead beside him, was running at an all-out sprint and looking back at all the other dogs like she had planned my demise and was thrilled to see that it was actually coming together.

"Kabob!" I yelled.

Kabob glanced back at me and tucked her little white-tipped tail down, along with her ears, picking up the pace. "She's almost off, guys!" she seemed to say, her energy informing the rest of the team. She loved this kind of shit.

"My sissy isn't listening to you," Littlehead said, glancing back.

"Kabob, woah," I said.

I swore to god she was shaking her head in defiance as she surged even faster.

"Fucking Ka-BOB!!!" I screamed.

She laughed maniacally, if dogs can do that, and essentially flipped me the bird.

With a powerful yank, I righted my dogsled and went to slam down on the metal brake bar, but I couldn't. An entire tree had somehow wedged itself into my handlebar and down through my brakes, all the way to the icy trail beneath the sled.

"How does this *happen*?" I yelled, ripping the tree out from the brake, threading it through the handlebar and throwing it into the woods.

I rubbed my elbow and felt a precise, wincing pain. This was not a great way to start a thousand-mile sled dog race. In another couple hundred miles, though, that elbow would be the least of my worries.

When I reached the checkpoint of Carmacks 150 miles later, people were scratching from the race all around me. One of them, Scott Smith, had been the 2013 Rookie of the Year. He told me it had been -68°F out on the trail on the way here, and his dogs weren't doing a good enough job eating to stay ahead of the amount of calories they were burning in the cold.

We rarely talked about scratching, because you didn't want to go into a race with a plan to not finish it, however subconsciously. But scratching was a totally respectable thing to do in most cases. When it came down to it, making the call to scratch from a race, after all of those years of effort to be there, was no small thing. And most mushers did it for the well-being of their dog teams. If it seemed like enough dogs weren't having fun anymore that you couldn't make it down the trail with the remainder, you scratched. One musher scratched because his sled had busted into pieces and he didn't have a backup. Another scratched because his dogs were blowing through food and, even with extras from other mushers, he didn't think he'd have enough to make it across the upcoming vast distances between checkpoints. But most mushers, it seemed, were scratching because of the extreme cold. I couldn't blame them. At my last camp, I had been too scared to fall asleep in the straw next to Hoss and Bullock, worried I would never wake up again.

I told Scott I was sorry he was scratching. Then I said, "You don't, by any chance, wear XXL Neos, do you?"

Laughing, Scott pointed to a pair of torn-up boots that were nestled beside a heater.

"One of the buckles is broken and they're pretty beat up," he said.

I hugged him.

"I think you just saved my feet."

I knew I was going to lose my sled the second I dropped down the cutbank and saw the fridge-size boulder of ice in the trail.

The whole incident happened in slow motion: the nose of the sled hit the side of the ice boulder; the sled corkscrewed into the air and landed on its side; I hit the ground with an epic body slam; my grip broke free from the handlebars; and my gleeful dogs dragged the sled right out of my reach. I heaved myself up onto my knees and caught Hoss's eye. He panicked, putting on the brakes with all four legs stiff, his shoulders hunched.

We have to stop! he said. *For* Mom!

In front of him, six pairs of dogs trotted beautifully forward. And at the head of that gorgeous train was Solo.

"Solo!" I yelled, pleading. "Solo, please wait, buddy! Please stop. *Woahhhh.*"

We were 250 miles into the race, and the temperature was steadily dropping as the trail dove deeper and deeper into the remote Yukon Territory.

Without breaking stride, Solo gave me a cool sidelong glance right in the eye, regarding me as though I were a total stranger. As though I were *annoying* him. He snootily raised his eyebrows, turned his head forward, and continued leading the team. The sled had righted itself, and the likelihood of it getting caught on something and stopping them slimmed with every step the dogs took away from me. I watched hopelessly as it banged and clattered against the jagged jumble ice, a type of river-freezing I had heard about before the race but had never experienced.

"Come ask me about this section of trail after the race," the Canadian trailbreaker had said during the prerace trail report, "and I'll tell you what I really think of it over a shot of whiskey." He had looked haggard and bruised, as though he and his crew had just emerged from battle. It had taken them an entire week to put in these five miles of trail. They had come at it with chain saws, axes, and hatchets.

Jumble ice formed when slabs of ice in the still-freezing river jammed into and upended each other. He explained that when rivers start to freeze in the fall, ice first forms at the shore and then extends out into the river. As water levels go up and down, some shore ice breaks off and floats downriver. Those flat sheets of ice can pile up and create a jumble of ice with sharp, jagged edges. And that's what I was looking at. An ocean of piled-up plates of ice spanning the Yukon from bank to bank. And out there in the middle of it, weaving through the chainsawed tunnel that was the trail, was my dog team, leaving me behind.

I wasn't allowed to sweat, because sweat soaks your clothes and freezes and causes hypothermia. But it was hard not to run desperately after them, because what if they got tangled up and someone ended up dragging? And also because everything I needed to keep myself alive was in that sled. I had firestarter and a snack and an extra headlamp in my parka, but that wouldn't last me for very long. So I took a deep breath and began to walk after my team. I shook away my mind's first instincts—panic, desperation—and actively replaced them with a practical to-do list: Keep walking. Do not sweat. Eat a snack. Twenty minutes later I emerged from a maze of towering ice piles and saw my sled wedged into a crack between two ice boulders. The dogs were barking and lunging, trying to free the sled and keep going. I walked straight up to Solo and Kabob.

"Guys, you have to listen to me," I said, crouching down. "This is serious, you cannot leave me like that again."

Solo put his paw on my arm. Kabob rubbed her head against my parka. Then, to my surprise, they lay down. All fourteen dogs stopped barking and either sat back on their haunches or lay down, crossed their paws, and waited. I wrenched the sled out from the crack in the ice and stepped on the metal bar brake, which promptly sheared right off my sled. For a moment, I just stared at it. Like my intense desire for this to not happen would somehow turn back time and make it un-happen. But you cannot outrun your problems on the Yukon Quest trail, nor can you hide from them or pretend they aren't happening. So I took out my ax and chopped a V into the river ice and placed my snowhook into the V, securing my sled. I looked up and the dogs remained exactly as they had been before—seated and resting. I dug through my sled bag and found my repair kit, grateful that I had just practiced using every tool inside in the weeks leading up to the race. It was −45°F and the sun was going down, creating a saturated, ink-stamp sky that ran the spectrum of all the purples. Nonetheless I took off my gloves and, barehanded, accomplished the tedious work of inserting a new bolt through the sled stanchion and then through the metal brake, securing it there with two washers and a nut and tightening it down with a socket and hex wrench respectively. I tested the brake and it hinged on its new bolt, but only begrudgingly. It would have to do for now.

"OK, guys," I said. "We're gonna do this, but we are gonna

do it *slowly*. OK, Kabob? Hoss, you're a good boy, you know what I'm talking about."

The dogs stood up and, very carefully, *walked* the remaining four miles of jumble ice maze. The sled flipped two more times and they stopped each time, looked back at me, and waited for me to right the sled and tell them we could go again.

Before the race, I hadn't realized that I could love them any more than I did. That I could build a bond with them stronger than the one we already had. When we pulled into McCabe Creek Dog Drop, one of the race veterinarians greeted me and asked how the run was.

"It was the best run of the race so far," I said, beaming. "Something happened out there, I don't know, they just…they understand me. They can read my mind."

I bedded down my dogs on fat spreads of straw, ladled out a hot meal, and turned to walk inside the family barn that served as a warming hut for weary mushers and race volunteers.

"Excuse me!" yelled a thickly accented voice in the dark.

"Excuse me, but, you have all fourteen dogs?"

"Yes," I said.

"How you do it? Through all the jumble ice, how you do it?"

A man emerged in the light of my headlamp. It was another musher, a French Canadian named Gaëtan. He looked so tired and so sincere, and very honestly shocked. He really wanted to know how I did it. He was already down to nine dogs. He was looking to me for advice.

I gazed down my string of dogs all in their red coats, noses tucked under tails, snoozing peacefully in seven perfect pairs. They looked so innocent. Their paws curled under, five dark little pads exposed. For all the ferocity and power and athleticism of these dogs, something about their paws broke my heart.

"They walked," I told him. "I asked them to walk, and they walked."

As I traveled over a string of frozen lakes on the way into Pelly Crossing, I felt a dangerous, creeping cold. It came up from under the ice and seeped into my boots and up my legs. It got into my tired brain and convinced it, over and over again, to shut down. To fall asleep. To succumb. That's why the checkpoint at Pelly Crossing was such a shock. It was bright lights and steam and lots of people and cameras. As I got checked in, a familiar voice said "Congratulations!" right into my ear and then it was gone. I pulled into the dog lot and parked beside two other resting teams. As I walked toward the community center to get water for my cooker, I passed Ryne bootying her dogs. It had been her voice. I thought I'd imagined it since Ryne was so far ahead of me, but it turned out she had given her dogs a bunch of extra rest here. I watched her leave, wondering if I would see her again.

After dog chores I was overwhelmed and beyond tired. The muscles holding up my eyelids had begun to twitch. My body wanted nothing more than to sleep. I walked into the community center and learned that another musher had scratched, ratcheting the total up to six, and we weren't even halfway done. I entered a dark room with gym mats on the floor and told a race volunteer to wake me up in 1.5 hours. In an instant, I was being awakened. I desperately wanted to go back to bed, but the enormity of packing my sled for 200 unsupported miles still loomed. I was about to mush from Pelly to Dawson, the halfway point of the race 210 miles away, without a single resupply, and it was –40°F. I still had fourteen dogs, who would need to be snacked every hour in those conditions. That's a lot of food.

I sat down at a plastic picnic table and got out a piece of paper and a pen. I wrote out everything I would need, ate some toast, and went back to my sled to get packing. My sled bag zippers were fragile in the cold, and as I yanked on one it popped right off. I cried as though I had just lost a friend.

The bricks of dog food weighed fifteen pounds each, and I laid them in the sled like sandbags, counting as I went along, checking things off my list. For a sleep-deprived brain, this is a very difficult task.

"How much food you got?" a harsh voice interrupted. I looked up and it was Bob McAlpine, one of the race judges.

"Uh...enough?" I said.

"What are you doin' here? You need to get a move on and catch up to the group ahead of you so you're not traveling alone."

Why does he think I needed to travel with other mushers? I thought. *Am I coming off as incompetent?*

"Well, I'm in the middle of packing for two hundred miles

and I still have fourteen dogs," I said brusquely, shoving gear into my sled bag. "I can't be rushed. I don't want to forget anything."

"Well, you're really burning daylight here," he said, shaking his head.

"It's nine a.m. I've only been here six hours," I said as calmly as I could. "I'm doing an equal run/rest schedule and it took me six hours to get here, so I'm not that far behind."

"Well, didn't you take a long rest at McCabe?" he asked skeptically. He wouldn't let it go, and I was beginning a downward spiral of anxiety from which I feared I wouldn't emerge.

"It took me five and a half hours to get to McCabe, and I rested there five and a half hours," I said.

"Huh," he said.

"Look, you're really stressing me out," I said. "I have a really good dog team, and we will catch up. I'm not just some rookie; I've done huge expeditions with these dogs."

I said the words to convince him I was capable, but also to remind myself, in the face of doubt, of all that I had accomplished. In the days it had taken me to arrive in Carmacks, I had only slept a few hours. I was raw, and it felt like my sanity was hanging on by a thread. I didn't understand why Bob was pushing me and all I knew was that I needed him to get away from me. I couldn't let his doubts about my capabilities work their way into my mind, because I knew that in my weakened state I could be convinced to believe them.

"I can't deal with you right now and I'd like you to leave," I said in a tone as devoid of emotion as I could muster.

I didn't want him to think I was a basket case, but also I had work to do and his interruptions were too much for my brain to handle.

He receded into the background, toward the steam of the checkpoint. All the focus I had mustered for the epic packing job rolled away with him. It was -38 degrees. I stuffed packages of booties into the busted sled bag with tears in my eyes, and the ziplock bags shattered in my hands from the cold. I began to doubt my ability to do this.

The sled was ridiculous by the time I was finished packing. It bulged out, corseted together with nylon tug lines zigzagging between one side of the sled and the other. My sleeping bag was attached to the top, just on the nose of the sled. A giant duffel bag holding half a bale of straw was bungeed atop the rest. The sled must have weighed close to four hundred pounds. I just stared at it. How in the fuck would we ever get this thing up the trail?

I trudged back inside, a little deflated. I needed warm food. I needed to put on my dried-out clothes. I scarfed a plate of eggs, then sat down to put on my layers. A woman with a camera approached me—one of the documentarians from a Canadian film company—and asked if she could have an interview.

"We want to talk to every musher in the race," she said, omitting the rest of the sentence "...not just the frontrunners."

I was officially the last thousand-mile musher. There was no one behind me. I was it. For seven hundred more miles.

"I'm really proud of my dogs and...even though a lot of people are scratching, um...(crying)...I am not gonna let them down," I said. "I'm a rookie and so this is my first thousand-mile race ever and I just wanted to finish. I didn't have any particular place in mind to finish, I just wanted to finish with my whole team. Which is kind of really hard to do (laughing). But so far, I'm doing it, so, it's been successful thus far. But we're only one-third of the way through."

The lady interviewing me told me that it was something special to still have all fourteen dogs in my team. That people were watching us and even looking up to us.

I steeled myself against the cold and marched out the door. Bob arrived at my sled just as I began to bootie my dogs.

"You'll have a head-on pass out there," he warned. "Jeff King just called from Stepping Stone and he's gonna scratch. Too cold. Not enough dog food..."

Was this guy pulling out all the stops to try to get me to quit or what? Andy pulled him aside and, explaining that Jeff was my mentor and that I was in a fragile mental state, firmly requested for him to leave me alone. Suddenly, instead of feeling defeated by Bob's insistent doubt, I was fuming. I had a renewed sense of purpose.

"I'll show you, motherfucker," I said under my breath.

I bootied my dogs with a smile on my face. A crowd had gathered to watch me depart. Photographers stationed themselves on various parts of the exit trail, knowing it would be the last time they'd see a musher for two hundred miles. I attached fourteen tug lines to fourteen barking dogs. I stepped onto my sled and said, "All right!" with relish. We were on the Yukon River once again, bound for Dawson City. For the first time in three hundred miles I stood on the runners instead of the brake. It was time to let the dogs fly.

I passed Rob Cooke in a blizzard on a mountaintop outside Stepping Stone. "You're fucking crazy!" he yelled into the wind as my four-hundred-pound sled dropped with a thunk into the waist-deep snow on the side of the trail. I laughed like a maniacal witch as wind swirled snow all around me and the dogs. I called up the dogs and we passed his team, chugging up the mountain as though the sled were weightless. By the time I reached Scroggie Creek Dog Drop—a seriously remote outpost on the edge of rugged Yukon River foothills—Ryne and I were running together. We carried on the tradition of writing our names in Sharpie on the plywood wall of a tiny ten-by-twelve-foot warming hut, right next to so many names of mushers past. Ryne left a little ahead of me, but said we should camp together somewhere in the Black Hills, around fifty miles outside of Dawson City.

Hours later, Ryne was there, just like she said she would be, with a big fire blazing next to her sled. She walked up and greeted me, pointing to a spot across the trail from her that would be good for my team. The dogs strained against their tug lines and pulled the hook a couple times before letting me tie them down, and Ryne marveled at that. I was annoyed. Kabob was going into heat and Solo was humping her any chance he could get. Everyone had too much rest and was misbehaving.

It was still forty below, and they were all *so* happy and eating well. Ryne went to cut more firewood, complaining about how dull her ax was, and I was happy to let her use mine.

"It's brand new. I just sharpened it, and cutting wood with this thing is like hitting a home run," I said, unsheathing the wood-handled Gransfors Bruks from its slot in my loaded sled.

Ryne took the ax and walked off into the woods.

When my cooker was acting up, Ryne offered hers. It didn't have any kind of regulator at the bottom like mine did. She just poured methanol right into the bottom and lit it up with a massive *whoosh*. It wasn't fuel efficient, but the water was boiling in minutes. She didn't care; we only had one more run before arriving in Dawson City, where we could restock with everything we could possibly need. We could use up all the fuel and it wouldn't matter.

I got the dogs settled and walked across the trail to Ryne's fire. We sat down together and talked while I ate my dinner. I offered to split my homemade cheesecake with her, and she enthusiastically accepted. Once we realized we shouldn't have heated up the cheesecake in the hot pot of water, it was too late. The gooey sweetness was already running down our fingers, and we laughed openmouthed as it ran down our faces. "We are disgusting!" I said. "I'm pretty sure I have shit on my hands, or at least raw meat." We licked our fingers anyway— we couldn't really pass up a single calorie at this point, but also the homemade blueberry goodness couldn't be wasted.

"It's pretty hilarious that we're the only two women left in this race and here we are, gabbing and eating cheesecake by a campfire," Ryne said.

We talked about how our dogs were doing, we told each other of our highs and lows, we asked each other's advice. It wasn't your average girl talk, but it was exactly the kind of girlfriendship we needed 450 miles into a dog race.

"I'm gonna sleep for an hour and then take off," Ryne said, rolling out her sleeping bag. She had a foam Z-Rest sleeping pad that took up barely any room in her sled and insulated her from the cold ground. I eyed it jealously, and felt a little sheepish about not bringing one of my own. It weighed nothing and would have saved me so much shivering. Instead I lay down on the straw with Hoss and Bullock, just as I had done so many other times before in this race. Headlamp off, I could see the shadow of Solo sitting upright, staring at Kabob.

"Solo, lay down and get some rest," I said.

He just looked at all the other males and growled, pre-emptively letting anyone who might care to challenge him know that Kabob was *his*, thank you very much.

I closed my eyes and Hoss began to snore. Then, Ryne was up.

"Ryne, I thought you were gonna sleep for an hour," I said.

"I did, didn't I?" she asked.

"Uh, no, you laid down for about five minutes," I said, laughing.

We both started cracking up.

"Man, I guess I just really want to get to Dawson," she said with a laugh.

She quickly booted up her team, then did something I had

never seen a musher do. Starting with her leaders, she ruffed up their fur and got right in their faces and said, "Ohhhhh, Katy! Who's a good girl? Ohhhhh, Fire, who's a good girrrrrl!!" in the most high-pitched cheerleader voice I had ever heard. I was shocked. She moved down the line. "Ham, who's a guh-boy? Ruuucuuuu, who's a guh-boy??" The dogs were loving it. They wagged their tails and began to bark and lunge into their harnesses. By the time she got to her wheel dogs, the whole team was howling. She picked up her snow hook and off she went. "See you in Dawson!" she yelled. I watched her headlamp disappear into the night.

Less than an hour later, we were on the trail, too. I knew I should have slept more, but it was too cold and we were so close to seeing Andy and getting to sleep in a warm hotel bed. The draw of Dawson was too strong. We were on the move, but my eyes began to close and I awakened with a jolt as I tipped over the handlebar of my sled. I looked up to see my entire dog team in a ball. They had stopped and the sled had kept on going because I had failed to step on the brake. When I slow-motion-bumped into Hoss and Bullock, I had woken myself up. But then, to my horror, I saw a wolf about twenty feet in front of my dogs.

"Hey!" I screamed. "Get outta here! Get the fuck outta here!"

I knew mushers saw wolves all the time on the Quest, but this one was within striking distance of Littlehead, for Christ's sake. What if this one was rabid and out of its mind? What if this was the one time in history where a wolf got aggressive with a dog team? Quickly, I stomped my snow hook into the ground and began running to the front of the team. The dogs were oddly unreactive to this whole situation. Nobody even barked.

Because there was nothing there. The wolf had been a hallucination. And Littlehead gave me a withering look of disappointment. She shook her head at me. "Mom, what. the. fuck." And Littlehead *never* swore.

"Jesus, you guys, I am losing it," I said as I walked up and lined out my team and gave everyone a snack. "I just really need to lay down. Just for a minute."

I flopped on my back on top of my sled bag, arms outstretched at my sides and hanging off the sled. I have no idea how long I was there. I woke up with my hands numb and frozen. We started down the trail again and I became very confused. There was a little bit of light in the sky, but I didn't know if it was sunrise or sunset. I couldn't remember. Six hours later, we reached Dawson City. Under the halfway finish line, the dogs howled. They were ready to keep going. I was ready for a beer, a bath, and a bed. Even though this year the Quest was experimenting with a twenty-four-hour mandatory break instead of a thirty-six, I was still thankful that I now had an entire day to enjoy all of those things while Andy cared for the dogs.

I had left Dawson City two hours earlier, and even though my sled now felt like my home, I still felt torn from the comforts of civilization. The beer had been cold, the bubble bath divine, and the bed a deep well of sleep and rejuvenation. Dawson City felt like a hell of a good place for a finish line, I had joked. But in all honesty, ten people had now scratched from the race and a small part of me wanted to be done with it, too. I shook off thoughts of quitting and got back on my sled, which at this point seemed like an outgrowth of my body. The first twenty miles down the Yukon were beautiful, with big, towering bluffs jutting out from bends in the river. When darkness fell, the same Yukon became less of a concrete geological feature and more a gut-dropping feeling of cold and distance. Like calling out into an enormous, frozen echo chamber, but never hearing your voice come back. I clicked my headlamp up to its highest power and turned my head, but the light never landed on anything.

Thirty-five miles outside of Dawson, Norton stepped in a perfectly paw-width crack in the river ice, tweaking his shoulder. He was limping, but pulling ahead straight as an arrow in true Norty fashion.

"Norty," I said. "Buddy, I'm gonna have to carry you."

I stopped the team and sat down on my sled. The next time I could drop a dog with a veterinarian would be in Eagle, more than one hundred miles from here. Should I turn around and take him back to Dawson? If I did that, it would be the end of my race, for sure. Leaving Dawson once was hard enough. I looked at Norty, who was by now impatiently whining to keep on going. We were fifteen miles from Clinton Creek Hospitality Stop—the home of a couple who lived on the Fortymile River year-round. I walked up to Norty and stretched out his leg, forward and backward, and he didn't utter a single squeak.

"OK, bud, we'll go nice and slow and see how you do for a little while," I told him.

Norton faced forward and lunged into his harness.

A couple miles after turning onto the Fortymile River from the Yukon, I spotted a dog team camped on the river. The race officials had told us that Clinton Creek Hospitality Stop was way up off the river, that our dogs wouldn't have to camp on the ice. I was confused. I parked my team beside the other dog team, took off everyone's booties, grabbed my cook pot, and looked upward. A long, steep pathway had been kicked into the snow up to the door of a cabin. I trudged up the trail and knocked on the door, turning to look back at the dogs.

The door opened and I was greeted with a four-voice-strong, "Heyyyy!!!!"

Four stumbling men with their arms around each other welcomed me into the smoke-filled cabin.

"Um, hi," I said, barely containing my disappointment. "Is this the...hospitality stop?"

"No! Mushers just keep stopping here," one of the men said, laughing. "We just rented this place out for the weekend. Here, have some spaghetti!"

I looked over at the day-old pot on the stove and almost vomited in my mouth. Beside the stove were dozens of empty bottles of beer. And in the back, snoring away, was Nic Vanier, the musher whose dogs were parked out on the river.

I was turning over the possibility of actually getting any rest here, when a knock came at the front door. It was Earl, an old sourdough-looking guy with a Kris Kringle beard and sparkling eyes. He and his wife Sandy ran the real hospitality stop.

"Kristin," he said. "We've been watching you on the tracker and waiting for you. We were wondering why all the mushers kept stopping short."

I closed the door behind me, coughing out the stale smoke, and said, "Thank god. I was worried this was the only place we could stop. But, I already took off all my dogs' booties and bedded them down. I don't know if I can ask them to get up and keep going."

Earl looked at me and said, "It's two more miles up the river. There's homemade sourdough bread there. Moose stew. Homemade cheesecake. Blueberry pancakes."

My stomach rumbled.

"OK," I said. "I'll give it a shot."

I trudged back down and looked reluctantly at my sleeping dogs. As Earl waited patiently on his snowmachine, I repacked my sled and reattached all the tug lines. The dogs popped up right out of their straw and lunged forward, happy to continue. I couldn't believe it. Would I ever see the tired limit of these dogs? I knew right then I was the weakest link in this team.

We followed Earl underneath a low bridge and then turned up a steep driveway, past a blinking neon pink LIVE NUDES sign in the front yard. I laughed out loud, because fucking seriously?

As I took all the tugs off my dogs and bedded them down

in straw again, Earl said, "You know who's been waiting in here for twenty-four hours for another musher to come along? Lance Mackey! He wants to travel with you."

Lance Mackey was a legend. There's a saying in Alaska: "Superman wears Lance Mackey pajamas." Lance Mackey was the only musher in history to win four Yukon Quests and four Iditarods back to back. It is a feat that likely will never be matched. And he did it all while battling cancer.

I went inside the thick-logged trapper cabin where Lance was asleep in Earl and Sandy's bed. His seal fur hat and red one-piece snow suit were hanging over the fire on a drying rack made of antlers. I was about to eat the aforementioned homemade sourdough bread and moose stew, and even a salad for Christ's sake, all the way out here. And Lance Fuckin' Mackey wanted to travel the Yukon Quest trail with me. Life could be a whole lot worse.

In the morning, I bootied up my dogs and Lance told me to go on ahead, he would catch up to me in a bit. Unlike on the yawning Yukon River, the world of the Fortymile was finite, with high, narrow walls twisting and turning ahead of my team. Towering trees and angulated rocks were caked with snow, and the tracks of wild animals perforated the riverbank. I was overcome with the feeling that civilization was far, far behind me. The river ice tilted down into swirling roils of dark water, and I kept one foot on the high-side runner and one foot on the trail to prevent my sled from sliding down into it. On that tilted trail, it became clear that Norton was going to have to ride in the sled. His gait was abrupt and I knew his shoulder was bothering him. I woahed my team to a halt and kicked in my snow hook, then proceeded with one of the most disheartening tasks ever—unpacking my sled and completely repacking it in a way that left room for a giant, seventy-pound dog to travel comfortably.

I loaded almost everything into a boxy gray duffel bag, which I bungeed down over the nose of my sled. This way, Norton would be right in front of me and I could reach into the bag and calm him down if he tried to escape (most dogs do). The downside to this setup was that I would now have no steering capability. Typically, mushers load the heaviest, clumsiest objects into the back of their sled and the lightest objects over the nose. This gives them a lot of control, because all of the weight is right in front of them in the beefiest part of the sled. The upturned nose of the sled doesn't bear any of that weight and thus does not become an accidental pivot point. I was essentially doing the opposite so I could carry Norty. I loaded up the nose of the sled with hundreds of pounds of meat and kibble. Then I went to Norton, unclipped his neckline, and walked him back. Norty pranced with head and tail held high, confused. I crouched down and lifted him up, bringing him over the opening in my sled bag and setting him down on a bed of insulated dog coats. He scrambled to escape, putting his front legs straight out and craning his neck, heaving himself up and out of the sled bag.

"No, Norton," I said. "You're gonna go for a ride in here. I don't want you to hurt your shoulder."

Just to illustrate how far gone my sanity was, let it be known that I was actively attempting to reason with this dog.

I hauled him up and set him down over and over again. Finally, I clipped his collar into a neckline that was tied to the bottom of my sled bag and encouraged him to curl up in a ball and lay down on the bed I had made him. I zipped up the one working zipper almost all the way to the top of the sled bag, leaving room for his head to stick out so he could see.

"Arrrrrrr!" Norty yelped. "Awoooooo!"

He was desperate.

"All right guys, let's go!" I yelled to the dogs, hoping that once the sled was in motion Norton would calm down and maybe fall asleep.

The second the sled lurched forward, Norty panicked. He threw his head up with all of his might and emerged through the sled bag with a ripping sound, as though being birthed.

The sled was sliding down toward the open water of the Fortymile River and, at the same time as I tried to steer it to the uphill side of the trail (impossible), I was also pushing Norton's head back down into the bag as sternly and gently as possible. We were officially a moving shit show.

After two miles of battling Norton and the sled, I stopped. I put in my snow hook. I stood over Norton and then crouched down to his level. He eyed me distrustfully from the sled bag.

"Norton," I said. "I know how much you hate this. I know

you still think you can pull. But you are making this miserable for *everybody*."

Norton glared.

"Now, I want you to lay down in here," I said, patting the dog coats beneath his paws, "and be quiet, and be a good boy. Do you hear me, you stubborn son of a bitch?"

I looked him in the eye for a solid minute. I put my hands on my hips and let him know I was not fucking around. He turned away from me and licked his snout.

"Good," I said.

I got back on the sled, pulled the snow hook, and within ten minutes, Norton was lying down and letting us take him down the trail. I reached into the sled bag and massaged Norton's shoulder as we glided along. The dogs warmed into their gaits and began sniffing the air. The river was quiet and sunlight filtered through the boughs of giant spruce. The dogs began to run faster and I detected movement on the periphery. I couldn't tell if I was making it up again, but the dogs confirmed that wolves were in the woods, running alongside us at the top of a high riverbank. They were playful and seemed excited to welcome their cousins into this part of their world. I felt a rare sense of privilege, not only to witness the wolves dancing in the sun but also to be allowed a primordial sense of wildness myself. With the exception of the improvements in our gear—the material of our parkas, metal on our sleds, and nylon of the dogs' harnesses—we could be travelers a hundred years ago, driving our dogs down this same trail, enjoying the same hospitality, trailing the ancestors of these wolves.

Suddenly, a sign appeared in the distance. Trail markers glinted in the middle of the river, marking the quietest border between nations. Out in the wilderness we passed from Canada into Alaska and not a single person was there to bear witness. It was a seamless transition and a meaningless one in the best sense. In the northern reaches of our two countries, it was hard to differentiate one from the other. The same magic was in the air.

"You want some of my straw?" Lance finally asked. He had been eyeing my dogs, who were bedded down on a bridge over the Fortymile—a spot fifty miles from Clinton Creek where we agreed to camp together. Ahead of mine, his dogs snoozed in a line. It was finally warming up—maybe −20°F now—but I had accidentally used my entire bale of straw during my wrong cabin detour before the last hospitality stop. I had tried to gather up as much straw as I could back at Clinton Creek to carry with me, but it wasn't enough for the thirteen-dog team I had left (I'd dropped Kabob the Temptress back in Dawson).

"Sure," I said, a little embarrassed. "Thanks a lot."

The water in my cook pot was getting hot, so I dropped in a vacuum-sealed meal my friend Jill had made me—an English muffin breakfast sandwich. After about ten minutes I retrieved it from the near-boiling water and opened it up.

"Want some?" I asked Lance. "It's a breakfast sandwich."

"Aw, that's my favorite!" he said.

I just gave him the whole thing, which he ate very slowly. It ended up being frozen a bit in the middle—a typical musher meal on the trail. But I didn't realize until later that Lance didn't really have any teeth. He'd had throat cancer, which had spread to his jaw, which made a lot of his teeth fall out. A thick, raised scar wormed down his neck. Later, one of my uncles would say, "We Googled him, and boy he looked scarier than hell! But we were sure glad he was traveling with you."

"What do you think I should do with this dog?" I asked, pointing to Norton. "He tweaked his shoulder and he was limping earlier, but he still really wants to run. He was a huge pain in the ass to carry—he weighs seventy pounds."

Lance thought about it. We were about to go up and over American Summit—a 3,420-foot bare backbone of a mountain that towered over some of the most remote country on the continent. The sidehills, we had heard, were terrifying. If you didn't keep your sled on the uphill side of the trail, you could slide down the side of the mountain—*alllll* the way down—and then have to trudge all the way back up with a fully loaded sled and a bunch of freaked-out dogs.

"It's mostly uphill," he said. "That would give him a chance to warm up into his shoulder. We won't be going very fast, and the likelihood of him injuring it worse is pretty low."

As we left, I put a shoulder coat on Norton and slid a chemical handwarmer into the sleeve over the strained muscle. After about five miles, Norton actually looked great! I was surprised, and also grateful that I wasn't carrying him thousands of feet up the mountain.

The trees began to thin out as wind lifted up the fur on the dogs' tails and then set it back down. Up ahead of me, Lance was stopped. He shined his headlamp backward, then began to walk toward me.

"Hey, you wanna do a snack trade?" he yelled. "I'm sick of eating smoked salmon!"

"Sure!" I yelled back, laughing. Traveling with Lance was going to be awesome. "How about pork cookies!"

"What the hell is that?" he asked, coming closer.

I explained that pork cookies were a gingerbread-type cookie that my friend Lynn made, and they were loaded up with bacon fat, chocolate chips, and bits of bacon so they wouldn't actually freeze. Plus they were packed with calories.

"Oh, fuck yeah," he said.

I covertly checked to see if they'd be easy to chew by giving them a gentle squeeze and making sure they weren't solid in the middle, like the breakfast sandwich had been. They broke in half in my hand. Perfect.

Lance handed over the salmon and then took off. I could feel that the summit was just ahead. There was no cover anymore and we were awfully high up.

We came around a corner and into a sideways wind that swept the snow on the mountain into a smooth, hard cone. And it was a cone we had to traverse along the side of. Lance's headlamp was already a mile ahead—a tiny glowing point way out there that was fuzzed and dimmed by snowy wind gusts. Instantly, I was gripped with fear.

I stuck my foot out onto the uphill side of the mountain,

trying to keep some traction as the sled runners slid down. I shined my headlamp down over the edge—big mistake. My heart pounded. My dread and anxiety went straight up the gangline to Littlehead, running in lead. She was on the right side, paired with Solo. The trail markers glinted on the uphill side of the trail, and after about a hundred feet Littlehead began to arc up toward them. At first, I was worried she was Littleheading out. But then I realized that when she'd see the trail markers coming, she would launch into a gallop, pulling with all her might up, up, up, to keep us on the trail. Hoss looked back at me, eyes wide, and yanked the sled uphill. Every time he felt it sliding down, he'd turn back and look at it, as if doing a complicated physics calculation, then pull at the perfect angle and get the sled back on the trail.

"I'm a big brave dog," I said. "I'm a big brave dog. I'm a big brave dog."

The mantra had come out of nowhere. It was a thing Anna, one of my campers, used to say when she was doing something terrifying—crossing a steep snowfield or negotiating sliding scree. It was like the spirit of all those girls came to me at a time when I was deeply afraid and infused me with strength. I said it over and over again until I believed it.

In four miles, we were back in the trees again. I ran up to Littlehead and hugged her hard. I threw my arms around Hoss and he licked the frost off my hat. Everyone wagged their tails and silently leaned into their harnesses. I was surprised to see that nobody was the least bit fazed by what we had just done. I walked back to the sled. My legs were wobbly. It was the first time I realized how much fear could drain me, how much it lingered in my body after the fact, but how easily it had disappeared completely from the minds of my dogs, if it had ever entered in the first place.

Over the next three hundred miles, Lance and I traveled the trail together. He always slept longer than me, and on the floor of whatever checkpoint or hospitality stop we were at, he would dream like a dog, four paws running. He had one brown lead dog named Stiffy and eight black team dogs he called the Ninjas. I would always leave before him but he inevitably caught up to me and passed. Silently, Stiffy and the Ninjas would trail me until the second before they'd pass me from behind. That's when Stiffy would let out a high-pitched, rapid-fire bark that made me scream and jump out of my boots. Lance would laugh till tears were in his eyes.

"Fuckin' love that dog!" he'd say as they trotted on past, leaving a trail of white grape-flavored cigarette smoke or marijuana, depending.

I left Norty with the veterinarians in Eagle—they could find nothing wrong with him, but I didn't want to chance it— and while there, Lance started calling my overloaded sled the "Chest Freezer." He later snapped a picture of me mushing down the Yukon with my head barely peeking over the top of it. Probably for blackmail later.

We went through forty straight miles of jumble ice on the

way to Circle. When we left Circle together, me out front as usual, even though my dogs were going about three miles per hour to get out all their pees and poops, I tripped on my brake and fell. I held on to the brake bar with my hands and dragged behind the dogs, eventually pulling myself up onto my knees. I looked behind me and Lance was sitting down on his tail-dragger with one foot in the air, hanging over the side of his sled clapping and laughing hysterically.

All the time, he said, "This is my most fun Yukon Quest ever."

By the time we got to Central we had caught back up with Ryne, though Lance had arrived an hour or two ahead of me and Ryne was two hours ahead of him. I told Ryne I was surprised not to see her at Clinton Creek and asked why she hadn't camped there. She said she never saw a cabin, just a flashing light with a stripper on it, so she knew she was hallucinating and proceeded down the river a few miles to camp.

The three of us slept in the dark musher sleeping area, while outside the aurora snaked like a bright green cobra, bobbing and weaving, swiveling its hooded head. I gave the race volunteer my wake-up time to put on the dry erase board and I saw Ryne and Lance would be waking up hours ahead of me. I felt dread seep in because I knew it meant I would have to go over Eagle Summit alone.

Eight hundred miles into the Yukon Quest is a mountain every bit as steep and daunting as its lore makes it out to be.

Eagle Summit. A six-mile ascent ever upward, climaxing with a four-story near-vertical headwall that's the stuff of legend. For the eight hundred miles preceding it, the specter of it looms at the fore of mushers' brains. And the stories of coming all that way, getting right up to the base of it, and having a dog team turn around and take you on an elevator-drop hell-ride are numerous and all true.

So when I woke up in Central a few hours later and looked around the musher sleeping area, I was confused to see Lance's sealskin hat and coat still hanging above the heater. I stumbled out into the bar and grill that served as a checkpoint and rubbed my eyes. Lance was there, eating eggs.

"I couldn't leave you *now*," he said.

I just shook my head.

"Thank you," I said without elaborating. He knew what it meant.

We struck out from Central together, Lance in front this time, but once we began the six-mile ascent of Eagle Summit and approached treeline, he was gone. Below the summit, it was a perfect, still morning. The sky was electric winter blue. I took his departure as a vote of confidence. He was telling me, "You've got this, all on your own."

I turned toward the mountain and ran behind my sled, pushing hard and calling up the dogs. I looked back and saw how the entire landscape—as far as the eye could see—was one giant funnel for bringing water down into the Yukon.

We made it up the first pitch and came face-to-face with the summit headwall, catching a mouthful of wind. It was partway up that four-story face that Solo decided he didn't want to be in lead anymore. He casually walked off the side of the trail and rolled in the snow.

"All right, bud!" I yelled. "Ready?"

Solo wandered back onto the trail, took a few steps, and began turning back toward me.

"No, no!" I screamed, my voice swallowed by wind. If Solo turned the team around it would be a disaster, and I tried to wipe away the image of a tangled ball of dogs falling down the face of a mountain while I dragged behind them. I was panicking and clawing my way up to the front of the team on all fours, kicking my toes into the mountain, but Littlehead was calm. She was behind Solo, in the swing position, and she was leaning solidly forward, holding the line taut. I unclipped her neckline and she migrated to the front of the team as if drawn up by a magnet.

"Ready, Littlehead?" I said. I stepped aside as she took up the gangline alone, facing forward and never looking back. For a moment I stared at her from behind. I could see the headwall of Eagle Summit in between her ears. She was unwavering. She owned her decision. After all, females could be brave. The team advanced like a steam engine. Two by two the dogs roared past me and I grabbed on to the handlebar, got behind the sled, and pushed as my boots grappled for purchase on the slick vertical trail.

We made the summit as sunshine spilled across the horizon line, blinding us. I ran to the front of the team and fell to my knees beside Littlehead. I thanked her through sniveling sobs and she licked my tears. She then stepped back into the team where she had been before the climb. As if to say, this was my accomplishment, but it was ours, too.

The reflective trail markers blinked in the arc of my headlamp and by now the dogs instinctively drove toward them. We had been on the trail for a week and a half, and for the past 850 miles the trail markers had been a torch light to follow, this lone constant in a maze of wildly changing extremes. They twinkled along the edge of a steep trail lined with trees and then the trees fell away. The dogs surged forward and I set my toes on the drag brake, laughing a little. We had 150 miles to go and my twelve dogs were sprinting up Rosebud Summit, chasing caribou in the dark. Their noses were lifted, nostrils drawing in some tantalizing current and turning it into energy, and I could feel it.

I lifted my head, too, and saw those glittering trail markers ascend perilously upward. Rosebud Summit was the notoriously under-described neighbor to Eagle Summit. I'd overheard a musher in the past saying, "Fuck Eagle, why didn't anyone tell me about Rosebud?" Rosebud Summit was more like a series of summits connected by a sinuous ridgeline. And running the trail this direction, from Whitehorse to Fairbanks, meant mushers had to go down the most dangerous part—two big drops, one right after the other, interrupted only momentarily by a ninety-degree turn around a fat spruce tree. But I was still on the ascent, and the trail markers outlined various lanes on a narrow gravel summit virtually free of any kind of shoulder. I stomped my sharpest snow hook into the frozen gravel and walked ahead of my dogs, making the mistake of shining my light down either side of the knife-edged ridge. I walked back and knelt down next to Solo and Littlehead. I told Solo I needed him to be on his A game up here. Obviously, Littlehead needed no such encouragement. I stepped back onto the runners and pulled up the hook and the dogs continued to surge along, ears forward, intent on hunting. I stopped them again and again and reminded them that here is where we will take it easy. Here is where we will walk.

It felt like we had gained well over a thousand feet in elevation when I saw the trail markers pitch unbelievably upward again. I turned my headlamp on its highest setting to be sure, but the reflective markers stayed the same brightness. I shined the light back onto my dogs and realized it was glittering stars perched just above the horizon line, mimicking the lathes, tricking me. We had reached the top. A faint aurora swirled its green scarf around us. It felt like we were floating. My gut turned sour, recognizing before the rest of me that something bad was happening. I looked ahead and watched my dogs disappear over the mountainside. We were falling.

The dogs were loping straight down the bare face of Rosebud. *No!* I thought, panicking. *There's no snow! This is wrong!*

The trail became a kind of chute, delineated on both sides by glowing trail markers. At first, we passed the markers in what felt like slow motion. The way a roller-coaster car seems to hover over the edge just before it drops. And then the sled began to vibrate as it picked up speed over the gravel. I balanced on the thin metal brake bar, digging its sharp teeth into the bare ground as heavily as I could. My knees were bent and I was tucked into the back of my sled, trying to become one with it. At that moment, the dogs swerved to the side of the trail to investigate a caribou carcass that had been wasted by hunters the week before, and my sled fishtailed, catching an edge hard and flipping. My body landed on the ground but my hands still gripped the handlebar. I dragged for a hundred feet or so and the dogs came to a stop. I stomped a snow hook into the ground and turned the sled back onto its runners. The pitch was so steep that the sled glided forward past its bridle and hung there against the snow hook line. I couldn't believe this was the trail. Surely there had to be a better way to get down this mountain. I took a few deep breaths and pulled the hook.

Within seconds we reached warp speed again, the incandescent trail markers creating a blurred and brilliant boundary for this uncontrollable hell. The sled was vibrating so hard that the scene before me took on a flip book–like quality: My wheel dogs, Hoss and Bullock, were nearly crouched with their front legs outstretched, pushing hard into the earth, trying to stop. Hoss and Bullock looked back nervously. Hoss and Bullock started to fall. In front of them, Ox and Iron started to fall. The sled began to overtake the dogs. I flipped it on purpose this time, hoping the friction of the sled on its side would slow it down enough to keep from running over my team. I landed hard on my right elbow for the fifth time over the course of the race and the pain was a hard flash of light. The trail took a sharp right turn and we came to a stop beneath a sizable tree.

I lay under the sled for a few moments, stifling sobs. *What's the point of crying? Nobody cares. Nobody can hear you.* I crawled out from under the sled and walked up to Solo, apologizing to all the dogs that I couldn't keep them safe. He jumped on me, wagging his tail, licking the tears off my face.

"Mom, I am having the *best* time," he said.

On the way into Fairbanks, thick clouds hovered above us and acted like a mirror reflecting back the light of the city. That's how I knew the finish line was near. Civilization, with all its buzzing and noise, ruled again. People shined their car headlights on us as we passed by, yelling and cheering, "Way to go, Kristin! You're almost there!" The dogs and I seemed suddenly out of place. Running along the Chena River past the lights emanating from expensive, three-story houses; past Fort Wainwright thrumming with helicopter blades chopping the air; past cars swooshing by on icy roads. We were a creature from bygone days emerging in a new century.

Rounding the final bend in the Chena, I could just make out the distant banner backlit by super-bright spotlights. A crowd of people ringed neatly around fencing. The Fairbanks finish line. In the same moment I felt both a jolt of relief and a paralyzing hesitation. I subconsciously slowed my team, wanting to hold on to what we had built, formed, endured. What we had become. This very private, intense, insular journey was about to end very publicly indeed. And the moment that line was crossed, all those people would beg to be let in.

A few hundred feet from the finish line, a figure stepped out from the dark. It was Jess.

"Krissy, I just wanted to tell you before you get in there how proud I am of you," she said, barely getting her arms around me in my huge parka. "You did it!"

I shook my head and thanked her for being there to see us come in. For being there since the very beginning.

We crossed the finish line and the cameras and microphones pointed. I posed for a photo with Littlehead and Solo. I closed my eyes and disappeared into Andy's arms. I stood on a podium and answered questions from fans. I hugged Brent, who had won. I joked with Lance. (Ryne had finished hours ago and was back home already, but her house was right near the Quest trail and as I had mushed past she had run out and given me a hot dog.) Mom and Dad stood on my dogsled and rode with Andy back up to the truck. Mike Ellis emptied out my sled and loaded it on top of the dog box. Everyone around me was talking and laughing and drinking ice cold beers. I smiled huge and exhaled, my gaze turned to where the spotlight landed on the snow. At its edge was the darkness on the frozen river that led to the Yukon and to all the wildness that filled and formed my heart.

PART 9

Shovel, Scrape, Start a Fire

A t the end of April, the hillsides burst with green. Well, not actually burst with green but the very beginnings of the tips of green buds were peeking out of woody stems. Spring was emergent, but underfoot the earth was still frozen hard and ice covered the ground in slick, melting patches. The varied thrushes had just begun their otherworldly, electric whistle and high above, as if to call Moose home, bellowed the raucous yet sweet chorus of sandhill cranes returning to their nesting grounds. It was the end of April, and Moose was dead.

At the beginning of March, Moose had been running up and down the stairs at our neighbors' house, where I was staying while I recovered from a knee injury that happened right after I finished the Quest. The neighbors were out of town and they had indoor plumbing and all the amenities on the first floor, which was important since I could no longer make it up our ladder to the bedroom back at home. Thundering loudly, his heavy paws bearing the weight of his hundred-pound body, Moose went up and down and back up again. I was staying in bed an awful lot, and Moose crawled up next to me on top of the covers and made himself small enough to fit. When he wasn't resting his giant head in such a way that his exhalations through puffed cheeks feathered sweetly against my hand, he was at it on that stairway. Up and down, up and down in gallant, weighty leaps. Either that or he was trying to get Maximus to play with him as he slid awkwardly across the smooth wooden floor. A lot like a moose calf, actually. Long, spindly legs failing to keep up with the rest of him. Maximus's deep brown eyes never strayed from mine. *Is this guy ever going to grow up?* they asked.

At the beginning of April, Moose had a limp. Likely he slipped on the ice around the cabin and strained his knee in some way. The limp got worse and he stopped putting weight on his leg, and the way his hip looked, it may have been dislocated. He was clearly in a lot of pain, and the only thing that gave him comfort was a combination of drugs that left him a little dazed and dreaming wild, active dreams. There, in that unconscious world, his body could do all the things it had ever been able to do—maybe more. And then the drugs would wear off and the pain would come again. It was definitely time for an X-ray.

It was too much for the big Moose to stay perfectly still for such a precise procedure, especially when it hurt. So our vet Jayne gave him a sedative as I rubbed his velvety, palm-size ears between my fingers and Andy rested his head on Moose's back. Our arms were around him as he drifted off to sleep, his heavy head cradled in the crook of my elbow. We lay him on his side and took a picture of his knee, Andy and Jayne in their hefty lead aprons and me outside the door. The picture was good and there was no cancer in the knee, as Jayne had suspected. Now it was time for the hip. Carefully, Jayne and Andy turned Moose onto his back. Andy's arms were under Moose's front legs, which stuck straight out into the air. He took up the whole table. As Jayne pulled his back legs into position, we heard a loud pop. Collectively, we gasped. Maybe his hip was out of socket after all, and now it had been reset! Still, my heart raced in reaction to the sickening sound. I felt a little dizzy. The picture was taken and as it developed we gathered around the sleeping Moose.

"Oh!" Jayne said.

"Well?" we asked. "Was that it? Is the hip back in place now?"

"That's where his cancer is," she said, frowning.

"What about his hip?" we asked. "Did you pop it back in?"

"It...broke," she said.

You didn't have to be a veterinarian to see that his hip was a crumbling mess. It didn't even resemble the ball and socket joint it used to be. There on the light box, where the phosphorescent-looking white of bone should have been, it was just...black. The cancer had started in the marrow and silently, painlessly worked its way to the nerve-riddled sheath that encases the bone. And that's when it started to hurt. And by then it was already too late, as it had likely spread to his lungs and maybe other places, too. We just stared at the picture, our minds filling in that negative space where the bone used to be and wishing it back to normal. Rewinding and finding a way to will back time. Surely this was not our reality.

All of us, the three of us humans, had just spent a week together in the Arctic. Everyone's faces were still deeply browned and freckled by the sun except for where our sunglasses had been. Jayne's eyes closed as she turned to us. Our veterinarian and our good friend. Our adventure companion. She said, "We can't let him wake up from this. He'll be in so much pain." The tears welled up and then slid down her cheeks as we stared at her with our mouths open.

"I was not prepared for that, Jayne," I said, shocked. "I am not prepared for this."

It was supposed to be a routine X-ray. That's all. Just an ordinary, everyday type of doctor's visit. But there Moose was, lying on the table, so big his paws hung off the side. He was slowly, incrementally, coming out from under the power of the sedative. He was going to start waking up soon. Maybe in about fifteen minutes.

"Did he feel any of that?" we asked, crying. Did he feel the hip break for what looked like the third time? The spiderweb of cracks in the failing bone.

"No," she said. "The last thing he'll remember is falling asleep in your arms."

And we weren't sad for his last moments then. We weren't scared or anxious. We were stroking his ears, cooing him to sleep, laughing at him fighting it, catching him and slowly lowering him down to the floor.

Back at home, at the trailhead, we parked the truck. Andy left me with Moose as he walked down the trail to retrieve the black jet sled and a blanket. I pulled back the jackets we had put over Moose, who was lying in the backseat. I stroked Moose's fur. Felt his ears again. The last of his living warmth was still there, but he didn't respond to my touch. My fingers, all my senses, were so surprised at the strangeness of that. We got him home and wrapped his body in a blanket and covered him with a tarp and put him under the house.

We walked to the bluff overlooking the creek and followed its contours on the old game trail to a dead tree. At the tree we turned right and walked about fifty feet through the woods to a clearing. There, a sign marked Willa's grave—she had died of cancer the year before. And beside there is where we started to dig.

We took turns. Andy pierced the mossy tundra with the sharp nose of the shovel and jumped it down through the first layer of earth, perforating a perfect rectangle and ripping it up in pads. He saved the top layer so it could be replaced. So the sphagnum could reroot and grow there again.

A breeze blew from out on the creek and spread through the trees like an invisible, rushing wave. Not the applause it would have been in leafy summer, but a clean spring wind through mostly naked branches. Just a day ago, Moose and I stood on this same bluff as the wind blew a symphony of colors and details and scents into his searching, curious nostrils. The rich stimulation made him forget his pain and he trotted excitedly for a moment, head lifted, until he remembered the limitations of his body.

The *clank, clank, clank* of the shovel hitting hard, claylike permafrost brought me back to now.

"Want me to try for a bit?" I asked Andy.

I picked up the heavy yellow Pulaski and methodically slammed its black steel adz into the frozen earth, scraping and scraping toward me. Scrape-pull, scrape-pull, scrape-pull, scrape-pull. Relentless and rhythmic like a steam engine. The progress we made could have been measured in milli-meters.

"We're going to have to start a fire," I said.

The brush was old and dry, but the flames started slowly. Encircling the branches and glowing there, but not incinerating them. In a while, though, the orange-yellow heat was magnetic and we stared into it, adding more and more brush. The old snow around the shallow pit began to melt, and quiet rivulets of water snaked down the earthen walls and pooled underneath the tinder. Heat radiated in thick, clear, wavy bands as tongues of flame snapped at the cool air, popping like a powerful jaw snapping shut once and for all.

It took two days to dig Moose's grave. Shovel, scrape, start a fire, let it cool, shovel, scrape, start a fire, let it cool. Over and over until it was three feet deep. We would have to build it up higher, too, maybe by a couple feet. And by the time it was finished, the grave would be the size of a human's. We went to the house and pulled the sled out from under it. Its weight flattened the tundra as we slid it down the path to the clearing. We each grabbed two corners of the blanket and lifted Moose out of the sled, lowering him carefully into the box in the ground. I pulled back the blanket and rubbed his soft ears one more time. I touched his cheek and it was cold and stiff. Not alive, like my fingers had expected.

"This isn't you," I told him. "You are so alive, still, Moose. This is just your body, this isn't you."

His lip was dry and curled up against his teeth and I didn't fix it. It didn't matter. We put his purple octopus toy in the box as our tears dripped onto the blanket. *Moose. Mooooooose.* The word was emanating from Andy's lungs in a baleful, animal-like crooning. We hesitated to put the lid on, to drive the screws in with the loud drill as we hunched over and mud slid off our wet boots. But then, what did it matter? He was already gone. Putting the lid on the box and then putting the dirt on the lid and then putting the carpets of tundra back on top of the dirt was all just a ceremony. It wasn't going to be the thing that ended him.

"Where do you think Moose is, right now?" I asked Andy.

"Oh, probably at Eight Mile Lake, with the cranes," he said.

"That's it! That's exactly where he is. He always wanted to fly with them," I said.

He was so fascinated by the flight of big, heaving birds, intently wanting to understand how they got themselves off the ground and then actually flew so many thousands of miles.

There was a time when Moose was a puppy, maybe four months old, and he was captivated by the wild turkeys out the window at my old cabin in the Bitterroot Valley of Montana. Alfred and I would let him go out onto the porch and he'd sit and watch, his giant ears quivering, gathering information.

Until one day he couldn't take it anymore and he leaped off the porch and galloped into the middle of the flock of big birds. All at once they began to run and then to flap loudly and then, to Moose's great incredulity, they began to levitate. As they gained speed, Moose lost momentum, slowing as though he was suddenly submerged in water. And then he sat, looking up in disbelief as turkeys flew away from him in every direction.

Our neighbors made their way down the trail as mud sucked at their boots. We gathered around Moose's grave shoulder to shoulder and said good-bye to him. Everyone poured one gulp of beer onto the ground, and then we turned and walked single file down the narrow game trail, the sun filtering in through the branches and alighting in everyone's hair.

Eleven days later I sat on a pallet as the nine-o'clock sun highlighted the new leaves, turning them golden. I looked across the wide expanse of the creek bottom, following it down to the decaying shelf ice and then back up through the copses of tall birch trees. Light green of birch, dark green of spruce, thrushes striking their single, melancholy chords, insects' gossamer wings glowing as they flitted through all that space. I was covered in mud again, and charcoal, too. Another two days of digging a grave. Another two days of shovel, scrape, start a fire. Our bodies were like machines, going through the muscle memory motions, while our minds tried to understand our reality.

"I can't believe we're doing this again," we'd say.

And then one of us would step out of the muddy rectangle while the other one stepped in.

Inside the cabin, Maximus lay cramping as fluids from a bag trickled through a long, clear tube into his body. Four days after Moose died, he had walked out of the house, stumbled down the stairs, and collapsed. After a week of tests and drugs and IVs and much-hated car rides, it was clear that Maximus was done. And I had promised him years ago, after he trembled so hard at the vet's office, after he got sick over and over on that long car ride to Alaska, that his life would never end that way.

And so I sat on the pallet at the edge of the bluff and I waited. I was worried the thrushes would stop singing. Maybe fly away and never come back. As the shot rang out I felt I could see the trajectory of its sound echoing out across all that space. My heart raced and my mind deflected a panic back to my heart and I stood up and ran through the trees.

"Andy!" I screamed.

"Wait," he said.

His voice trembled, trying to hide a worry, I knew. And I saw the white of his shirt and I saw him kneeling over the fallen-down white of Maximus's fur, all through the blurry filter of tears and trees. I turned away and listened. It was quiet. And then the sobs, the lonesome, inaccessible sobs of someone who had to kill an animal for the first time.

The drill drove the screws through the plywood and our tears fell onto the box. The mud clunked onto the lid, a hollow resonance. As the mud piled higher and higher over the grave, the thrushes' whistles pierced the air, ringing electric against my eardrums.

The waning sun came back to life against the late evening clouds and colored them neon. Unbelievably, the sun went down at the usual time. It didn't set on the wrong side of the world or just hang there, unmoving, crystallized or paralyzed, like I thought it should. There were three graves, right in a row, and the sun was going to set on this day and then, inevitably, unfairly, rise on another one in the morning. From the east. At the usual time.

PART 10

The Iditarod

In 2016 I was a Yukon Quest veteran and an Iditarod rookie. There was hardly any snow on the ground, but Iditarod officials had decided the race would not take an alternate course, rather it would take the traditional, historic route that winds from Willow north across the brutal and unforgiving Alaska Range and out to the sea coast via the Yukon River. I had fifteen eager dogs in my team, twelve of whom had just completed the Yukon Quest with Andy three weeks ago, making us one of very few kennels in the sport to compete in both one-thousand-mile races back to back. The dogs were more powerful than they had ever been, and I was worried I wouldn't be able to control my team, especially on what had been reported as hundreds of miles of snowless trail. In my head, I was coming up with every excuse to not compete. Now that I was here, I didn't actually want to do this.

A week ago I went on my last big training run. I drove six hours out to Eureka, Alaska, where 2015 Yukon Quest champion Brent Sass lived on a remote homestead. Brent was six feet tall, with a ponytail of greasy brown hair, pierced ears, and thick, black-rimmed eyeglasses. He was loud. So loud, that every time he posted a video on Facebook we would automatically turn the volume all the way down. And he was pretty famous. He was one of the first long-distance dog mushers to warm to social media, and had tens of thousands of followers. Through his pictures and videos, he let people into his life on an off-the-grid homestead on Joe Bush Creek in Eureka, Alaska, three hours outside Fairbanks. People were fascinated. He was the only person for miles save for a few miners and trappers. And he had an overwhelmingly devoted following of single, middle-aged women that I dubbed the Cat Lady Army, or CLA. The CLA knitted him knickknacks, sent him care packages of candy in the mail, and sometimes even showed up on his doorstep.

Brent's personality was inescapably magnetic. He drew people in. But also, he lived all the way out there, hours from civilization, alone with sixty-five dogs for a reason. He loved being self-sufficient, not having to rely on anyone or anything but his own ingenuity. His place had no electricity, rather it ran on generators and solar panels and diesel fuel. If his road washed out, he had to rebuild it himself, but first he'd have to fix the ancient excavator that came with the place. And the women who showed up to woo their fantasy of a mountain man inevitably left with the realization that this dude was, in reality, an unwashed, sweatpants-wearing maniac who worked nonstop for twenty hours a day and subsisted on four hours of sleep and a diet of gummy worms. Brent strode about the homestead with purpose, always with a tool in hand, headed to fiddle with something. He narrated, out loud, what he was about to do and then what he would do after that, and after that. There was always something to fix—a generator, a well pump. There was always something to finagle—a satellite dish for Internet. And after that, there were always dogs to feed, and there were always dogs to train. He was, after all, running a competitive thousand-mile race team. Time didn't exist out there at Joe Bush Creek. The endless litany of chores were the hours of the day.

Andy and Brent went to high school together in Minnesota,

but they never met until they were both dog mushers in Alaska. The first time we followed the Yukon Quest and the first time we heard of Brent, Andy said, "That name sounds so familiar."

He took out his high school yearbook, and there Brent was, in the class below him. A super geeky, skinny cross-country running and skiing star.

The first time I talked to Brent, I interviewed him for a freelance article I was writing about mushing and climate change, and he told me the story of a trip gone wrong where extreme temperatures caused water to flow over a frozen river (a phenomenon known as overflow) and essentially drown one of his snowmachines that was carrying an enormous load of gear. Instead of watching the machine sink farther and farther down into the John River, way north of the Arctic Circle, he took nine of his best dogs and hooked them up to the bumper of the machine. It took three tries, but on the third all nine dogs and human and machine fired at the exact right moment and launched themselves out of the river. Dogs were always more reliable than any machine, he'd said.

The next time we talked to Brent was a year later, when he wrote us and asked if we would be interested in training a team of his yearlings for the winter. We would familiarize them with the harness and sled, we would get them running up to forty miles a day, and we would do a lot of camping. We would be getting them ready for an April expedition up in the Arctic. In exchange for all of that, we could keep half of them. Those dogs later became the core of our race team.

Now, all these years later, Brent was one of my very best friends. His stream-of-consciousness texting, riddled with typos, was a new language I was fluent in. Often, these cryptic messages spoke of deep concern for the longevity of whatever handler he had hired for the winter.

Not lookin' good, he would write. I bet you this one goes to town and never comes back.

Or, He's not even scooping the puppy pen, head is definitely not in the game.

Eventually, I gave all of his handlers the blanket nickname Flight Risk.

Sometimes, I'd get a message from Brent's InReach, a GPS device a lot of mushers carry because we live and travel in places without cell phone reception:

My tires just passed me on the Elliott Highway. Can you email my handlers and tell them I won't be home til tomorrow?

Or, best of all, the novel-length text message rant:

Brent: Aaa Fuck got the place back to myself! Why the fuck don't I have a reality show and at least be making some money from all this Fucking drama! I Wanna Fucking kick Nikoli square in the nut sack like 50 times but had a good chat with Montana. He first tried to lay it on my To decided if he was the right person. I flipped it back and just told him flat out thus is a dog world you gotta life for getting up everyday to spend time with them. If you don't it's going to be hard to live and thrive here. He admitted he had no desire to play with pups and run 3 days a week was enough. Blows my mind . . . but he's just not that doggy person we talked about . . . No doubt I could improve living conditions but

I give them all the freedom to make it the way they want it around here. And the ones that make it are motivated enough to make it homey. Dude I got some stories for you, but that's another time. AnywAys I'm not a home maker never Fucking will be! And you also nailed it on how I am Around here that's why I can't be a Fucking homemaker! But I do empower people and give them a chance to grab ahold. The ones that don't grab ahold don't make it. They have to be just like me they have to be "running around to and fro with this running commentary in your head that's one giant to do list, and you just naturally live it there" that's the type of person who makes it. Of course at a much lower degree then me but you still have to think that way Around here. I've scene it about 25 percent of the time over the last 5 years. All various levels of skill but if their doggy and have the ability to care And apply themselves they don't have to be very skilled. I had a girl who couldn't drive dogs but loved feeding and picking up After them and came to work everyday with a smile and that was my first year here! It was hell compared to now...She was not smart, extremely uncoordinated and had no common sense but she listened well and loved it here! It was crazy! Fuck sorry venting a little here! Basically just wanted to thank you for being honest and pointing all that out. Your totally right but for that to even work you gotta have the right people to start with. These guys were not the right people. And I knew it deep down but had To go with it to recover from the Tim fiasco! Seriously you can't make this shit up! I'll be running 3 Teams a day walking puppies, feeding 60 dogs, and keeping the homestead alive daily for a while. Still beats managing people who don't wanna be here!

Rant over we hope you've enjoyed this presentation of brents
Fucked up life, we thank you for listening. For more titles like this
one go to shitshowforever.com

By the way no one owns shitshowforever.com

Me: Dude, Jesus Christ.

Brent's texts were, a lot of the time, his only conversations.
He would go weeks out there without talking to anyone but
himself or his dogs. And sometimes, in the middle of winter, he
would go out on runs through remote country on dangerous
trails with nobody to notice whether or not he came back home.
One time, he was running a sixteen-dog team with a fancy new
four-wheeler with four seats, a window, and a steering wheel—
essentially a small truck—before there was enough snow to run
on a dogsled. It was extremely cold, −30°F, and there was a thick
ice fog. Brent didn't see that the whole team had run up onto
a five-foot-high glacier of ice that had grown out of the side of
a road cut. The water had oozed out of the ground and frozen,
over and over again, until it grew over the entire road and
slanted at a perilous tilt, abruptly ending in a cliff. And before
he even realized what was happening, the quarter-ton four-
wheeler was slipping off the face of the glacier and flipping over.
Brent closed his eyes and tried to relax, knowing the impact
that would come. Jumping ship was not an option—that would
leave the dogs in even greater danger. He was slammed into
the ground, hard. And with some alarm he realized the vehicle
had landed on his feet, pinning him there against the ice. The
temperature was falling, and he couldn't reach his GPS to send
for help. It was the middle of the night.

Brent started reaching, digging around at the mess of shit that had come tumbling out of the storage compartment in the hood: three Hydroflask water bottles, food, oil, battery charger, extra clothes, random tools, dog booties—all the things mushers carry with them on a long run. He was enclosed on all sides by the roof and the windshield, surrounded by junk.

He put the handle of his knife in his mouth. ("You know, like in the movies," he said later.) This was going to hurt like hell and he had no idea what the dogs' condition or status was. ("I was seriously concerned about them," he said. "For all I knew the main line broke and they were gone. It had been totally silent since I crashed.") And he didn't want to be yelling and screaming and getting them all worked up. He grabbed one of his legs with his hands and yanked as hard as he could. His bare foot came out of his smashed boot, which still gripped his sock. With the impact of the fall, his boot had chipped out the ice a little bit, leaving a gap between the roll bar of the machine and the ice. He looked around for something he could wedge under there, and his eyes settled on one of the Hydroflasks—a stainless steel vacuum-sealed thermos with a double wall.

"It was rugged enough to take a beating and I could get it jammed between the roll bar and the ice," he said.

He took his one loose leg and pounded on the flask to get it jammed under.

"That took just a little pressure off," he said. "My first leg was stuck just smashing my foot, so it gave some. That's what allowed me to rip it out."

But his other leg was still pinned above the ankle, so

yanking that out was not so easy. He jammed in the second Hydroflask.

"The circulation in my foot was not good," he said. "The first flask released the pressure, the second one lifted it just enough to repeat the leg removal, which also left the sock and boot behind, but now I was free."

He popped up and the dogs were all curled up on the ice, calmly waiting for Brent to tell them what to do next. They were totally fine. But the four-wheeler was in dire straits. First, Brent cut down several small trees with an ax to use as lever poles to get the machine upright. He eventually succeeded, only to find out that two tires had blown off their rims. He got those back on with a ratchet strap and a little air compressor he had. The oil had spilled out while the machine was on its side. He had extra oil. The battery was dead. He had a battery charger. But the machine was still on slippery glare ice, on which he wouldn't be able to drive. So he took his ax and clear-cut three hundred to four hundred yards of willows and trees down in the ditch so he could drive the machine around the bulbous ice patch and back up onto the gravel on the other side. First, he had to get the dogs off the machine. He took a chance and let all sixteen loose, confident that they wouldn't fight or run off. They didn't.

After getting the machine back up onto the gravel road, he looked at his watch. It had been exactly four hours since the crash. "It could have easily resulted in death," he said. "Had I hit my head and got knocked out, I would have froze to death. I was a long ways out a trail that no one was going to go down."

So now here we were, a week from the 2016 Iditarod. Brent was running the race along with me, and was confident that 150 miles with him and his team would help me get my head in the game before the big race. It had been a long season—the longest Andy and I had ever had in our nascent mushing career—and I was ready for it to be over. I arrived at the pullout where Brent parks his truck and hooked up my fifteen dogs to mush a six-mile trail in to his house. It was dark and windy. I clipped the first ninety-degree turn onto his trail and immediately flipped my sled, getting caught in a stand of thick willows and alders. The dogs yanked the sled loose and I dove on top of the sled, dragging behind the team (I know, seriously). Even with some steep hills in their path, the dogs never lost power or momentum. I dragged for a mile or more, snow piling into my coat and friction pulling my pants down. I held on for as long as I could, until my hands could literally no longer grip, and then the sled slipped away from me. I calmly said "woahhh" to the dogs while running after them frantically. I ran about one mile, then came around a corner to the sound of my team barking and a snowmachine headlight shining brightly in my face. Brent's handler, Tim, had caught my team. I was back on the trail in a minute's time, arriving at Brent's with record speed as my dogs thrummed into the darkness. They were terrifyingly strong.

Once there, I couldn't hide my reluctance at hooking up this team and training on Eureka's infamously technical trails. Brent laughed at me and told me to suck it up. Over the course of the next two days, I ate shit on a high mountain pass and was dragged behind my sled again and I broke my handlebar in half, but I never lost my team. I managed technical trails through burns and wind drifts and glaciated sidehills, and kept it together. When we came flying around a steep turn in the middle of the night, I could hear the wind rubbing the broomlike birch branches against one another, creaking eerily. We stopped in front of an abandoned log cabin, which had a similarly abandoned dog yard.

"Do you know what this is?" Brent yelled from up in front of me, his dogs eating snow and watching the trail ahead. "This is Susan's place. Four Iditarod championships. Soak up the energy here!"

Susan Butcher is one of Alaska's most celebrated mushers. She is one of six mushers in history to have four Iditarod championships (Rick Swenson holds the record at five wins) and is the only woman to hold such a record. Her winning streak in the 1980s prompted the slogan "Alaska: Where men are men and women win the Iditarod." I never got to meet her, because she died of leukemia in 2006. But now I was standing on my sled runners outside her homestead, overwhelmed with emotion. Energy rippled through me like a ghost and tears began to flow. I think it was Susan, telling me how lucky I was that I was allowed to do this thing she loved. This thing she would never, ever be able to do again. It was a calm but firm presence, goading but not ridiculing, urging me to savor any opportunity to see this country. To travel with these dogs. To live.

I clutched what Susan gave me and held it close as I put on my race bib at the Iditarod start a week later in Willow. I convinced myself over and over that I could do this. Jeff wrote "Calm, Assertive, Relax" in Sharpie on the left arm of my parka. He wrote "Kick Me" on the back, and I couldn't argue with him. I needed nothing more than I needed a kick in the ass. Even though I was about to embark on the race about which I had dreamed for so many years—the race that sparked the will to start my very own kennel—I was exhausted. It was exhilarating to see Andy finish the Quest a few weeks ago and it was thrilling to know that we were going to do the two big ones back to back. But also, the work it took to accomplish these things was burning me out. We were broke all the time. Nothing in our lives really worked, except for the dogs. They were the only things that were well cared for. I wasn't sure if all the glories of the trail were worth the effort we were putting in. I knew by now there was no such thing as doing things the easy way, but I was getting tired of the hard way. Besides, what kind of glory would I find out there if there wasn't any snow? All I felt was impending danger.

Libby Riddles, the first woman to ever win the Iditarod, took a selfie with me just before I hooked up my team. All the greats were there to encourage me. Nonetheless, I was ashen and petrified as I led each muscular, barking athlete to the line and watched the power amplify with every harness clipped in.

I stepped onto the runners and proceeded to the start line. There was no turning back now. I thought of a saying I'd heard in the past: "Sometimes the fear won't go away, so you'll have to do it afraid."

As the announcer counted down the seconds, everything around me became a silent movie. My dogs' mouths opening and closing, tongues lolling, thousands of fans lined up against the neon orange fencing of the start chute, my mom with her mouth pinched closed, taking on my fear as her own. Andy kissing me good-bye. Five people held on to my sled and then five people let go and I felt the thin metal bar of the claw brake under my feet swaying back and forth on the ice and hoped the bolt holding it to the sled wouldn't shear off. (It wouldn't for six hundred miles.)

It was hot—almost 40°F—and the sun bleached out the white mountainous landscape of the Alaska Range peaks soaring to the cerulean blue sky and made everything a homogenous, sparkling, blanched canvas. I could feel my cheeks burning, and the dogs were thirsty and hot. I stopped every chance I could to let them roll in the snow and cool off, but we couldn't stop for long. Their power and enthusiasm were almost uncontrollable, and soon enough we were mushing on the super wide Yentna River in the dark. There were dog teams all around me as multiple trails came abreast and drew apart again and again. I couldn't tell which trail was the right one. My headlamp wasn't strong enough to see from one bank to the other. As Yentna, the first checkpoint of the race, came into view, I thought about my next steps. I had a chance to be competitive, so my race plan had me blowing through this checkpoint and camping out on the trail in another twenty miles. Ryne and I had spoken earlier, and she had encouraged me to run with her on a more scaled-back race plan, but I was hell-bent on trying to push myself to the limit. Now though, I was almost in a panic. I couldn't even see. And if I looked down for a second to get out a new headlamp and missed where I was supposed to camp on an unfamiliar trail...I couldn't risk that. So I decided to stop and rest for a few hours at Yentna and gather myself together. I fed the dogs, put in my earplugs, and closed my eyes. Before I fell asleep, I felt a deep disappointment. One run into this race and already, things weren't going according to plan. When my timer went off an hour later, I looked up to see Ryne's purple parka hanging on a nearby sled. I walked over to her just as she was waking up from a nap. "OK," I said. "Let's run together."

On Rainy Pass, Ryne's team was silhouetted against the pale yellow dawn as we crisscrossed from one side of the steep-walled pass to the other, our teams snaking silently beneath the highest mountains on the continent. The serene beauty was enough to make me forget what I was about to do. Dalzell Creek descends from Rainy Pass through the infamous Dalzell Gorge—one of the most dangerous sections of trail in the entire race—before it joins the Tatina River outside the checkpoint of Rohn. And the terrain was beginning to funnel us down. Ryne and I stopped to talk.

"We should probably get some distance between us so we don't run over each other going down the gorge," Ryne said.

"OK," I said, my voice trembling. "But if there's anywhere that you think I could die, would you stop and wait for me?"

"OK," Ryne said.

Ryne had run this race before, when she worked for Aliy Zirkle, so she didn't have the same fear of the unknown that was presently consuming me.

Ryne took off and I waited a few minutes. Jeff's voice was in my head, describing the trail, telling me when I would probably want to stop and take the tug lines off half my dogs to inhibit the power of my team as we descended into the gorge. I slowed my team to a stop as the trail began to climb steeply up the right side of the canyon. Here is where Jeff had said to take a breath, because things were about to get ugly. Shaking, I ran up and unclipped half the dogs' tug lines, so they could only pull on their collars and not with the full power of their muscular bodies. *OK*, I thought to myself. *Here we fuckin' go.*

We sidehilled along the canyon, green tundra peeking up through splotches of snow, the smell of earth having been clawed up by all the brakes that went before us. The trail was getting narrower, and I could see it take a blind turn before what must be some kind of elevator drop. Just before my dogs disappeared from sight, I could hear Ryne's team far below, barking impatiently. This was a place where Ryne thought I could die.

The next moment, I was falling straight down a dirt chute as trees whirred past on either side, their branches littering the trail. A head-size rock got caught in my metal brake as we came clattering down to the bottom, taking a hard left turn directly into the back of Ryne's dogsled. We nodded to each other and off she went.

What happened next was a series of skidding, slippery power turns on ice, high above open water on Dalzell Creek. The sled bounced off a giant wooden tree root and slammed onto the ice just as I realized the dogs were already halfway across the creek on a narrow ice bridge. The sled skidded along the ice and slammed into a manmade bumper of tree branches and other detritus the trail-breaking crew had assembled to keep mushers from slipping over the lip of the bridge and into the water.

Over and over again. Over and over, a realization that the dogs were all one with each other and the sled and we were all one thing moving in unison, with one instinctive brain guiding our reflexes, unifying our reactions. I had never been so present in all of my life. The fear had loosened its grip and turned into deep concentration. My body had relaxed and become a part of something bigger than itself.

We wound through a hallway of stout trees and exited onto the smooth, white Tatina River. In what felt like an instant, the Dalzell Gorge was over. We had made it without a scratch. I stretched my arms above my head and exhaled, looking past my lead dogs for the first time in hours. I had been in a funk the whole race because fear had created a knot in my stomach and a well of reasons to quit that wouldn't go away. Brown, bare-shouldered mountains rose thousands of feet above us, checked with patches of snow. Polychromatic boulders seemed to shimmer in the sun, and the sky was deep blue against all those siennas and tans and terra cottas. We were mushing through a new wilderness. Over new mountains and new rivers. It was what we lived for. The snowlessness gnawed at me a little, but I pulled into Rohn on a wave of relief. We had made it over the Alaska Range. The hard part was over.

After exactly six hours of rest we left Rohn on a couple inches of hardened snow. *OK*, I thought. *We're more than two hundred miles into this race. Not a lot of stopping power but everyone is mellow and traveling at a nice, consistent speed. We're going to be fine.* The snow thinned down to half an inch. And then a powdery mix of snow and dirt. Finally, as my dogsled clattered noisily down the dirt trail, bouncing off roots and rocks and gaining speed, I realized we were not going to be fine at all. The dogs were hunting something and, despite my years of training telling me to stay calm, talk low and sweetly to slow them down, the panic was rising in me along with the pitch and intensity of their unified yelps. Fifteen noses and tails were held high in warning, and in a synchronized burst they lunged forward and exploded into a dead run. I stood helplessly on the impotent drag brake bereft of its stopping power on the snowless trail. A cloud of dust rose around the team and dirt clogged my eyes and mouth. This place—the Burn—reminded me of the dinosaur death scene in the animated movie *Fantasia*. With bubbling primordial mud pits and stinking piles of dung left behind by prehistoric creatures. The dogs' noses ran wild and we went faster and faster, dirt clogging the runners and engulfing us in a brown cloud, and then we came upon the leviathan, one that belonged to another time. The massive head melding into rough-hided shoulders. The thick horns honed to deadly points. The four-foot-long face on a fifteen-foot-tall body. Even above the clattering of my sled on rocks and dirt, I could hear that gut-wrenching grunt as the giant male wood bison wheeled and ran alongside us and then ahead of us. And when it stopped broadside in the trail and the team dragged the sled forward with more power than ever, I felt an irrevocable sense of doom. This was the end. My fifteen dogs and I were no match for this two-thousand-pound beast from another world. We were going to collide and there was nothing I could do about it. I didn't even try to woah the dogs anymore and instead resigned myself to narrating out loud, "Well, this is happening." And then the crash.

The bison rolled his eyes and snorted and stomped. And I couldn't stop. The dogs leaped up onto the beast as Loretta turned her head back to face me. I could see the whites of her eyes. I screamed at her "You did this!" I hoped the dogs weren't hurt and that nobody was tangled, but I was helpless to do a single thing except hold on and breathe, breathe in the dust and not let go. I couldn't stop the sled and I couldn't run up and check on anyone. And just as though all of my fears had manifested themselves into an omnipotent force, the bison turned away from the dogs and ran into the woods. My relief was short-lived, as fourteen of my fifteen dogs leaped to follow him. They yanked on their necklines, rearing onto their hind legs and banging, banging into their harnesses, yelping shrilly. Solo was the only one who continued straight down the trail, pulling the gangline with all of his might, singlehandedly keeping us from darting into the woods and going on a hell ride of disastrous proportions. Finally, by brute stubbornness, he convinced the rest of the team that we should stay on the trail.

Over every rise and past every bend in the trail was the specter of another bison to chase. I thought, *Surely this couldn't happen again, right, Universe? You wouldn't put another bison for us to hit in the middle of this burned-out, snowless trail, it would just be too cruel.* But I had learned that the universe didn't care about odds, or danger, or dust in my eyes. It didn't care about the safety of my dogs. And seemingly impossible things—things that were never supposed to happen—happened without consideration for our fears and desires. And we would have to deal with them nonetheless.

I entered the checkpoint of Ruby dragging behind my dogsled down a dirt road (I mean...it just *never* ends). I had made a wrong turn and, by the time my leaders realized it and corrected it, the sled was pinned up against a power pole and Hoss was pinned, too. A native woman came running out of her house to help me, but as soon as we got the dogs lined out and the sled unpinned and Hoss unstuck, the dogs were making a run for it and I was not prepared. I dove onto the sled and it flipped onto its side as we left this woman's front yard. Solo and Loretta turned onto the dirt road leading into town, ignoring my muffled request for them to stop. Ragged and defeated from the hot, five-mile-an-hour slog of a run we had just endured, I almost didn't care about how embarrassing this was. "Woah," I said, halfheartedly, as my parka got ripped to shreds on the gravel road. "Woah," I said as the towns-people gawked. Finally I got up onto my knees on the drag brake and stepped onto the runners. I had arrived at Ruby—a tiny village in the Alaskan Interior—and nobody was there to check me in. "Um, hello?" I yelled, peering over a mountain of open drop bags heaped one over the other like a crazy landfill. People milled about, but nobody paid attention to me. I parked my team on a residential side street as a drunk wandered through, leering at me and my dogs. I walked into the community center that served as checkpoint headquarters and began to fill the water pot. I looked up and saw a white piece of paper taped to the wall. It said,

```
         FOR IMMEDIATE RELEASE
            March 12, 2016
   Zirkle, King, and their teams purposefully
             hit by snowmachiner


Anchorage, Alaska—Early this morning, as
Aliy Zirkle (bib #13) was making her way to-
wards the Nulato checkpoint, a snowmachiner
repeatedly attempted to harm her and her
```

team. One dog received a non-life-threatening
injury. Upon arrival at the Nulato checkpoint, Zirkle reported the incident to race
officials and a report was filed with the
Alaska State Troopers. Contact was also made
with the village police officer in Nulato.
Jeff King (bib #61), who was behind Zirkle,
experienced a similar incident 12 miles prior
to his arrival at the Nulato checkpoint.
This incident resulted in the death of Nash,
a three year-old male. In addition, Crosby,
a three-year-old male, and Banjo, a two-
year-old male, received non-life-threatening
injuries. King requested and received medical
attention at the checkpoint. The suspect has
been identified by the village police officer
in Nulato, and authorities are conducting
an investigation. Regrettably, this incident
very much alters the race of the two mushers
competing for a win; however, both are going
to continue on their way toward Nome.

My breath caught in my throat and I cried, open-mouthed
and horrified and loudly, out into the room full of people. I
set my water bucket on the floor. I read the words over and
over again: "resulted in the death of Nash." Nash and Crosby
were Solo's half brothers. Banjo's brother Lefty was just outside
the door, dozing in the straw with the rest of my team. I

thought of the horror of a snowmachine racing at Jeff, swiping his sled, killing his dog. This was a thing that was never, ever supposed to happen.

I walked outside and, immediately upon the sight of me, Ryne rushed over. She put her arms around me and we burst into tears. "I know," she said as we both shook. As Jeff was my mentor—the one who gave me my first dogs and got me started down the path of racing—Aliy was hers. We pulled away to look each other in the face. I was sunburned and snotty. Ryne's eyes were swollen and tired. I told Ryne about how terrible my run in here was, and she told me how someone else had broken into her drop bags and taken all of her dog food. And now this tragedy with Aliy and Jeff. The Iditarod was supposed to be a vaunted, iconic event, with the mushers as its celebrities and the sled dogs as its superheroes. People around the world watched the trackers attached to our dogsleds and their dreams went with us down the trail. But maybe, it seemed, the people right here in these villages didn't see us that way. Maybe we were unwelcome outsiders. How on earth could someone chase down an Iditarod musher with a snowmachine? How on earth could someone run over a dog team at 100 miles per hour? Jeff would arrive in Nulato with a dead dog and the bumper of a drunk's snowmachine in his sled after it had hit his team so hard it busted off. Aliy would arrive in Nulato so far beyond shaken that she could no longer speak. The same drunk had driven at her for two hours, revving his engine and charging and veering off last-minute, inches from her dogs.

"He was trying to kill me," she said, the color drained from her face. "And he kept coming back. Over and over again, he kept coming back."

Around us, people were scratching or thinking about scratching. It was all too much. It wasn't supposed to be like this. We fed and watered our dogs, got them bedded down, and decided to take a good, long rest. If we knew anything at all, it was that the world was a much better place when you woke up well rested. As we loaded our arms up with wet gear in need of drying, I turned to face the village. We were parked on a street that ran parallel to the river. The Yukon River. High, snowy mountains rose straight from the riverbank like a mantle. The Yukon was an old friend, and we had made it to its shores.

Most of mushing is without an audience. So after leaving Galena, the next checkpoint after Ruby, when I nailed a particularly technical portage, barely skimming past a giant tree before jetting straight off a cliff cutbank and landing on ice, I was surprised when my private self-congratulation was suddenly met with cheers and claps. I looked up to see a family on snowmachines, who greeted me and pointed the way to Nulato. The encounter gave me a lift. My dogs had been traveling slowly, without pep, and I knew it was because of my own downtrodden energy that stuck with me after all that had happened in Ruby. Ryne was hours ahead of me now, and Sarah Stokey, an enthusiastic rookie who had dreamed of running the Iditarod her whole life but who was now having leader issues, was not far behind me on the trail. Solo had developed a sore right wrist on the run to Ruby and, though it was already showing improvement, I wanted him to save up all of his amazing leader powers for the Bering Sea coast—the final and most unforgiving hurdle of the Iditarod trail before reaching the finish line in Nome.

So, I had Loretta and Kabob in lead, and Kabob just wasn't feeling it. I didn't blame her.

I stopped the team and pulled out a bag of frozen salmon cut into palm-sized, inch-thick snacks. The dogs wagged their tails and licked their chops. After everyone had a tasty treat I walked back up to Kabob and Loretta and looked into their eyes. I thought about all my travels with Ryne. Before she left every camp, she ran through the team with a bolt of energy, ruffing up all the dogs' fur, scratching their chins and butts, getting them going. "Who's a good boy?!" she would yell to Ruku, Kindi, Ham. "That's my good girl!" she would shout to Fire, Katy, Janna. She was effusive. I always laughed at her because her normally deep voice would go up at least two octaves; her enthusiasm had a Valley Girl kind of bent. But now that I thought about it, her pep rallies totally worked. By the time she had gotten back to her sled, everyone in the team was barking, howling, wagging their tails. I thought I would give it a try.

I crouched down to eye level with Kabob and Loretta, mother and daughter. Their eyes had the same glowy, brown sweetness. Loretta stamped impatiently, leaning forward in her harness, but Kabob needed some encouragement. I looked her deep in the eye and I said, "Mama, I need you right now. I am so sorry I haven't been doing a good job of keeping things positive. You deserve that from me. There is nobody else who can lead this team like you can right now. We just need to make it to the next checkpoint and then you can take a break from lead. But right now, I need *you*. OK?" I stood up and beamed at her. I smiled at all the dogs and then started dancing, right there in the trail. "Woohoo!" I yelled. "We're doin' this, guys! We're running the fucking *Iditarod*! You guys are amazing! We've got this!" I ran down the line and ruffed up everyone's fur with two gloved hands.

Kabob leaned into her harness and let out a high-pitched war cry that I had never heard before. She yelled with her whole mouth open, her tiny white teeth coming to points beside her pink tongue, her eyes shining, her tail pointing down. "Awawawawa!" she yelled. And Loretta, Buck, Tex, Hank, Dolly, Patsy, Solo, Ferlin, Ox, Iron, Hoss, and Bullock barked and yipped. From the middle of the team, Solo threw his head back into a howl and the rest of the team joined. I was in awe of them. I ran back to my sled and stepped on the runners, pulling up the snow hook with another "Woohoo!" and just like that, we were off.

We sped down the smooth, fast trail and wound a big S over an ice bridge where the Koyukuk River joined the Yukon. Behind me, two snowmachines entered the trail just as I wound out of sight. I assumed they were trailbreakers or locals, making sure the mushers stayed on the trail since the route was a little confusing right there. A wrong turn could lead to the village of Koyukuk, where the path was well traveled—not only did it split the distance between the villages of Galena and Nulato, but it also had the only liquor store for hundreds of miles in any direction.

Two hours later, the sun had set and my dogs were traveling beautifully. I looked down at the glare ice on the Yukon—black and bottomless, giant bubbles trapped and frozen, aquamarine breaks and cracks in the ice. The trail alternated between glassy ice and smooth snow. It was about twenty below and I felt mindless, in a reverie of sorts, when suddenly I heard yelling. I looked behind me and it was Sarah.

"What?" I yelled back to her, taking down the hood of my parka so I could hear her better.

"I've been trying to catch you for hours!" she shouted. "Did those snowmachiners back there bother you?"

"No!" I yelled, confused. "I think they were trailbreakers."

"They grabbed my ass!" she yelled.

Immediately I set my foot on the brake and came to a hard stop on the ice.

"What?" I asked. "Are you fucking serious?"

"Yeah," she said. "One of them blocked the trail, so I slowed down to see if everything was OK and that's when the other one grabbed my ass and tried to pull me off my sled. Thank god my dogs read the situation... they picked up the pace and got around the snowmachine that was blocking the trail and got us out of there."

My eyes were wide and my emotions alternated between

blood-boiling anger and icy fear. I took a breath and tried to think practically.

"OK, let's stick together and go as fast as we can into Nulato," I said. "You stay right here, right up on my ass. My dogs are used to training with two teams right together."

I looked around and shined my headlamp in all directions. I waited for Sarah to snack her dogs and then we traveled together down the trail.

My mind was racing, and after a few minutes I grabbed my sharpest snow hook—the one Cody said had sliced through someone's femoral artery and almost killed a man—and I yelled back to Sarah, "What's your plan?"

"What?" she asked, our runners scratching along the ice of the Yukon River.

"What's your plan?" I yelled again. "We need to be ready for them if they come back. And if they do I'm gonna gouge someone with this snow hook, swing at them with my ax, and let Hoss and Bullock loose. What are you gonna do?"

Sarah bent forward against her handlebar and began rifling through her sled bag, headlamp beam swallowed in the swales of fabric. We should have been focused on surviving in -20 degree temperatures, on traveling a hundred miles a day through unforgiving wild land, on keeping our dogs healthy and exemplifying the pioneer know-how and spirit of thousand-mile mushers. Instead, we were fearing sexual harassment, violence, and rape. Instead, we were fearing what men thought our bodies owed them. How on earth could they watch us go by, these icons of the northland driving powerful dog teams, and have the nerve to reach out and touch one of us? Have such a feeling of entitlement over us as to grab one of our asses? To violate? If they could do that to a total stranger, to a professional athlete passing by on a dogsled, what were they doing to the women in their lives, in their schools, in their houses? I turned forward and watched the backs of my dogs, then saw their ears perk up as six snowmachine lights gathered together and took off up the riverbank, then came circling back. Under my beaver fur hat, my scalp prickled. The hair on the back of my neck stood up. Behind me, Sarah's voice. "I have an ax and a snow hook," she said.

"Good," I said. "They're coming."

The machines came from the front and the back. The one behind us caught up more quickly than those ahead, and as the sled came alongside my team I threw my beaver gauntlets behind my back and unsheathed my sharpened ax. I kept my team in my peripheral vision as I turned to face the snow-machiner, heart thumping. I saw the wrinkled face of an old native woman and let out a breath of relief. The snowmachines up ahead fanned out and sped past us on either side. They weren't coming for us.

In Nulato, Sarah reported what happened to a race judge and then to the Alaska State Troopers. "Their eyes looked really messed up," she said, "like they were on something." She gave the race specific directions to not generate a press release. She didn't want this to be a blemish on her rookie Iditarod. She didn't want to be known as "that girl." To be humiliated, because that's what reporting and publicizing sexual harassment would do to her. And just like Jeff and Aliy, she would swallow the invasive, pervasive fear and keep on going. But unlike Jeff and Aliy, Sarah wasn't attacked at random. She was attacked because she was a woman. And the thought of what those men could have done to her if they had succeeded in pulling her off her sled would haunt me all the way to Nome.

The beauty of the trail outside Kaltag slowly began to wipe away the trauma. The trail undulated through a landscape that was yawning. Trees began to fall away as bare hills first encircled us and then spread away, like arms opening. Ryne and I were traveling together again, and we planned to mush to Old Woman Cabin, a shelter a little more than halfway between the Yukon River village of Kaltag and the Bering Sea coastal village of Unalakleet. After the sun set, the aurora ripped across the sky. It was like we were in a comic strip. The outline of every *Pow! Bang!* and *Zap!* was superimposed onto the black and glowing, pulsing.

The cabin was in a protected spot on the trail, surrounded by trees. I parked my dogs at the edge of a dark meadow alongside a handful of other teams and gave them food, bedded them down in fresh straw, massaged their feet. Ryne and the other mushers had finished up their chores twenty minutes ago and now it was just me, crouched down on the straw and taking moments to stare at that unreal sky, the purple, green, blue, and white aurora. It was so bright I had to squint. I knew I should be more efficient, that I needed to capitalize on rest, but I couldn't help staring. I blinked in disbelief, then felt the presence at the edge of the black woods across the meadow. Immediately the dogs stood, ears perked, and began to growl a warning.

I knew it was the Old Woman, and the skin on the back of my neck prickled. Legend had it that she had died in an avalanche and, though her body perished under the snow, her spirit had never left. Nobody could agree on whether she was good or bad, but many veteran mushers had felt her presence or even seen her on the side of the trail. I gathered my vet supplies and stumbled into the dark, warm cabin. I tiptoed over snoring bodies and made my way to the back wall. Ryne was tucked behind a table and had saved me a spot. I crawled into my sleeping bag and set a timer for two hours. A chill crept in from the cold floor, but I couldn't know if it was really cold seeping in from the outside or the feeling that we were all being watched.

Later I found out that Old Woman Cabin was Susan Butcher's favorite place on the trail, and that her ashes were spread there. Maybe the spirit I felt there was hers, yearning after each of us, luring us in.

The Bering Sea coast was an otherworldly place. The trail wound in and out of piles of driftwood, snarling my sled brake. The trail skimmed over sand dunes dusted with snow. I was on the beach, but I was also on a dogsled mushing alongside the ocean. And then, to my utter disappointment and even anger, I was on dirt. Again. I had thirteen dogs now—still an overwhelming amount of power—and I was mushing up a dirt trail among sunlit tussocks when Loretta decided she really wanted to check out whatever was happening over *there*, twenty feet or so off the trail atop a small knoll. And what was there to stop her? The dogs could stay on the trail or they could go off on the barren tundra and what was the difference, really, when there was no snow? No way to stop? I became furious. Not only with Loretta for sniffing out a ground squirrel den, but also with the Iditarod Trail Committee for letting us mush on hundreds of miles of snowless trail.

"Goddammit, Loretta!" I screamed, my voice breaking. "God Damn You!"

I stomped my sharpest snow hook into a mound of grass and ran up to the front of my team. I grabbed Loretta up by the harness straps and shook her.

"What are you doing?!" I yelled. "You need to stay on the *trail*!"

All the dogs were afraid of me now. They lowered themselves down onto the ground, cowed. Immediately I felt awful and began to cry. What the fuck was *I* doing? These dogs hadn't asked for this. *I* asked *them* to do this. Not the other way around. Like Jeff had always taught me, "It's never the dog's fault." Loretta was just being a dog, and a thing that dogs do is sniff after ground squirrels when given the chance. I sat down on the ground next to Loretta and put my arms around her. I held her to me and buried my face in her fur.

"I'm sorry," I said, right into her skin. "Loretta, I'm so sorry. You have done so much for me. You have brought me here."

I stood up and sighed.

"Goddammit guys, I am really sorry. This whole thing is so fucked."

I turned and looked around me. The sun was just on the other side of our hill, and light was raking across the tall grasses and glinting off the frozen ocean. The wind ruffled the dogs' fur and dried out my eyes. I reached into my pocket for my piece-of-shit iPod and saw that it had a tiny bit of battery life left. I scrolled to the song "Animal Life" by Shearwater. I ran my hand along my neck underneath my balaclava to insert each earbud, stepped onto the runners, and pressed play.

I remembered the feeling of putting in earbuds in the newsroom where I used to work, back in Montana. The bullpen was hectic, jam-packed with reporters interviewing people, typing frantically, hurrying to file reports before the deadline. There I would sit, staring at a computer screen, typing out the stories of other peoples' lives every day. Wondering when the moment would come that I would get up from my office chair, walk out of the newsroom, and live a life worth writing about.

As the opening lines commenced—a single guitar that

readied me for the imminent sweep and build of the song—I
suddenly felt better. The dogs had more bounce in their step.
We were moving forward on the trail, not sideways onto the
tundra. I looked at the back of every single dog. These dogs
were my family. God I loved them so much. And they had
brought me here, to this incredible place right above the sea.
We climbed higher up onto the Blueberry Hills. The music
in my earbuds was quiet, pensive. The dogs were trotting so
smoothly that I could have balanced glasses of water on top of
them and they wouldn't have spilled a drop.

The music began to build. I could feel my heart lifting as
my eyes began to blur with tears. We were coming around a
corner and the sun lit up my dogs two by two by two as we
slowly advanced, climbing ever higher. We rounded the bend
and the sunlight blinded and dazzled me. The music smashed
onto my eardrums.

Charging down the maw of the ocean
I wanna come close, I wanna come closer
I held your name inside my mouth through all the days out
  wandering
But called out from the mouth of oblivion
Cast away like dogs from the shelter
I shed the dulling armor plates
That once collected radiance
And surging at the blood's perimeter
The half-remembered wild interior
Of an animal life

The ocean was frozen piles of glinting diamonds. And there upon them, just offshore, were hulking, cliff-faced islands perched upon the stilled sea, as if hovering. Wildness filled my heart. This is who and what and where we were: wild, and animals, and no place that felt like earth. The primordial part of me that had always yearned to be let out—that had always longed to know what it looked and felt like away from all the roads and civilization and scheduled ordinariness—that was the only part of me now. And the dogs were who they always were, without costume or false pretense, and I was one of them now. My animal life not half-remembered, but instead fully realized.

We climbed to a lofty height as the sky turned red. The trail reached a pinnacle and held us at its height for a moment before dropping us down a dizzying descent of switchbacks bookended with 180-degree turns. I wasn't afraid of those things anymore—the reckless speed, the technical trail. I looked out across the coastline in disbelief. It stretched north-ward, forever. The ocean was a mirror that reflected burning red and velvet lavender. The mountains were a serrated maw opening. We were at the outer edge of a wilderness that had no end. We were coming in for a landing.

Ryne and I left Shaktoolik to cross Norton Sound just before daybreak. The dogs were surging because the trail exuded odors they had never smelled before. A cutting, salty cold came up through the ice to envelop us. We were on pack ice now, mushing across the open ocean, and the freezing, bottomless sea was only feet below our runners. My team was at its best that time of day—the coldest and darkest part, just before the dawn. And we jetted out across the Sound at eleven miles per hour, chasing sunrise. The sea began to light up, a dull blue now instead of endless black. And it had an end, a perimeter. And that perimeter was slowly changing from black to pale yellow to deep, glowing crimson. Now the sky was ablaze with sunrise, except for its outer edge, which was rich navy punctuated with stars. The sled rose up and down with frozen ocean waves. And when we got to the very middle of the Sound, I stopped my team, gave them a meat snack, and ran back to Ryne.

"Now's the time for Ol' Bob!" I said.

Ryne had been carrying the ashes of a complete stranger—a guy named Bob—in her dogsled this whole time. Iditarod mushers often get surprising, personal requests like this. The trail is a dream to most people. And so Ryne had been asked by someone to carry their loved one's ashes and spread them out here.

"I just spread him a few minutes ago!" Ryne said, laughing. "It is so beautiful here."

"Well how about a dance party, to warm up?"

I pulled the headphones out of my iPod and put on Mark Ronson featuring Mystikal "Feel Right" and we bounced around in our giant parkas, bibs, and boots, laughing hysterically in the middle of the frozen ocean.

"This song is fucking perfect!" Ryne said.

Once we were satisfactorily warm, we jumped back on our dogsleds and mushed into the rising sun. Soon after, it overflowed the lip of the horizon and spilled out across our teams and the world, turning everything blue and white. The dogs slowed their pace with the growing warmth. A shock of red appeared out of the corner of my eye, and the dogs sped up as two massive foxes with luxurious crimson coats chased each other a few yards from the trail. We must be getting close to land, I thought with a sigh. The stories we'd heard of crossing Norton Sound were more than terrifying, they were life-threatening. People had floated away on blocks of pack ice that had broken loose. People had gotten caught in ground blizzards and blown out to sea, or anchored down their sleds and crawled inside and almost frozen to death. People got lost out there. But this time, we were the lucky ones.

We mushed from Koyuk to Elim in the dark, and my dogs chased a rabbit down a plowed road while I desperately dragged my snow hook in the wall of snow at my side, trying to slow them down. I stopped them long enough for Ryne to catch up to me and, crying, told her that I hated my dogs and that they were trying to kill me. Ryne began to laugh. "Kristin, this far into a race I think a lot of mushers would kill to have this problem."

We left White Mountain for the finish line at sunset. We had been timing most of our runs this way—resting during the heat of the day and mushing during the night, when it was colder and better for the dogs. It got dark quickly, and I turned my headlamp on right as we were going down a rollicking trail that wound in and out of big sand dunes and spat us out on a massive, polished lagoon. There were no trail markers here anymore—the wind blew one direction here and it had blown every dog team before us into those trail markers, leaving none standing. The wind also left no snow whatsoever, only a big, black, slippery mirror run through with white, puckered cracks. Solo took up his harness with the excitement and confidence of a kid knowing he was about to hit a home run. Regular trails were boring. This here was a challenge worth perking up for. His head lifted and his ears turned back, toward me. We were ready.

We crashed onto the ice and immediately began to fishtail. The dogs, still wearing booties, began to slip-slide, rapidly shortening their steps to stay upright and avoid going belly-down on the ice. I shined my headlamp across the lagoon to see where the scratch track of the snowmachine had gone. It was maybe twenty feet to the right of where we were.

"Gee!" I yelled to Solo.

Immediately, he edged right.

"Yep, that's it, buddy! Gee!"

More pulling to the right. The rest of the dogs were doing a hell of a job staying upright, and the sled had stopped fishtailing and was now pulling straight as an arrow behind them.

"Almost there, Solo. Gee!"

Solo perked up and saw the scratch track, steering us onto

the inch-deep grooves in the ice and lowering his nose down to sniff it. Yep, other dogs have been here. Assured, the whole team settled into a steady pace, gripping the grooves in the ice. Every fifty feet or so, the scratch track would disappear and we would be on the smooth, rounded surface once again, doing some slippery route-finding. But this was Solo's delight. I could feel his energy and it lit me up. I swelled with pride.

"We're almost there, you guys! We have twenty miles and then we're in Nome, at the finish line of the fucking Iditarod! Oh, dogs, you are so amazing. We've got this, guys."

Tails were wagging, eyes were glimmering, and a light was beaming down on us from way up high. I thought it must be a lighthouse. The trail was aiming straight at the light, and I couldn't believe we were about to climb a hill that high. The light spun around and around as the dogs dug in and I pushed the sled with all my might. They surged up the final pitch of Cape Nome. When the wind was still for a moment, we heard dogs barking. The light was Ryne! She had been waiting for us. I put in my hooks and walked up to her.

"Let's have a ceremonial bib putting-on," she said, handing me her race bib. She stood on her runners and held her arms out in a T. I put the bib over her head and clasped the plastic buckles and she did the same for me. Then we turned off our headlamps and looked up.

The moon was out but it wasn't full. It cast just enough green light to see the tall, snow-covered mountains surrounding Nome slope down to the ocean. But the aurora was a weaving, dancing river just above our heads. It pulsed and glided in numerous strands. Green, white, purple, and red. It felt like we could reach our hands straight up and dip them into the light. Headlamps off, we glided down the backside of Cape Nome, the dark shadows of our dogs trotting before us and melding into one, sinuous being. The shattered-glass northern lights dancing overhead.

A few miles before we reached Nome, I saw the taillights of a truck and couldn't believe my eyes. It was the first automobile I had seen in eleven days, and in my head Moose's voice said, "Look, Mama! A ve-hicle." I laughed out loud. *Oh, Moose, I am so happy you're here with me now, seeing all of this*, I thought. I felt his joyful spirit keenly. I turned onto Front Street right behind Ryne and we both stopped and lined out our dogs. The fans waiting in Nome were excited to get to see us race to the finish line, side by side, and all began cheering and clapping. It was 4:30 in the morning so most of them were our parents and fellow mushers who had already finished.

"Ready?!" Ryne said, looking at me.

"Yes!" I screamed, and off we went.

We raced each other with earnest competitive enthusiasm—ridiculous for fifty-sixth and fifty-seventh place—and were running beside our sleds and calling up our dogs. Never one to miss such an opportunity, Solo took the lead with relish, and we finished two seconds ahead of Ryne, gliding under the burled arch in Nome, lit up by a blinding spotlight. An announcer's voice boomed on a loudspeaker, but I couldn't hear anything that she said. I ran to Andy and hugged him so hard. I buried my head in my dad's shoulder and swallowed up my mom in a hug. I told them, "That is the most fucked-up thing I have ever done in my life." Then my dogs began to bark. They lunged into their harnesses and yipped impatiently. They began to howl. They wanted to keep going. I got back on the sled and looked nervously at the plowed, concrete road ahead of me that was glazed in ice. The turn for the Nome dog lot was one hundred feet away and I wasn't confident about getting there. An entire team of people ran alongside my dog team to ensure we made the turn and we still missed it. The dogs were completely amped.

"Woah! *Woooooahhhh*, you assholes!" I yelled, my voice echoing off empty downtown buildings.

The dogs slowed enough to make a turn in the back entrance, and once they saw all the beds Andy had made for them, and the hot meal ladled out into their bowls, they decided maybe it wasn't such a bad thing to be done with this madness.

Mom and Dad walked me back to the house of our host family in Nome. I sat down at the dinner table and pulled off my boots and socks. Whispering, I told them about the buffalo. I told them about the snowmachiners. I told them about the Dalzell Gorge and the Coast. They told me it could wait until the morning, after I got some sleep, but I couldn't stop talking. It was the opposite of my Yukon Quest finish. I couldn't wait to let them in. I told them all the things I wished I could have told someone I loved right as they were happening. My eyes were swollen and dried out by wind. My cheeks were frost-nipped and peeling. My face was red and puffy. My hair was in a greasy knot. I had lost ten pounds since I saw them at the start line. I needed sleep desperately, but equally as desperate was my need to unburden myself of everything that happened.

In a pink-walled bathroom I filled up a deep, green tub with hot water and got in. Nothing could take away the cold that had seeped into my body over the last eleven days. Andy had returned from caring for the dogs and I asked him to heat up a teakettle and pour the boiling hot water into my tub. I must have soaked in there for an hour. I thought about what I had just done and what it had taken to get there. The obsessive, difficult work that required so much of us for so many years of our life. I felt satisfied. I felt relief and pride. But I also felt something else. Something kind of like moving on. Like I got what I came for, after all these years. When I got out of the bath, I walked into a dark, back bedroom and sunk into a soft, comfortable bed with clean sheets and a big quilt. Andy's warm body was by my side. I slept for six hours straight—more than I had slept in a row for the last two weeks—and woke up with midday sun streaming in through lace-curtained windows. We looked each other in the eyes and held each other's bodies. We made love quietly—people were having breakfast on the other side of the door. "Let's have a baby," I whispered, unable to contain my grin. "Let's make a baby right now."

EPILOGUE

In December we left the windows uncovered, and from my pillow I watched the stars blink brightly from a deep black sky. To the east it looked like someone had sloshed a bucket of pale green paint onto a black wall and then the color oozed and slid slowly downward. Without warning, the color brightened and lurched, stabbing upward, coruscating to the north. It was like watching the keys while some invisible hand played the piano. Under that electric aurora the dogs were stirring. Norton bellowed out a low, throaty baritone, followed by Lefty and then Ox. Kitty joined in with her jarring alto and then came the puppies' straining yips, sounding more and more like adults with each passing day. Even in the dark, I knew each dog's voice. When the canine chorus reached its peak in a perfect thirty-one-dog harmony, my stomach lit up, mimicking the sky. Energy rippled across the dome of my belly. I rested my hand over its voluminous curve and under my palm burst unpredictable waves and flourishes.

It was 15 degrees below zero and I heaved my massive body out of bed to pee. I had no idea what time it was because time didn't exist in winter in Alaska. Four in the afternoon looked the same as seven in the morning, which looked the same as midnight. The only thing that changed was the position of the stars wheeling overhead. I stepped carefully down the ladder-steep stairs from the bedroom loft, trying not to wake Andy. I reached the plywood landing and took one last big step over Zigzag, curled on her dog bed. In twenty feet I was at the front door, pulling aside the wool blanket that hung over the door to keep the draft at bay. Outside, the snow squeaked under my down booties as the temperature continued its downward plunge. I crunched through the three or four inches of snow that fell a few days ago—the season's first snowfall—and thought of Decembers past. More normal years, where the first snow fell in September and we were on dogsleds well before Halloween. At this time last year we were running sixty miles a day, training for back-to-back thousand-mile races across the Yukon Territory and across Alaska. This year, we ambled across the tundra with our pack of three-month-old puppies as our neighbors clattered by stubbornly on the gravel road, letting their dogsleds get beat to hell out on the uncovered tussocks the size of basketballs. Andy chopped firewood and perma-chinked drafty spots along the walls of our one-room log cabin and hauled water every other day. From nails in the rafters hung dog harnesses in need of repair and also a bouncy swing for a new baby. Upstairs under the window, across from our bed, was a little wooden crib that could be rocked back and forth. Andy had built a shelf alongside it full of minute onesies and miniature knitted sweaters and sleeper sacks and diapers. Once a week or so, we would pull out a teeny pair of footie pajamas and marvel that any human could ever be small enough to wear them. Yesterday I watched Andy's face as he held up a pink fleece number and then cradled it to his chest—his blue eyes glowing, the skin around them crinkled in straight, emanating lines. Neither of us had those lines when we first met six and a half years ago. Our faces hadn't yet been weathered by wind and sun and a dozen thousand miles of being on a dogsled.

Like most dog mushers that time of year, we were the constant fixers of broken things. We had one fully functioning vehicle and two partially working ones, with a fourth in the shop whose repairs were worth more than the value of the thing in its entirety. We had thirty-one dogs to feed and unpaid maternity leave and an open pantry with boxes and cans tumbling out of it. Four dog beds took up most of the real estate in our small cabin, and on frigid nights we could feel the heat from the woodstove on one cheek and the cold creeping in from the windowpane on the other. But outside, the puppies contentedly slept on top of each other in their houses. They closed their eyes and exhaled, burrowing their chins down on the heads and bellies and backs of their littermates. The adult dogs play-bowed and barked and howled excitedly, exalting in an uproar when Andy brought out their harnesses and took them on a run. Clumps of snow from our last and only storm clung to spruce boughs and stayed cemented in the crotches of birch branches. Unbelievably, the Healy winds hadn't knocked them to the ground in sheets and sprays. It was cold and clear, brighter than day when the moon was full, the spruce casting long shadows on a sparkling silver lawn.

I didn't sleep anymore. The baby in my belly was too big, stuffed underneath my rib cage. My hips fell asleep as I tossed from one side to the other. Andy couldn't sleep, either. I told him he ought to take the couch downstairs and get some rest, but he didn't want to leave my side. He rooted into my curved back, putting his warm hand on my moving belly, calming the baby into peaceful sleep.

That part of pregnancy was like the end of training. We'd packed all the drop bags, made a race plan, gotten ourselves and the dogs as prepared as we ever would be, and now the race was only days away and we were thinking about the start line. We were thinking about hooking up that finely tuned dog team and the announcer saying 3...2...1...*go*! But like any other musher, we'd so much rather be doing the thing than thinking about doing the thing. We were people of action, but all we could do was wait.

In the delivery room, my body debuted an awful power. I had been in labor for twenty hours and the pain was overtaking me. I tried to crawl out of it, clawing the back of the hospital bed and lunging toward the door. I thought that it would break me. My midwife said, "Kristin, I know you are in pain, but you can't escape it. You have to go there. You have to go into it. The only way out is through."

And then I closed my eyes and it was Littlehead, taking up the gangline on Eagle Summit. It was one dog lunging into her harness, silhouetted against blinding sun. I heaved a final time and Ada was through the bones and screaming into the world. Andy caught her slippery body. Andy felt her wet swirl of hair. Andy looked into her eyes and then he handed her up between my legs and into my arms. She was my accomplishment, but she was ours, too.

Just like so many other times in my life, it was the end of

one journey and the beginning of another. I didn't know how to be a mother, but the knowledge must be innate somewhere inside myself of how to be *her* mother. Just like when I first arrived in Alaska, I was, at once, lost and found. I had to utilize every skill I had, but also I had to let go of so much.

Alaska had taught me well about letting go: How I had to in order to move on, how I absolutely never should. How I had to be brave and purposeful, and also how clarity almost always came to me by wandering aimlessly. I learned to be certain of my heart, and also what a nourishing garden uncertainty could prove to be. And how, looking back, the painful rites of passage—divorce, childbirth, journeys into the unknown—seemed so necessary in carving my particular mold.

I held Ada to my breast and saw my life as a landscape. The river of my own will had carved it like the Nenana had the valley I called home. Its topography was varied, marked by the wide open plains of an imaginative childhood filled with long grasses and soaring Texas oak trees; by wild Montana peaks jutting, angular and unfamiliar, from the flat ground—a gateway to unexplored territory; by geologies representative of important people, influencing each bend in the river. It was a satisfying panorama to behold, and I would change none of it. It was resoundingly authentic, and my sorrows were as much of a force there as my hallelujahs. It was a wonder to me that my own personal landscape was best illuminated in the crepuscular tinge of the Alaskan winter—a time where I could sit alone for a spell and hold my own hand and become as much of a comfort to myself as a good friend. It was a wonder how I could find myself in that vast space, and then how I could find Andy. All that lonesome time on the trail was everything a lifetime could throw at me—heartbreak, defeat, exhaustion, injury, failure; but it was also renewal, disbelief, beauty beyond imagining. And always, at the end of it all, were the dogs who brought me home.

ACKNOWLEDGMENTS

Without the love and support of my parents, I never could have lived the life described in this book. And now that I am a parent, I am in awe of their courage in letting me go to follow my heart to the literal ends of the earth. Mom and Dad, thank you.

My siblings—Ryan, Kalin, Jared, and Jordan—have met every hardship of mine with humor, support, and love, just as they have celebrated my successes as though they were their own. Thank you, guys.

Cheley Colorado Camps, and more specifically, Girls' Trail's End Ranch, was the forge that shaped me. Thank you, Don, Carole, Brooke, and Jeff for continuing to provide an opportunity for girls to develop their courage, to be fearless for one another, and to lead. Thank you to all my fellow campers and counselors at GTE for fostering a loving community that empowers women.

Nancy Smith, Julie Zobal, Jeff Hull, and Sharon Barrett were some of the teachers and professors who challenged me, developed my writing skills, and ultimately encouraged me to write this book. Thank you for your support and persistence. You have one of the most underacknowledged, incredibly important jobs in the world, and I appreciate each of you so much.

Stacey, Lindsay, Kelly, Maria, Ali, and Liz—thank you for pulling me through the devastating heartbreak of divorce. Someone once told me, "The power of women will get you through this." Thank you for exemplifying that, and for being a port in the storm for me so many times.

Jessie—I wouldn't be here in Alaska without you. Thank you for so many things, but most important for the fateful phone call that changed my life. And Karen, thank you for offering me the job all those years ago. The dogs you introduced me to were the missing puzzle piece in my heart.

The rangers with whom I have traveled the Denali backcountry—most especially Tay-Tay, Dirty D, and Eleanor—thank you for being by my side through every humbling challenge and mountaintop triumph. I love you girls.

Jeff, Brent, Paige, Cody, Mike, Sue, Lance, Laura, and Mandy—thank you for every lesson, every adventure, and every single day of your friendship. Nothing means more than the kinship shared with the other people who have traveled a thousand miles on a dogsled. And Ryne, you were there for every one of those miles. Thank you for being my sidekick on the biggest adventures of my lifetime so far. I love all of you.

Claude, Jen, Bob, and Chrissy—thank you for creating a second home for us and, in turn, for becoming our family. Lynn, Bub, Jill, Carl, and all the crazy bastards on Regulus—thank you for your love and friendship.

Thank you to Katie Orlinsky and Scott Chesney for your gorgeous photos, and for braving the lonesome trail to capture our adventures.

The dogs can't read, so thanking them might be silly, but I am nothing without them. They are the filling in my heart.

Ali Frick, thank you for that fateful walk across the Brooklyn Bridge. And Whitney Frick, thank you for believing in me and my story. Thank you for introducing me to Brettne.

Brettne Bloom, this book would never have come into existence without your tireless passion and commitment. You are singlehandedly responsible for putting together the Dream Team!

Maddie Caldwell, you know all the words, thoughts, feelings, and dreams inside my brain. I can follow your intuition and trust it as though it were my own. What a gift it has been to work with you.

AP, my love, what a life we have created together. Thank you for being my partner in every last endeavor. I so often forget that you are a separate person from me. And Ada, it blows my mind to think that one day you'll be old enough to read this. And then, later, you'll be old enough to follow your heart on all the perilous journeys that beckon.